BORDER ENVIRONMENTS

Spector Books CRA Press

Edited by Riccardo Badano, Tomas Percival,
and Susan Schuppli

CASE STUDIES

FIELD NOTES

Series Forward

This book series situates you, the reader, at our Roundtable in the Centre for Research Architecture on the third floor of the aptly named Richard Hoggart building at Goldsmiths, University of London. Gathered 'around' this table you will find yourself amongst a group of spatial practitioners and researchers who convene to work together, sharing their projects and insights. These assemblies have produced a space of critical encounter and pedagogical experimentation with the objective of developing new investigative methods and speculative insights aimed at responding to and intervening into the urgent political conditions of our time. Students work collaboratively with their peers as well as with the affected communities in which their research projects are embedded. Staff and guests bring critical ideas and key works into this context.

This Roundtable, which we now seek to re-animate through a series of written reflections, investigative accounts, and documented fieldworks, as well as transcribed conversations and glossaries is both the spatial form that organises our encounters non-hierarchically and the material surface upon which projects are laid out and ideas debated. As this book series unfolds across its thematic issues we invite you to become a part of this lively environment that has nourished us intellectually and shaped us politically.

Across the series we have sought to foreground the distinctive pedagogy and field of research that distinguishes the Centre for Research Architecture. Since its founding in 2005, the Centre has brought together a diverse group of architects, artists, urbanists, geographers, lawyers, scientists, journalists, and activists to work on expanded notions of space. Projects in the Centre address contemporary struggles and conflicts as they register themselves in the transformation of environments: shifting scales and intensities from the architectural and urban to that of territorial and planetary processes, from the micro-scale of buildings and infrastructure to the macro-scale of borders and global flows. In the Centre, space is analysed as an elastic medium that is constantly reshaped by political and mediatic forces. To address such complex interrelations, our researchers have necessarily developed diverse creative and practical approaches for conducting their fieldwork and developing their conceptual frameworks. The book series explores these spatial entanglements by drawing upon contributions from current as well as former graduate students and staff, many of whom have gone on to establish investigative agencies and teach in programmes directly inspired by our work. It also includes the research of collaborators, friends, and thinkers who have informed and motivated our interventions.

Alongside spatial reformulations, the Centre has also developed specific aesthetic considerations. In conceptualising the books and laying out contributions, we have tried to retain the inventiveness of these methods and practices. Images, audio recordings, videos, maps, and other media take on specific roles within each of the projects presented. In particular, many audio-visual materials become fields of investigation in and of themselves. Alongside their means of production, their modes of circulation, and their networks of exchange, such media are treated as sites of research that open areas of investigation and intervention. The quality of a photograph, the metadata of a file, the resolution of a satellite image, the frequency of an audio recording, all become registers of the complex politics of events. To transform this mode of 'investigative aesthetics' into book format, we worked with Ariadna Serrahima (Oficina de disseny), to develop a number of design strategies to help readers identify the different roles that materials play throughout its pages.

These highlight the interrogation of media that 'do not speak for themselves' but rather need to be patiently studied and carefully narrated in order to make their specific political claims.

Each book in the thematic series brings together a heterogeneous range of materials and contributions, with a particular attention to collective modes of knowledge production. As stated, our aim is to invite the reader into this ever-evolving pedagogical context. For those of us studying and working in the Centre for Research Architecture, the book series offers another iteration of this generative assembly in which knowledge is co-produced, shared, and mobilised. Publishing is for us, an extension of our Roundtable forums. In this regard, each book is a collection that engages with current spatial processes and research practices and the series is a critical reflection on how these act and are acted upon in the world. Here, we must thank Spector Books for providing the framework and context for this endeavour and for their guidance and expertise on translating these projects into book form.

Riccardo Badano, Tomas Percival, and Susan Schuppli
10 October 2022, London

Border Environments
Lorenzo Pezzani, Tomas Percival, and Riccardo Badano

A conservation project on the site of a longstanding migant encampment in northern France attempts to encourage the reappearance of a protected orchid by erasing the traces of its most recent inhabitants, re-instating the line between native and alien forms of life. U.S. Border Patrol off-road incursions in the Sonoran Desert endanger the fragile soil ecologies of this desertic area, while pushing migrants into more and more remote crossing points. The quality of air inhaled in South London becomes a differential of inequality, and air pollution comes to be a causal effect, alongside colonial legacies of displacement and structural racism, in violence against racialised communities.

Located at the conjecture of borders and environments, each of the stories and projects in this publication contributes to producing a distinctive understanding of the intersection of these seemingly incommensurate terms. Over the last years, an emergent literature has highlighted the link between practices of border control and environments. Some of the earliest theorisations of this relationship have come from studies of the U.S.-Mexico border, where the notion of "prevention through deterrence" was adopted by U.S. border guards as early as 1994.[1] This enforcement strategy called for the deployment of massive numbers of agents as well as so-called 'tactical infrastructure' (e.g., surveillance technologies, sections of walls or fences) along the sections of the border that are easiest to cross, usually around urban areas. This militarisation of specific sections of the border, in turn, has led migrants to attempt to cross in desertic areas such as the Sonoran Desert that, due to extreme heat and scarce access to food and water, are more difficult to traverse, often leading to their disappearance and death.[2] Against the "methodological humanism"[3] of most migration and border research, critical accounts of "prevention through deterrence" have foregrounded how the desert and its geophysical characteristics—or its geopower, as coined by Elisabeth Grosz to underline how geographic environments are endowed with "forces contained in matter that precede, enable, facilitate, provoke and restrict 'life'".[4-5] Others have also successfully shown how the harsh terrain of Southern Arizona has been mobilised as a "moral alibi" for border violence, with state actors attempting to deflect responsibility for migrants deaths by pointing to the harshness of the landscape as the main culprit.[6] In sum, all of these

1 On this, see: Joseph Nevins, *Dying to Live: A Story of U.S. Immigration in an Age of Global Apartheid* (City Lights Books, 2008); Jason De Leon, *The Land of Open Graves: Living and Dying on the Migrant Trail* (Oakland, California: University of California Press, 2015); Geoffrey Alan Boyce, "The Rugged Border: Surveillance, Policing and the Dynamic Materiality of the US/Mexico Frontier," *Environment and Planning D: Society and Space* 34, no. 2 (April 2016): 245–62; Geoffrey Alan Boyce, Samuel N. Chambers, and Sarah Launius, "Bodily Inertia and the Weaponization of the Sonoran Desert in U.S. Boundary Enforcement: A GIS Modelling of Migration Routes through Arizona's Altar Valley," *Journal on Migration and Human Security* 7, no. 1 (March 2019): 23–35; Tara Plath, "An Elusive Viewshed: An Investigation of United States' Border Patrol Rescue Beacons in Arizona's Western Desert," *PLOT(S)*, Volume VII (2020).

2 While the declared aim of this tactic was to facilitate border enforcement by deterring potential migrants from attempting the perilous crossing and by pushing others into places where they are slower, what it has de facto produced is a massive humanitarian crisis of death and disappearance at the border.

3 Juanita Sundberg, "Animating United States-Mexico Border Studies," *Public Political Ecology Lab* (blog), 14 May 2014, http://ppel.arizona.edu/?p=633.

4 Duncan Depledge, "Geopolitical Material: Assemblages of Geopower and the Constitution of the Geopolitical Stage," *Political Geography* 45, no. 2 (March 2015): 91–92.

5 See also: William Walters, Charles Heller, and Lorenzo Pezzani, eds., *Viapolitics. Borders, Migration, and the Power of Locomotion* (Durham, North Carolina: Duke University Press, 2021).

6 See: Roxanne Lynn Doty, "Bare Life: Border-Crossing Deaths and Spaces of Moral Alibi," Environment and Planning D: Society and Space 29, no. 4(2011): 599-612; 599-612; Jill M. Williams, 'From Humanitarian Exceptionalism to Contingent Care: Care and Enforcement at the Humanitarian Border', *Political Geography* 47 (July 2015): 11-20.

studies have crucially highlighted how "nonhuman actors—plants, animals, and biophysical processes—are constitutive of boundary making" in the same ways in which border guards, national and international institutions, legal frameworks and surveillance systems are.[7]

Needless to say, the weaponisation of hazardous terrains for the purpose of border enforcement is not confined to the U.S. and Mexico. A growing body of literature has focused on similar phenomena taking place across the desertic region separating Sub-Saharan and Northern Africa, the rugged mountain passes and tumultuous rives in the Alps or Zagros mountains, or the oceans surrounding Australia, the USA, Europe and the Arabian Peninsula. Yet, in some of these works, an excessive focus on the harshness and hostility of these terrains tends to abstract "complex, bio-diverse ecology[ies]" into a "static image of wilderness [...] as lethal and naturally unsuited to migrants".[8] This process of abstraction erases centuries of Indigenous inhabitation and trans-regional exchange. In doing so, it does not only risk reproducing (neo-)colonial narratives which, in order to justify violent dispossession and the genocide of Indigenous populations, have consistently described these areas as empty, remote, and unliveable. It also risks being co-opted into racialised conservationist narratives that describe migrants as a threat to the environment and the objects they leave behind as hazardous "trash".[9] In order to counter the process of abstraction at work in such narratives, it is critical to account for the veritable process of design that is at stake in the becoming borders of oceans, deserts, and mountain ranges. As Pezzani has argued in more detail elsewhere, and as the texts presented in this volume try to do, it is through very specific practices, protocols, and laws that certain geophysical characteristics have been weaponised against specific categories of people and rendered hostile to them.[10] Emphasising the way in which legal geographies, surveillance technologies, and bureaucratic protocols have indeed turned certain environments into rugged borders is thus a critical antidote to reductionist understanding of natural environments: it exposes the structural violence of bordering practices, while simultaneously making it possible to account for the wealth of intergenerational knowledge that over centuries has allowed Indigenous people to develop intimate relations with these fragile ecologies and their rich biodiversity. Following these prompts, the contributions to this volume seek to question and rethink both terms that make up its title. Environment, here, does not simply refer to the "environs of humans" (that which is around and outside of us) but rather to a dynamic, socionatural space: "a society of societies, an international arena, a cosmopoliteia"[11] that is composed by multi-scalar and multi-temporal interactions across a range of human and more-than-human entities. Crucially, the environment here is not simply the inert background instrumentalized by border control; due to its "stubborn materiality",[12] it participates in and comes to matter to practices of border enforcement, enhancing or inhibiting detection capabilities depending on meteorological

7 Juanita Sundberg, "Diabolic Caminos in the Desert and Cat Fights on the Río: A Posthumanist Political Ecology of Boundary Enforcement in the United States–Mexico Borderlands," *Annals of the Association of American Geographers* 101, no. 2 (March 2011): 318–36.

8 Pietro Autorino, "'No Exponga Su Vida a Los Elementos': the Political Ecology of the US-Mexico Border in the Sonoran Desert," (University of Heidelberg, 2017).

9 See: Vicki Squire, "Desert 'Trash': Posthumanism, Border Struggles, and Humanitarian Politics," *Political Geography* 39 (March 2014): 11–21; Pietro Autorino, "'No Exponga Su Vida a Los Elementos': the Political Ecology of the US-Mexico Border in the Sonoran Desert," (University of Heidelberg, 2017).

10 Lorenzo Pezzani, 'Hostile Environments', *E-Flux Architecture*, 15 May 2020, https://www.e-flux.com/architecture/at-the-border/325761/hostile-environments/.

11 Deborah Danowski and Eduardo Viveiros de Castro, *The Ends of the World* (Malden, Massachusetts: Polity Press, 2016).

12 Stefanos Levidis, "Border Natures. The Environment as Weapon at the Edges of Greece," PhD diss., (Goldsmiths, University of London, 2021).

and sociotechnical conditions (the presence of waves, fog, heat, etc.), and moving according to seasonal rhythms as well as slow geological transformations.[13] As a "synthesis of nature, space, technology and law", border environments represent an inversion, a critical "turning inside-out" of the concept of "natural border".[14] The latter—a well-known trope of the modern era—provided the conceptual justification to the idea that borders are somehow the political expression of naturally existing, geophysically determined boundaries. As such, it "formed part of a constitutive myth of the state" and served to legitimize and rationalise the territorial claims of the then emerging European (empire-)states.[15] Thinking through the notion of border environments is instead a way to denaturalise the very existence of borders, point to their constructedness and instability, and to the violence required to keep them in place. By working through this concept, this publication attempts to capture this diffused and pervasive nature of contemporary borders beyond the linear metaphors that have been inherited from Westphalian mythologies of sovereign territoriality. Far from being a line without thickness demarcating the edges of territorial states, border environments are complex "atmosphere[s] of surveillance" that have infiltrated the most elementary infrastructures of living: a form of racialised violence that has become, in terms proposed by Christina Sharpe, as pervasive as the weather.[16] This refers not only to how bordering practices have weaponised the weather itself, and people have been made to die of cold or heat across global borders, but also to the ways in which, more generally, the border becomes a pervasive environment that subtracts life-sustaining resources (from water, food and clean air to rescue and healthcare provisions) and exposes migrants to harsh socio-natural conditions (chronic food and sleep deprivation, the lack of access to any social support, etc.). In all such cases, the environment stops being simply a site of border control, and rather becomes one of its modes of operation.

Thinking about border environments, finally, also allows us to go beyond deterministic ways of thinking about the relation between environmental and border violence. Mainstream conversations about the potential for environmental damage to fuel a sharp increase in population movements worldwide often tend to institute a mechanical relationship between environmental degradation and migration, painting apocalyptic scenarios of mass displacement. The seriousness of the current ecological crisis, however, should not deter us from scrutinising how the alarmist tones of these technocratic arguments have fuelled an approach that sees migration as a key threat to global stability, one to be tackled from a security perspective.[17] Against this "naturalization of causes," it is imperative to foreground the complex structures of causality that connect, in non-linear ways, individ-

13 Geoffrey A Boyce, "The Rugged Border: Surveillance, Policing and the Dynamic Materiality of the U.S./Mexico Frontier," *Environment and Planning D: Society and Space* 34, no. 2 (April 2016): 245–62; Philip Steinberg and Kimberley Peters, "Wet Ontologies, Fluid Spaces: Giving Depth to Volume through Oceanic Thinking," *Environment and Planning D: Society and Space* 33, no. 2 (April 2015): 247–264; Marco Ferrari, Elisa Pasqual, and Andrea Bagnato, *A Moving Border: Alpine Cartographies of Climate Change* (New York: Columbia Books on Architecture and the City, 2019); Bhaskar Sarkar, "On No Man's (Is)Land: Futurities at the Border," *Transnational Cinemas* 9, no. 1 (January 2018): 47–67.

14 Stefanos Levidis, "Border Natures. The Environment as Weapon at the Edges of Greece," PhD diss., (Goldsmiths, University of London, 2021).

15 Peter Sahlins, "Natural Frontiers Revisited: France's Boundaries since the Seventeenth Century," *American Historical Review* 95, no. 5 (December 1990): 1424.

16 Darren Ellis, Ian Tucker, and David Harper, "The Affective Atmospheres of Surveillance," *Theory and Psychology* 23, no. 6 (December 2013): 716–731; Christina Elizabeth Sharpe, *In the Wake: On Blackness and Being* (Durham, North Carolina: Duke University Press, 2016).

17 It is not a coincidence, in this sense, that the very expression "environmental refugee" was initially formulated in the context of neo-Malthusian debates on population growth and resource scarcity in the wake of the 1973 oil crisis. See: James Morrissey, "Environmental Change and Forced Migration: A State of the Art Review," (Refugee Studies Centre, University of Oxford, January 2009).

ual desires with complex social, cultural, and economic conditions, and ultimately lead to decisions about whether or not to stay or move.[18] Here, climate itself "is difficult to tease apart from other variables (cultural, political, economic) [...] not simply because these factors are entangled, but because all these aspects of collective life always already bear the trace of climatic and environmental change," and are thus "even more deeply implicated with politics, ethics and culture than we usually imagine".[19] Thinking about border environments is an attempt to foreground the very geohistorical conditions that have made the environmental crisis not only possible but inevitable, going deeper into the roots that connect (neo-)colonial extractive practices and migration as part of the same historical continuum. As Rob Nixon has suggested, displacement should not simply be understood as "the movement of people from their places of belonging," but also as "the loss of the land and resources beneath them, a loss that leaves communities stranded in a place stripped of the very characteristics that made it inhabitable".[20] These forms of "accumulation by displacement" are visible in many contemporary borderzones, where contested political ecologies are deeply intertwined with histories of dispossession and migration.[21] Accounting for the extractive and developmental processes that have indeed turned these fragile ecologies into toxic sacrifice zones, where migrants are often detained or simply exiled, is thus another critical task.[22]

The contributions in this book try to render justice to this complexity, spanning a variety of approaches and methods: from forensic investigations to visual essays, from grounded fieldwork to digital witnessing, from legal case studies to geological analyses, from practical projects to critical and theoretical reflections. In bringing together this diversity of approaches, this publication aims to highlight the procedures, investigative techniques, and processes that each author has had to develop in response to the specificity of the geographical, social, political, material, and economic conditions investigated. Due to its cross-disciplinary, practice-based ethos, the Centre for Research Architecture has been an ideal incubator for many of these projects.

One key issue that emerges clearly in this publication is the increasing weaponization of semi-natural landscapes in the process of border-making. In this regard, Stefanos Levidis examines the construction of so-called 'natural' borders across the shifting geography of the Aegean Sea by looking at how waves and wakes generated by Greek coastguard vessels have been used as a technology to push-back migrants' boats, with deadly consequences. Susan Schuppli's essay on 'hypothermic tactics' examines the politics of 'cold' across a series of cases and contexts. She investigates how low temperatures have been utilised to police Indigenous communities in Canada, govern migrants held in detention centres along the U.S.-Mexico border, and disband protestors opposing the Dakota Access Pipeline. The mobilisation of temperature highlights the continuity between structural racism, longstanding inequalities, and colonial extractive practices.

18 Marco Armiero and Richard Tucker, eds., *Environmental History of Modern Migrations*, (London; New York, NY: Routledge, 2017). See also: Giovanni Bettini, "Climate Barbarians at the Gate? A Critique of Apocalyptic Narratives on "Climate Refugees"", *Geoforum* 45, n.4 (March 2013): 63–72.

19 Nigel Clark, "Strangers on a Strange Planet: On Hospitality and Holocene Climate Change," in *Life Adrift: Climate Change, Migration*, Critique, ed. Andrew Baldwin and Giovanni Bettini (London; New York: Rowman & Littlefield International, 2017), 131–50.

20 Rob Nixon, *Slow Violence and the Environmentalism of the Poor* (Cambridge, MA: Harvard University Press, 2011), 19. Thanks to Nishat Awan for pointing me to this formulation.

21 Farshad Araghi, "Accumulation by Displacement: Global Enclosures, Food Crisis, and the Ecological Contradictions of Capitalism," *Review (Fernand Braudel Center)* 32, no. 1 (2009): 113–46.

22 Steve Lerner, *Sacrifice Zones: The Front Lines of Toxic Chemical Exposure in the United States* (Cambridge: MIT Press, 2010).

Following the propagations of state violence across border landscapes, several of the authors explore the entanglement between humanitarian initiatives and security imperatives. Dimitra Andritsou's research into fires in the migrant detention camp of Moria, Greece, looks at more than one hundred outbreaks that affected the UN-run structure since 2013 until it was eventually burnt to the ground in 2020. In doing so, she addresses fires not as isolated accidents but as a structural mode of migrant management. The 'smouldering ground' asylum seekers were forced to inhabit is analysed as a multi-scalar site where faulty infrastructures, EU policies, planned over-population, and the climate crisis are co-opted to enable and justify both a regime of forced evictions and the criminalisation of solidarity. In parallel, Tara Plath's project mapping the location of the so-called Rescue Beacons scattered across the Arizona desert, examines the ambiguity of supposedly humanitarian initiatives as they conceal a strengthening of border logics. Her first-hand account of activist and solidarity work, alongside digital techniques deployed to map the beacon's secret locations, exposed the complexity of both researching and challenging this complex network of bordering practices.

The notion of border environments brings to the fore how ecological conservation and restoration initiatives can be co-opted to displace and restrict rights. Hanna Rullman & Faiza Ahmad Kahn's video documentary *Habitat 2190* (2019), transposed here into printed matter, explores the overlap between conservation and securitisation at the site previously occupied by the notorious 'Jungle', in Calais, France. The project examines notions of nativity and belonging through the restoration of the long-disappeared Liparis loeselii orchid from the site, in the context of the displacement of the informal camp which provided temporary shelter to hundreds of asylum seekers.

The question of posthuman politics and the role of more-that-human actors animates a sequence of contributions. Juanita Sundberg's extensive essay on the politics of soil at the U.S-Mexico border highlights how both geological and geopolitical events have reconfigured the desert. Her text analyses how the desert mediates imperial and bordering objectives in the present and how the activities of U.S. Border Patrol transform this 'soilscape'. Sundberg demonstrates how this landscape is transformed by bordering activities that destabilise the very terrain and material strata upon which enforcement takes place re-producing the desert, while also damaging the lives of Indigenous communities and migrants. Similarly, Gabrielle Wolf's engages with the more-than-human at the U.S.-Mexico border. Her contribution examines the materiality of the border infrastructure itself and unpacks how, in addition to state security agendas, various environmental factors—including animals and microbes, water and Saguaro cacti, and even condor faeces and urine—play an active role in co-producing the border, while also disrupting its operations. Areej Ashhab looks at instances in which trees have become political agents and storytelling devices to address the violence imposed by settler-colonialism in Palestine. Foregrounding her methodology of walking this political space, she negotiates the separation between access to the land and traditional land practices. Ashhab's essay narrates the history of the present through what she calls 'the fast-growing tree with the flying seeds, erect trunk and hemispherical crown', an unexpected actor in the Israeli colonisation of the Palestinian landscape. Ishita Sharma's reflections draw upon her fieldwork and archival research into the Kutch region, an alternatively desertic and aquatic geography stretching between India and Pakistan. Her essay looks at how geological forces, seismic activity, degrees of wetness, and changing environmental conditions, alongside colonial legacies and histories, have come to play a role in determining the socio-political trajectory of the region.

Mustapha Jundi's contribution examines the contested border geographies between Lebanon and Israel, focusing on debates over Karstic water flows crisscrossing the Levantine area. His distinct methodological approach explores the possibilities of researching a transborder condition from a distance, when proximity and access to the site is made impossible. How does the researcher attune with the inaccessible bordersite? What kind of dissonance can be generative when confronting unknowability? Working on questions of subsistence and surplus, Avi Varma reflects on the notion of the everyday border through an engagement with the agrarian crisis in the Punjab region of India and the possibility of collective assembly and study in relation to the farmer's protests. Varma's notion of the border is informed by socialities engaged in ecological, epistemic, and anti-colonial struggles.

To explore collaborative modes of researching and writing, the Border Ecology Network—a self-organised collective of researchers, artists, activists, and other practitioners—have developed a sui generis glossary in which each entry, rather than providing a univocal definition, explores a specific lens by which to understand the conjuncture of ecology and politics. In this way, the collective contribution is an attempt to highlight lines of inquiry, semantic continuities, and provocations for further research.

Nadine El-Enany's essay brings together the law, race, and the atmosphere to understand the environment as a medium for the propagation of complex causal forces and long histories of exclusion. Her essay examines how the health of racialised communities is disproportionately impacted by environmental harm and examines the possibilities for justice available through and beyond the law. El-Enany explores the manifestations of environmental violence, specifically air pollution, that would not usually be understood through the prism of race. With this, she articulates the limits of legal frameworks as a recourse to accountability when making claims at the intersection of racial justice and environmental justice, and points to alternative possibilities.

Far from exhausting the issues addressed therein, this book begins to map a growing field of diverse but converging interests, while at the same time pointing to future potential pathways of research and practice. It aims to be a contribution to emerging lines of struggle that have highlighted the intersectionality of environmental and mobility justice, insisting "on the inseparability between environmental matters of concern and socio-political and economic frameworks of injustice".[23] As many of the works gathered here reveal, borders enact differential conditions of inclusion and exclusion across human as well as more-than-human entities, generating intensities of violence and cruelty against all those classified as alien, be they people, plants or entire ecologies. Therefore, the aim is to join the collective attempt to locate these multiple lines of intersection and articulate languages and practices that might be able to counter their violence. From calls to develop "a robust political language defending the right of people to migrate in anticipation of climate change",[24] to the assertion of a "right to the world" that might be able to combine a right to mobility with that to a just share of the Earth's resources,[25] there have been many attempts in this direction. While we cannot certainly claim that our intervention will be any more successful, we hope it will contribute to the growing awareness that if the environmental and migration crises are entangled, their solution must be too.

23 T.J. Demos, "Ecology-As-Intrasectionality," *Panorama: Journal of the Association of Historians of American Art* 5, no. 1 (Spring 2019).
24 Geoff Mann and Joel Wainwright, *Climate Leviathan: A Political Theory of Our Planetary Future* (London ; New York: Verso Books, 2018).
25 Joseph Nevins, "The Right to the World," *Antipode* 49, no. 5 (2017): 1349–67.

Works cited

Araghi, Farshad. "Accumulation by Displacement: Global Enclosures, Food Crisis, and the Ecological Contradictions of Capitalism." *Review (Fernand Braudel Center)* 32, no. 1 (2009): 113-146.

Armiero. Marco and Richard Tucker, eds. *Environmental History of Modern Migrations*. London ; New York, NY: Routledge, 2017.

Autorino, Pietro. "'No Exponga Su Vida a Los Elementos': the Political Ecology of the US-Mexico Border in the Sonoran Desert." University of Heidelberg, 2017.

Bettini, Giovanni. "Climate Barbarians at the Gate? A Critique of Apocalyptic Narraitves on "Climate Refugees"", Geoforum 45, no.4 (March 2013): 63-72.

Boyce, Geoffrey Alan. "The Rugged Border: Surveillance, Policing and the Dynamic Materiality of the US/Mexico Frontier." *Environment and Planning D: Society and Space* 34, no. 2 (April 2016): 245-262.

Boyce, Geoffrey Alan, Samuel N. Chambers, and Sarah Launius. "Bodily Inertia and the Weaponization of the Sonoran Desert in U.S. Boundary Enforcement: A GIS Modeling of Migration Routes through Arizona's Altar Valley." *Journal on Migration and Human Security* 7, no. 1 (March 2019) :23-35.

Clark, Nigel. "Strangers on a Strange Planet: On Hospitality and Holocene Climate Change." In *Life Adrift: Climate Change, Migration, Critique*, ed. Andrew Baldwin and Giovanni Bettini. London ; New York: Rowman & Littlefield International, 2017.

Danowski, Deborah and Eduardo Viveiros de Castro. *The Ends of the World.* Malden, Massachaussetts: Polity Press, 2016.

De Leon, Jason. *The Land of Open Graves: Living and Dying on the Migrant Trail.* Oakland, California: University of California Press, 2015.

Demos, T.J. "Ecology-As-Intrasectionality." *Panorama: Journal of the Association of Historians of American Art* 5, no. 1 (Spring 2019).

Depledge, Duncan. "Geopolitical Material: Assemblages of Geopower and the Constitution of the Geopolitical Stage." *Political Geography* 45, no. 2 (March 2015): 91-92.

Doty, Roxanne Lynn. "Bare Life: Border-Crossing Deaths and Spaces of Moral Alibi." *Environment and Planning D: Society and Space* 29, no.4 (2011).

Ellis, Darren, Ian Tucker, and David Harper. "The Affective Atmospheres of Surveillance." *Theory and Psychology* 23, no. 6 (December 2013): 716-731.

Ferrari, Marco, Elisa Pasqual and Andrea Bagnato. *A Moving Border: Alpine Cartographies of Climate Change.* New York: Columbia Books on Architecture and the City, 2019.

Lerner, Steve. *Sacrifice Zones: The Front Lines of Toxic Chemical Exposure in the United States.* Cambridge: MIT Press, 2010.

Levidis, Stefanos. "Border Natures. The Environment as Weapon at the Edges of Greece." PhD diss. Goldsmiths, University of London, 2021.

Mann, Geoff and Joel Wainwright. *Climate Leviathan: A Political Theory of Our Planetary Future.* London; New York: Verso Books, 2018.

Morrissey, James. "Environmental Change and Forced Migration: A State of the Art Review." Refugee Studies Centre, University of Oxford, January 2009.

Nevins, Joseph. *Dying to Live: A Story of U.S. Immigration in an Age of Global Apartheid.* City Lights Books, 2008.

Nevins, Joseph. "The Right to the World." *Antipode* 49, no.5 (2017): 1349-1367.

Nixon, Rob. *Slow Violence and the Environmentalism of the Poor.* Cambridge, MA: Harvard University Press, 2011.

Pezzani, Lorenzo. "Hostile Environments." *E-Flux Architecture*, 15 May 2020, https://www.e-flux.com/architecture/at-the-border/325761/hostile-environments/.

Plath, Tara. "An Elusive Viewshed: An Investigation of United States' Border Patrol Rescue Beacons in Arizona's Western Desert." *PLOT(S)*, Volume VII (2020).

Sahlins, Peter. "Natural Frontiers Revisited: France's Boundaries since the Seventeenth Century." *American Historical Review* 95, no. 5 (December 1990): 1423-1451.

Sarkar, Bhaskar. "On No Man's (Is)Land: Futurities at the Border." *Transnational Cinemas 9*, no. 1 (January 2018): 47-67.

Steinberg, Philip and Kimberley Peters. "Wet Ontologies, Fluid Spaces: Giving Depth to Volume through Oceanic Thinking," *Environment and Planning D: Society and Space* 33, no. 2 (April 2015): 247-264.

Sundberg, Juanita. "Animating United States-Mexico Border Studies", *Public Political Ecology Lab* (blog), 14 May 2014, http://ppel.arizona.edu/?p=633.

Sundberg, Juanita. "Diabolic Caminos in the Desert and Cat Fights on the Río: A Posthumanist Political Ecology of Boundary Enforcement in the United States–Mexico Borderlands." *Annals of the Association of American Geographers* 101, no. 2 (March 2011): 318-36.

Sharpe, Christina Elizabeth. *In the Wake: On Blackness and Being.* Durham: Duke University Press, 2016.

Walters, William, Charles Heller, and Lorenzo Pezzani, eds. *Viapolitics. Borders, Migration, and the Power of Locomotion.* Durham, North Carolina: Duke University Press, 2021.

Williams, Jill M. "From Humanitarian Exceptionalism to Contingent Care: Care and Enforcement at the Humanitarian Border." *Political Geography* 47 (July 2015): 11-20.

CASE STUDIES

Sharp Rocks, Dark Waves

Stefanos Levidis

"They Were Towing Us" Farmakonisi, 37°19'35.85"N, 27° 7'33.60"E

About two hours after leaving Turkey, we arrived within 80-100 metres from the island. We were so close we could hear the waves break against the rocks. Then, the engine stopped. It was then that the [Greek] Coast Guard vessel approached us. They shone a searchlight towards us and gestured to us to go back. We tried to explain, waving, that the engine is broken. We held our babies up in the air to show we were in need of help. The Coast Guard fired 4-5 warning shots to scare us off. Their vessel then circled us once, creating big waves, and then moved with great speed, first parallel and then diagonally to our bow, causing our vessels to collide.

What Bariali K. is describing here is an operation of "aggressive deterrence". The term (επιθετική αποτροπή in Greek) is colloquially used by the Greek Coast Guard to describe the process whereby their patrol speed boats manoeuvre dangerously close to the smaller, migrant vessels, with the purpose of creating waves that will act as a deterrent 'wall'. Faced with the risk of sinking, asylum seekers are eventually forced to turn back towards Turkey, without the Coast Guard ever having touched their vessel. This is an effective, if extremely dangerous, patrol technique that permits the Coast Guard to deny responsibility in the case of an accident; if something goes wrong, the waves are to blame. The boat Kadiri was on, however, with its broken engine, could not turn back.

The two vessels came side by side, with the Coast Guard's engine facing our bow. Two people disembarked on our boat, pointing their guns at us. They ordered us to move away from them, towards the stern. They then tied a rope to our bow, and started towing us with speed towards the Turkish coast, and away from the Greek island that was just in front of us. This lasted for about 15 minutes.[1]

What started as "aggressive deterrence" quickly escalated in a pushback operation, or, as is the case here, a "tow-back". Another survivor, Ahmadi M. continues:
The two coast guards stayed on our boat and kept pointing their guns at us. We were going so fast, our bow was almost in the air, and the waves caused by the Coast Guard started hitting our vessel, which was taking in water from the sides and from the stern. In the end, the bow broke off, from the force of the towing.[2]

Then, according to witness testimonies, the Coast Guard vessel approached the migrants' small wooden vessel again—a 9 metre long Turkish fishing

1 Maritime Court of Piraeus, "Testimony of Bariali K. to Military Judge B," January 30, 2014. Translated from Greek by the author.

2 Maritime Court of Piraeus, "Testimony of Ahmadi M. to Military Judge B," January 30, 2014. Translated from Greek by the author.

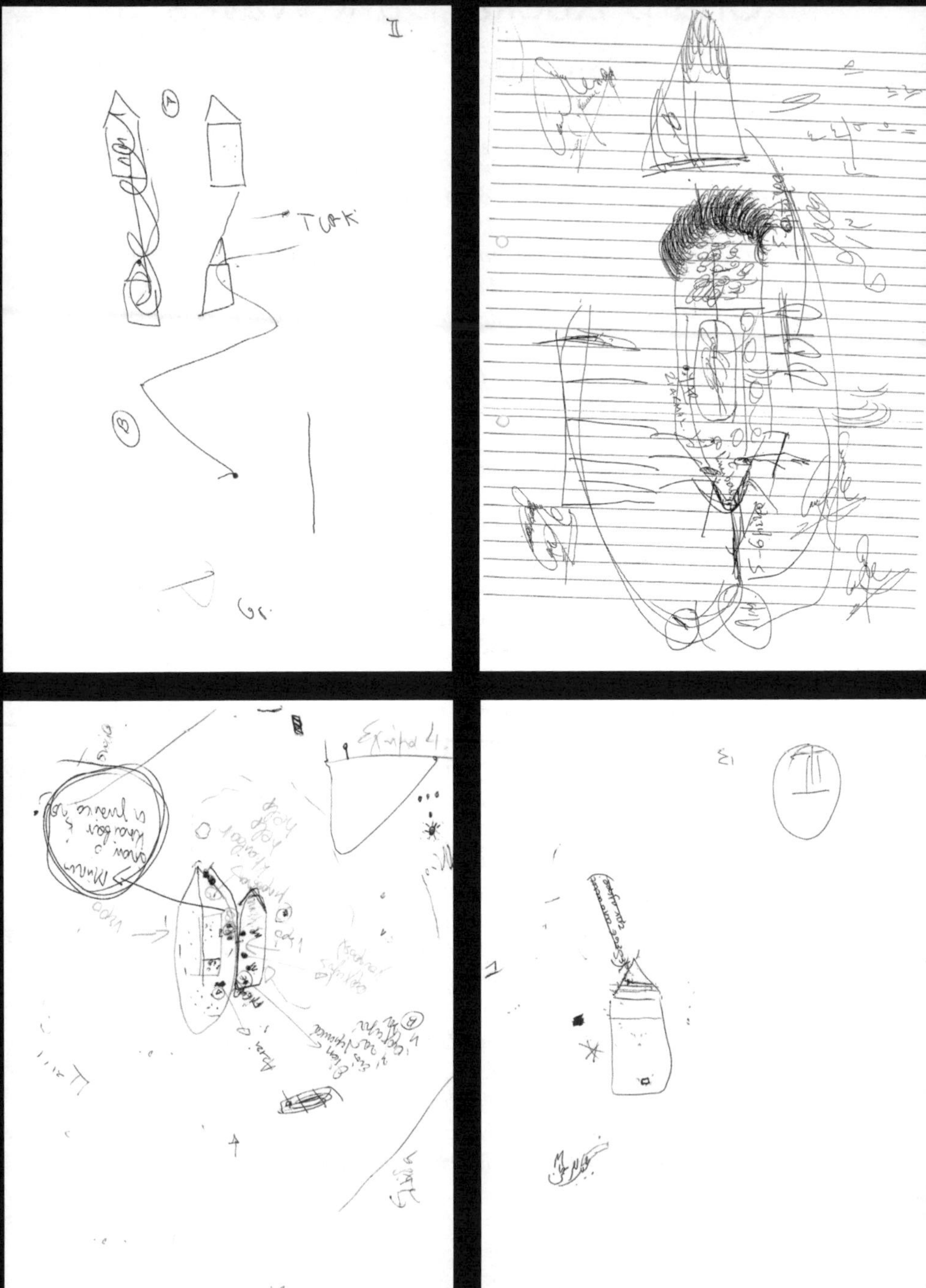

Sketches of the towing process made by survivors during interviews with their lawyers, January 2014.
Source: Farmakonisi case file.

boat called the *Göznuru*—and cut the rope. The *Göznuru* capsized and sank instantly, at 02:17, in the dark waters off the coast of Farmakonisi island, about 500 metres inside the Greek territorial waters, in the Dodecanese archipelago.

Once overboard, the migrants—Afghan and Syrian nationals—were treated with extreme violence; the coast guard crew reportedly kicked those who tried to climb onto their vessel back to sea and repeatedly told them to "fuck off" and "die".[3] Eventually, 14 people made it onto the Coast Guard vessel—the 24 metre long combat boat ΠΛΣ-*136*—before the rope that was used for the towing, loose in the sea, got pulled in by the jet and caused the left engine to overheat and catch fire. It was then that the captain left the scene, abandoning the rest of the migrants to drown. Eleven bodies were eventually retrieved from the sea of Farmakonisi; three women and eight children.[4]

"This Day, You Have to Forget it"
Agathonisi, 37°25'54.91"N, 27° 4'37.03"E

I tried to speak about this day, they say "this day, you have to forget it". They say "you called us today, not Friday". They were fighting between each other. They shout to each other. You can understand they were saying to each other, "why didn't you help?" You could tell they have a problem. We were saying to them "it was Friday", they were saying "no, it was Saturday".[5]

The "they" that Quassim is referring to is to the Greek Coast Guard on the small island of Agathonisi, also in the Greek Dodecanese. Quassim is one of the three survivors from a shipwreck that occurred in the early hours of Friday 16 March, 2018, in the waters south east of Agathonisi, and only 6 nautical miles north of the sinking location of the *Göznuru*.

The small fiberglass vessel left the Turkish coast near the port village of Mavisehir, setting its course to the Greek border. On board were 22 people: a family from Iraq, sitting at the bow, another family from Afghanistan, at the stern, and two Turkish smugglers. They were told the crossing to the island would take 10 minutes, without knowing exactly which island they were headed to. The sea was calm: winds in the Aegean usually subside at night, and pick up again in the morning. About an hour after they had left the Turkish shore, and some 1.5 nautical miles inside the Greek territorial waters, the boat engine stopped. The vessel started taking in water. The passengers panicked, one of the smugglers fell in the sea, and at around 06:45, the boat capsized.

Darab, a relative of the Afghan family who was following the vessel's location live on WhatsApp from his tent in the camp of Samos got in touch

3 IBID.

4 Death in Farmakonisi was extremely gendered. This is owing to the fact that, according to survivors' testimony, women and children were stowed in the hull, while men were on the deck. When the vessel capsized, the door to the deck was blocked and most women and children got trapped in the hull. In the central Mediterranean, a similar typology is seen to function through race. More affluent refugees from the Arab countries pay a higher fare to travel on the deck, while sub-Saharan Africans travel in the hull.

5 Author's interview with Quassim, a man from Iraq.

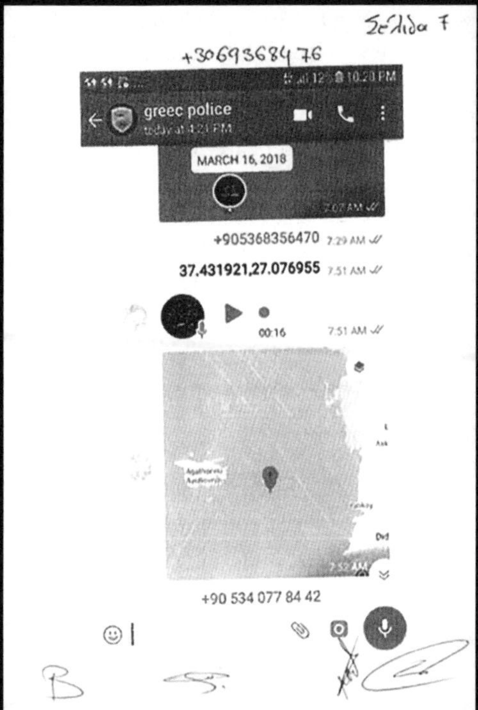

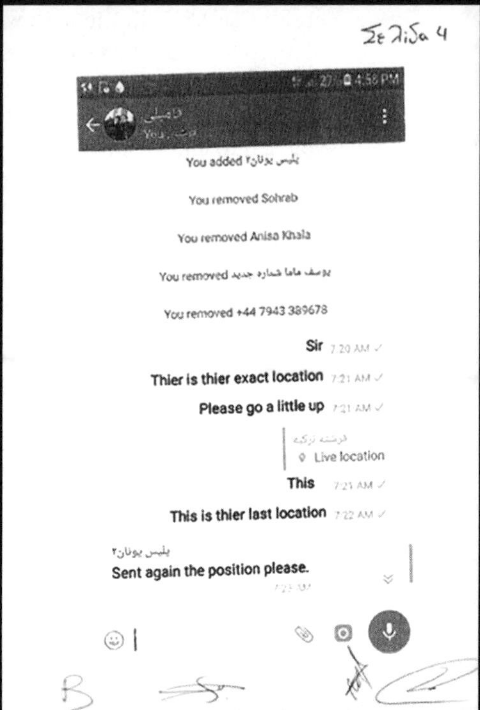

Messages sent by Darab to the Greek Maritime Rescue Coordination Centre reflect the geographical confusion which is the result of a combination between the authorities' unwillingness to rescue, and the complex and contested geography of the archipelago. Source: Agathonisi case file.

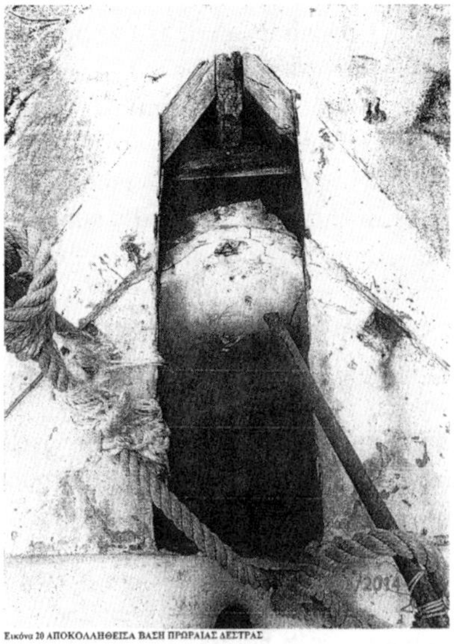

Εικόνα 20 ΑΠΟΚΟΛΛΗΘΕΙΣΑ ΒΑΣΗ ΠΡΩΡΑΙΑΣ ΔΕΣΤΡΑΣ

Εικόνα 21 ΚΟΡΑΚΙ ΠΛΩΡΗΣ

The broken bow of the Göznuru shows evidence of the violence of the towing. Forensic examination by naval architects and engineers, 7 February 2014. Source: Farmakonisi case file.

with the Greek authorities, to little avail. It was later revealed that three patrol vessels were deployed to the region, but these conducted a brief, and patchy, search operation. A full-scale operation was launched only after a local fisherman found bodies washing ashore the following morning, on 17 March. By that time, nineteen of the twenty-two passengers had died, and three survivors had made it to the shore on their own. One of the three survivors, Fahima, lost her four children in the shipwreck. Quassim lost his wife, his year-old daughter and his 6-year-old son.

Contrary to the shipwreck of Farmakonisi, where the Coast Guard violently towed the *Göznuru* into sinking, the sea in Agathonisi was weaponised in a more indirect and insidious way, after the boat's sinking, in the form of a deadly drift. As Fahima described in her testimony before the prosecutor,

We tried to stay close to each other but the pressure of the water caused us to drift apart. When the dawn broke I saw 4-5 life vests floating on the sea, without bodies. I didn't know how to swim, I just stayed afloat. Every one hour, I saw someone let go and disappear in the water. When the sun was high above our heads I realised that no-one from my family was alive.[6]

During their recollection of the events, the survivors used the position of the sun to situate events in time. In their perceptual frame, distorted by the forces of the sea but contained by the rhythmic movement of the sun, this deadly drift lasted for twelve hours, from sunrise to sundown. After they made it to the shore, they spent another twelve hours unassisted, from sundown to sunrise. This duration, from sunrise, to sundown, to sunrise again, is erased in official records: to cover for their insufficient response, the Greek authorities to this day deny the shipwreck occurred on Friday the 16th, and officially register it as having occurred the next day, Saturday the 17th. In many other maritime regions, such a denial might be more believable. But this excuse is not plausible in the dense, militarised, and thickly surveyed geography of the south-east Aegean. On the contrary, all three survivors to this day insist that a grey military vessel wearing a Greek flag approached them approximately one hour after they shipwrecked and stayed at a distance for hours, without offering assistance.[7]

The two shipwrecks, located six nautical miles and four years apart, bookend what came to be called the "refugee crisis", and, however similar their outcome, they demonstrate a shift in the ever-volatile migration management policies in the region. With push-back operations no longer occurring in the Aegean at the time,[8] and within the context of a society that had grown accustomed to the sight of death at sea after years of consecutive and inter-

6 Maritime Court of Piraeus, "Testimony of Fahima M., with translator," July 18, 2018. Translated from Greek by the author.

7 They did not know if the vessel had seen them or not, but they made several attempts to approach it and attract the crew's attention.

8 At the time of writing, this pattern has now changed once more, with pushbacks, or "drift-backs" – whereby asylum seekers are being loaded onto engineless life rafts by the Greek Coast Guard and cast adrift to Turkey – now a daily occurrence in the Aegean. This new practice is, for lack of space, not addressed further in this text but is the focus of an ongoing investigation by Forensic Architecture, accessible at aegean.forensic-architecture.org.

Quassim and Fahima both identified the same vessel, the British-built Vosper Thornycroft Open Sea Patrol Vessel "ΠΛΣ-50 Arkioi" as the vessel who approached them and did not offer assistance. To this day, the presence of this vessel in the vicinity of the shipwreck is unconfirmed. Source: Still from filmed interview conducted by the author.

The passengers onboard the vessel that sank outside Agathonisi recorded a video upon departure, stating the date and place, anticipating its evidentiary value. They were instructed to do so by people who had crossed before them. Source: Still from filmed interview conducted by the author.

secting "crises",[9] the more recent Agathonisi case demonstrates that non-assistance, as sanctioned by the 'deepstate' of the Greek navy and coast guard, emerged as the closest alternative. This suggests a shift from the more direct violence of the towing in Farmakonisi to "a form of violence that is exercised less by effecting a destructive force onto a given actor, than by creating the conditions in which the sea becomes a liquid trap and refraining to help those who are caught in it".[10]

Crucially, the two shipwrecks are among the most prominent incidents for which legal cases have been opened in the European Court of Human Rights against the Greek Coast Guard.[11] Having studied the court files for both cases thoroughly, conducted fieldwork, spatial analysis and interviews with the survivors,[12] and with permission from the lawyers to digitise and use the material in my research, I decided to attempt a close reading of the documents. I focus specifically on how questions of 'natural' violence appear in the files bestowing the Aegean archipelago with deadly agency, and how these are more often than not deflected onto, and summarily absorbed by, the body of the sea.

"Sharp like Razors"

During our interviews, Quassim and Fahima both described the rocky shores where they beached as "sharp like razors", difficult to hold onto and even harder to walk on. Sculpted by the sea, the Aegean rocks can certainly be hostile when walked on without the necessary equipment. However, more than the waves that

9 Here I am referring to what came to be called the "refugee crisis" in 2015-16, which saw more than a million people cross these borders into Europe, and several thousand more dying in their attempt to do so. I am also referring to the global "financial" or "debt crisis" of the late 2000s, for which Greece was one of the epicentres.

10 Lorenzo Pezzani, "Liquid Traces," in *Forensis, The Architecture of Public Truth*, ed., Forensic Architecture (Berlin: Sternberg, 2014), 671.

11 The Farmakonisi case, formally known as *Safi and others v Greece, or no.5418/15*, was submitted to the Maritime court of Piraeus by a consortium of lawyers representing the survivors in January 2014, and was dismissed by the prosecutor two months later. It was submitted again for litigation, this time at the ECHR where, in July 2022, more than eight years after the incident, Greece was found in violation of articles 2 (right to life) and 3 (prohibition of inhuman and degrading treatment) of the European Convention on Human Rights. In similar fashion, the Agathonisi case was also quickly shelved by the Greek state prosecutor, and was submitted to the European Court of Human Rights where, at the time of writing, it is pending resolution.

12 When the Agathonisi shipwreck occurred in March 2018, I met with two of the three survivors (the third, Saymaa, a woman from Iraq, asked to be repatriated immediately after the shipwreck) and a third relative, and conducted filmed, semi-structured interviews in an attempt to reconstruct the events, identify those responsible, and further support the survivors' testimony in court–the same court that had examined and dismissed the case of Farmakonisi four years earlier. In early May 2018, I travelled to Agathonisi, and the neighbouring, larger islands of Samos and Leros from where the criminally negligent rescue operation had been launched. I trekked all over the island to understand the terrain, documented military infrastructures that could have been used to spot and assist the shipwrecked people at sea, and looked for identifiable features in the survivors' testimonies, to "ground truth" them so as to prevent them from being discarded again as untrustworthy. I produced an investigative report attempting a spatio-temporal reconstruction of the shipwreck and the subsequent drift of migrants at sea which was submitted as evidence to the Maritime court of Piraeus and the ECHR. The testimony, maps, and photos presented here are part of the report.

break against them, it is these rocks' engulfment in territorial disputes[13] and histories of extraterritorial state violence and exile[14] that sharpens them into razors, dictating the way they are patrolled and managed against migrants today.

At their nearest - the 800-metre wide Mycale Strait between Samos island and the Turkish Dilek peninsula - the two countries' shores come so close that border crossers who wanted to avoid smugglers have successfully attempted to swim it, while Greek Coast Guards have been known to push people back to Turkey by throwing them overboard at the border line and forcing them to swim ashore. This narrow sub-archipelago of the Aegean sea, known as 'the Sea of Samos', stretching south of Samos surrounding both Farmakonisi and Agathonisi, along with a multitude of other smaller contested rocks and islets, is today largely restricted to civilian navigation, criss-crossed by Coast Guard patrols, and dotted with military installations. Any incident that occurs there—including migrant crossings and drownings—is considered a matter of "national security" for both littoral states, a deep mantle of secrecy cloaking these waters.[15]

In this dense and contested maritime space, attempts to place vessels and, indeed, blame for human rights violations often hinge on cartographic resolution. Such is the indeterminacy of these waters that the precise position of the border line itself is often subject to cartographic imprecisions, and therefore elusive to GPS navigation devices and the various online map platforms routinely used by migrants crossing it. This is confirmed by Darab, the relative of the Afghan family who was tracking the trajectory of the vessel from the Turkish coast to Agathonisi on Google Maps:

DARAB *When I saw this point here (points to map), I thought that they passed [the border]. Because I was just imagining with myself, I didn't know how much water was in the Turkish side and how much in the Greek side.*

ME *You didn't have a line [on your map]...*

DARAB *No, there was no line.*[16]

13 In what has come to be called 'the Aegean Dispute' between Greece and Turkey, the two littoral countries have been in disagreement over the precise course of the border line, the right to extend their territorial waters or station troops in their islands and shores, the sovereignty of numerous rocks and islets in the archipelago, as well as the precise limits of their overlapping contiguous, EEZ, SAR and FIR zones. As a result, sections of the maritime border remain de facto *grey*: unresolved, militarized, and only unilaterally respected.

14 First established in Roman times, prisons in the Aegean archipelago multiplied throughout the 20th century, as the islands became the quarantine zones *par excellence* of the successive military governments that assumed power in Greece from the 1920s onwards. There, "undesirables" – Pontic Greek refugees who fled Turkey after the 1922 Greek defeat in the minor Asian campaign; partisans of the DSE in the Greek Civil War; ethnic and religious minorities, and other dissidents were exiled. These islands often also functioned as labour camps, with inmates being forced to construct their own prisons, or monuments glorifying the Greek state. Following WWII, these were the only camps in Europe "this" side of the iron curtain. The practice survived until the fall of the colonels' junta in 1974, when the last island camp closed permanently, and the inmates were transferred to the mainland. Some of these islands remain off limits to the public, with the structures built by inmates still standing as architectural testimony to this not-so-distant exiled past. Their residue haunts contemporary Greek life and politics: In Greece, the phrase "to the dry islands" still survives as the synonym of isolation and exile, while refugee camps in the Aegean point to this ghostly continuum.

15 When I called the Leros Coast Guard to ask for permission to go spearfishing in Farmakonisi, it resulted in them taking my details and aggressively advising me to "go to one of the other rocks instead". The few images that can be found online come from videos of military drills or visits paid by high ranked army and government officials.

16 Author's interview with Darab.

It is through this entanglement of geography, territory, law and history, that migrant death in the Aegean is rendered possible today, designed into the archipelago's interstitial geography itself. The very matter of the archipelago - its waves, temperatures, rocks and currents – is enlisted to perform the work of border enforcement through legal, operational and military manoeuvres. Reflecting on a spatial and visual practice through which this matter can be decoded to reveal traces of state violence, the Aegean border will reveal itself, not as a line on the water surface, but as an ecology: a *border nature*.

Archipelagic Causality

The wreck of the *Göznuru* was lifted from its resting ground at a depth of seventy-four metres in the Aegean seabed, 2.4 nautical miles north-east of Farmakonisi, on February 18 by the oceanographic vessel Φ/Γ ΘΕΤΙΣ. When the naval architects who were contracted to forensically inspect the *Göznuru* for signs of contact with the Coast Guard vessel entered its hold, they found the body of a child that was trapped there during the sinking. Seven more bodies of women and children had already been retrieved by divers from inside the same hold and another two, belonging to a woman and a child, had been found floating a few miles north of the sinking location a day after the shipwreck, by the Turkish Coast Guard. A last body, belonging to a woman, was found several days later on a southern shore of Samos island, having been carried some 20 nautical miles north by the prevailing south-eastern winds. The coroner's reports are gruesome, detailing missing flesh, fish bites and accumulations of algae. They also lack a perpetrator, with the cause of death listed as "drowning in water" or "drowning due to excessive inhalation of water".[17]

Four years later, during the preliminary investigation into the Agathonisi shipwreck, the coroner at the General Hospital of Samos was similarly asked to determine "whether the deceased had died from natural, sudden, or violent causes". Using a blue ball-point pen to fill in the few blank spaces in a standardised form, the coroner filed the deaths under category 21, titled "regarding a violent death". Below category 21, the multiple-option box 'accident' was checked.

☒ *Accident*
☐ *Suicide*
☐ *Homicide*

Under "cause", he, like the coroner who had examined the Göznuru's bodies four years prior, wrote: "drowning inside sea water".[18] The answer, confined within the pre-determined linguistic boundaries and boxed-in answers of medico-operational bureaucracy, seemed pre-determined. Upon receiving these forms, the Coast Guard in Samos wrote to the registry office

17 Death Certificates issued in the island of Leros, 22/01/2014-17/02/2014. Translated from Greek by the author.

18 Death Certificates issued in the island of Samos, 20/03/2018. Translated from Greek by the author.

The rocky shores where the survivors of the Agathonisi shipwreck beached. In the background are the Turkish shores, May 2018. Source: Photograph by the author.

Lifejackets hanging from olive trees on the eastern shores of Agathonisi, May 2018. Source: Photograph by the author.

in Agathonisi to close the case: "His/Her death seems to have been caused *by* sea water".[19] At long last, the perpetrator had been found: sea water.

Reading through these seemingly mundane documents, one can sense the palpable anxiety of state actors to conceal their responsibility for deaths at sea. Questions of violence and agency are addressed and summarily answered, in boxes, photocopied and scanned time and again by court clerks to the point where they are barely legible. Following Susan Schuppli, the papers themselves serve as "material witnesses" to the event of evidence; they are mundane analogue codifications of border violence.[20]

A few days after the Farmakonisi incident, an anchor-man of the most popular channel at the time in Greek TV commented in the evening news: "I do not accept the responsibility. It is not our fault if they take their families

19 Letter from the Greek Coast Guard to the Agathonisi registry office, 23/03/2018. Italics added by author.

20 Susan Schuppli uses the term "material witness" to describe "non-human entities and machinic ecologies that archive their complex interactions with the world producing ontological transformations and informatic dispositions that can be forensically decoded and reassembled back into a history." Susan Schuppli, *Material Witness: Media, Forensics, Evidence*, (Cambridge, Massachusetts: MIT Press: 2020), 4.

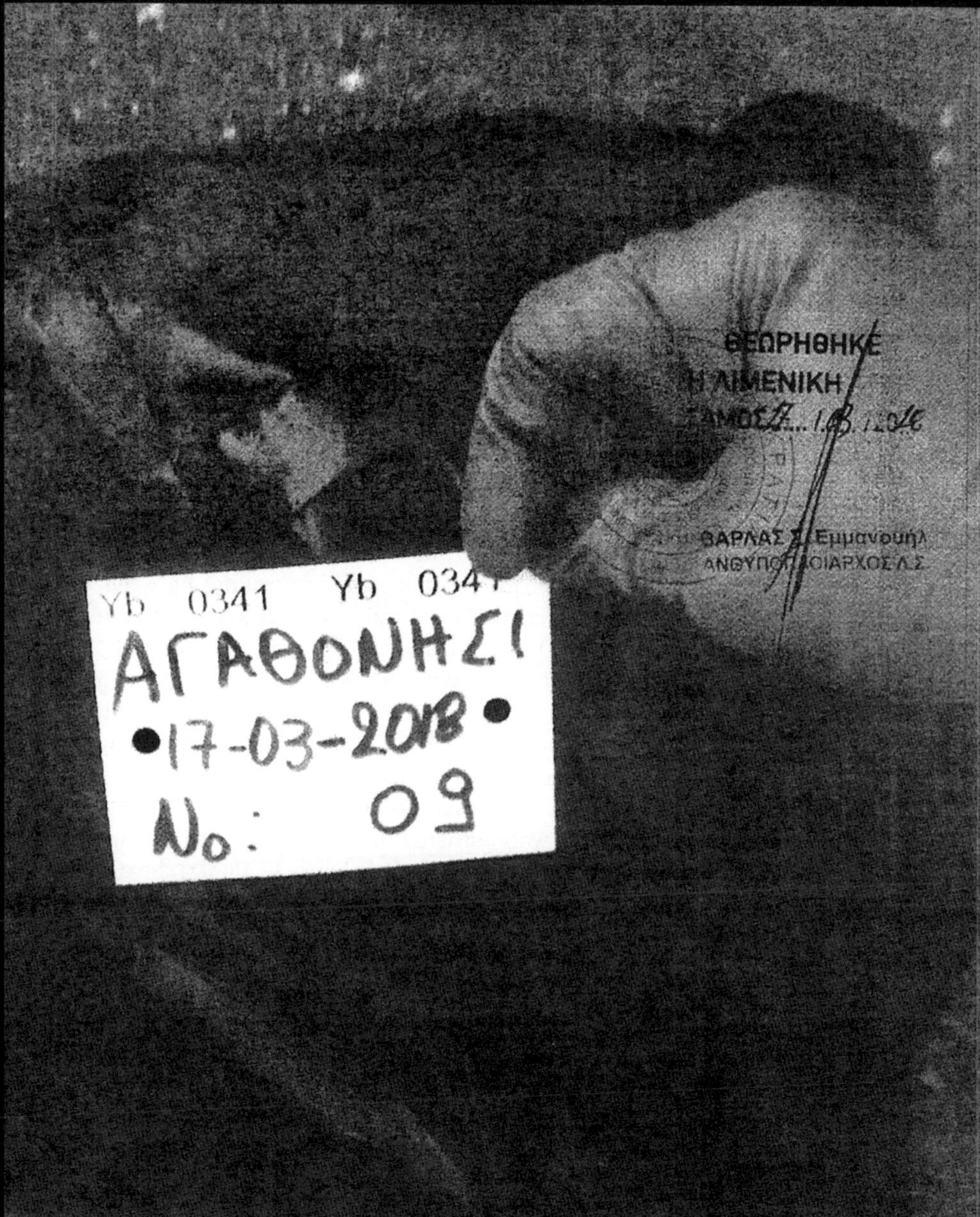

Cropped photo showing the gloved hand of a Coast Guard officer holding a tag for body No.9 from the Agathonissi shipwreck. Source: Agathonissi case file.

and try to cross the Aegean in a flimsy boat in mid-winter. Of course they will drown. I am not saying they *should* drown, but it isn't our fault".[21] Death "inside sea water", or *from* sea water is to be expected, the anchor-man shouts on the TV screen.[22] Operational and medical language here work in tandem with the cynical and xenophobic language of the media to register the saline waters of the Aegean as the victimizer of border crossers, and use it to obfuscate the actions, policies and legislations that work to weaponise it. Concealed by these reports are the ways in which sea water is actively enlisted in territorialising practices, and vested with violent agency to expand the capacities of border defence.

In the Aegean, the "pressure of the water" that Fahima described pulling the group apart in the sea off Agathonisi, carries not only bodies apart from each other but also contact further apart from trace,[23] distancing perpetrator from victim, and event from evidence. Any attempt to unpack these complex relationships of border causality and restore responsibility where this is due should stay close to the "melting" of cause and effect into each other, but also, specifically within the context of the archipelago, into the viscous body of the sea, over which these pelagic crossings (and stoppages) occur. To do that, we need to employ a mode of enquiry that is cyclical rather than lineal, rhythmic and abyssal, like the Aegean itself, rather than fixed in land, and encompassing its multiple intersections and interactions between bodies, sites, regions, legislations, territories, natural processes and situated histories and presents of exile.[24] Drawing from Eyal Weizman's concept of "field causality", an indirect, temporally distributed and "inherently spatial form of causality whose employment seeks to reconnect the multiple threads that linear juridical protocols have torn apart",[25] I will call this form of causality, both situated and mobile, and specific to the materially viscous "field" that is the Aegean archipelago, *archipelagic causality*. In what remains, I scrutinise the archipelagic forces that were enlisted to turn the sea into a weapon on the night of 21 January, 2014, and in the early hours of 16 March, 2018.

Winds, Currents, Temperatures

PROSECUTOR *Do you know how many hours you stayed in the sea?*

QUASSIM *Yes, I know that I stayed from 07:00 in the morning until just before it got dark,*

PROSECUTOR *This time of the year, the sea temperature is 16 degrees Celsius. How do you explain the fact that you survived for so many hours in the water?* [26]

21 Yannis Pretenderis on Mega Channel, 23/02/2014.

22 However questionable his motives and rhetoric, he is not far from the truth. In the Aegean Sea alone, 1964 people have drowned between 2014 and the first half of 2022, per IOM data. See *Missing Migrants*, missingmigrants.iom.int/region/mediterranean?migrant_route%5B%5D=1377,

23 Adrian Lahoud, "Floating Bodies," in *Forensis: The Architecture of Public Truth*, ed. Forensic Architecture (Berlin: Sternberg Press, 2014).

24 The Barbadian poet Kamau Brathwaite has called such an oceanic approach as *tidalectics*. Kamau Brathwaite, *The Arrivants: A New World Trilogy*, (Oxford: Oxford University Press, 1981).

25 Eyal Weizman, *Forensic Architecture*. (New York: Zone Books, 2017), 119.

26 'Testimony of Quassim S., with translator", July 17, 2018. Translated from Greek by the author.

The strategic use of the body of the sea to effect harm, and erase trails of responsibility for such harm, is evident in both court files. In the case of Agathonisi, as the above dialogue demonstrates, the main preoccupation of the state from the outset was to disprove the survivors' claim that the group could have spent twelve hours in the water, and twelve more on the island's rocky shores. In what unfolded more like an interrogation and less like the gathering of testimony, arguments to do with the material makeup and the bodily effects of the archipelago were used to frame the survivors' feat as an impossibility. Scrutinised against meteorological and cartographic data, the group's deadly drift was also used to contest the time and location of sinking. Pages upon pages of meteorological data forecasting wave heights, wind speeds and current directions were fed into a software designed for search and rescue, called SARIS,[27] to plot the possible drift trajectories of the survivors. The model determined that the coordinates given by the migrants as the location where their vessel sank were not correct, because in this case the people would have drifted north to the Turkish peninsula of Dilek instead of west, to the island.

However, both the software and the weather data that were fed into it failed to take into account the dense geography of the Aegean, and the effects of the scattered islands on the forces affecting the drift. Designed in the UK for coast guards that operate in the open ocean, the software returned trajectories of drift that cut over peninsulas and islands, continuing north-east into the Turkish mainland. Similarly, the meteorological reports covered large areas of the Aegean at a time, not accounting for the microclimatic conditions between the different islands. Pursuing accountability became, once again, a matter of resolution. With the help of a physical oceanographer, Dr. Richard Limeburner, we sourced additional meteorological data and performed our own counter-analysis, determining that the tool used by the Coast Guard to calculate the drift was inaccurate, and that the drift of the shipwrecked people to the eastern shores of Agathonisi was possible, occurring at a speed of 0.32 knots (0.16 metres per second).

More than just the drift trajectory, the three survivors' very ability to survive for twelve hours in the cold sea, and another twelve hours soaking wet on the shore was presented to them as evidence against their claims. The wetness of their clothes was perused, and deemed excessive for people who alleged to have spent twelve hours ashore. The *weathering* of the bodies that had drowned in the cold water was also used as evidence against the claims of the three survivors. The legal question became one of bodily thresholds vis-à-vis the forces of the sea.

Conjuring and assessing different types of expertise, the prosecutor concluded that the shipwreck had happened twenty-four hours later than when the survivors claimed, and that the people had drowned and drifted ashore a mere couple of hours after that[28]. The only experience that was not heeded was that of the people that experienced this deadly drift. Both survivors I spoke to

27 The "Search and Rescue Information systems" (SARIS) v2.0x. SARIS is a search planning tool designed for coastguards to plot search areas and target trajectories at sea according to oceanographic and meteorological data.

28 This conclusion was also inconsistent with the coroner's report who calculated that time to 8-10 hours.

remembered the cold vividly. They both separately recounted how, after hours of holding on to an inflatable ring, waiting for the currents to take them to the shore, their limbs went numb. Darab, who was in the island of Samos, told me that, as the hours passed, he was getting increasingly worried that his family would not survive in the cold water, and decided to go into the sea to feel the temperature for himself,
In the evening, once I got to Samos beach, I wanted to check how cold it is. So I go into the water, I put my head three times in the water, I realised it is very cold.

When I visited the island a month and a half later, in early May, also went into the sea. The waters were still freezing, causing pins and needles across my limbs.

Waves

In the Farmakonisi case file, the threshold shifts away from interrogations of bodily endurance to more straightforward questions of agency. Did the 1.5 metre high waves of the Aegean Sea sink the small vessel, as the coast guard claimed? Was death in the rough, 7-beaufort winter seas off Farmakonisi "to be expected"? Or were the waves released by the 24 metre long coast guard vessel's 1400 hp hydro-jet engines in full throttle to blame for the sinking, as the survivors claimed? With sovereign violence here mediated by the forces of the sea, were these engineered waves products of nature, or of culture? Can the two be distinguished in the context of the Aegean *border nature*?

Aegean waves are claimed and measured separately by both littoral countries.[29] As studies suggest, the shading effect of the Turkish coast and the Dodecanese island chain means that waves along the south-east Aegean border are smaller and less powerful than those that occur in the central and southern Greek Aegean.[30] These border waves are therefore less like mountain ridges and more like a rugged terrain of hills, depressions and ravines, forming not so much an unsurpassable sea wall, as an attritional, slow, and repetitive defensive architecture that, activated within littoral disputes and border patrol operations, can turn this liquid topography into a killing field.

Such an ability to quantify and calculate waves as liquid topographies has long been central to military projects. Through technologies like Argo floats, remote-sensing satellites, wave buoys, and ship sensors,[31] and despite

29 During the period of 1994-2000, Turkey carried out a NATO-funded project, called NATO TU-WAVES project, with the purpose of establishing "a reliable wave atlas" of the Turkish coast. On the Greek side, the Hellenic Centre for Marine Research also uses a combination of buoys, Argo floats, ferry box data and satellite imagery to "record the physical, biological and chemical parameters of the Greek seas." www.medcoast.net/modul/index/menu/NATO-TU-WAVES/91 and http://poseidon.hcmr.gr.

30 Maximum wave heights, above a mean height of 0.96 metres and a mean power of 5.2 kW/m, have been found to occur more frequently in the central Aegean, between the islands of Ikaria and Mykonos, some 50 nautical miles west of the location of the two shipwrecks, as well as at its the southern edge, between the islands of Karpathos, Kasos and Crete. Navid Jadidoleslam et al., "Wave power potential assessment of Aegean Sea with an integrated 15-year data," *Renewable Energy* 86 (February 2016): 1056.

31 Jennifer Gabrys, "Ocean Sensing and Navigating the End of this World," *e-flux*, June 2019, www.e-flux.com/journal/101/272633/ocean-sensing-and-navigating-the-end-of-this-world/.

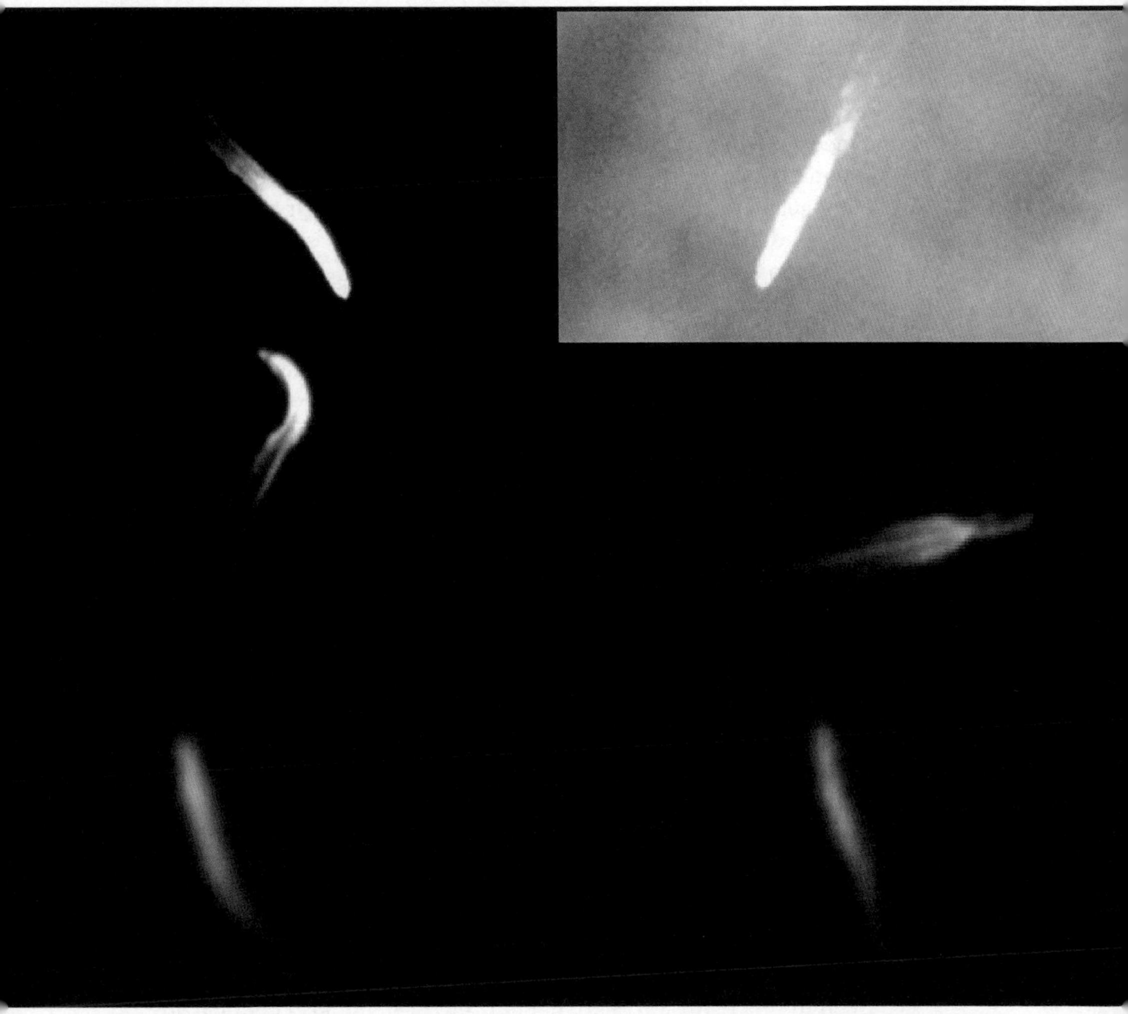

Wakes of coastguard Vessels on the sea around Agathonisi island, 16-17 March 2018. Source: Planet Labs.

their temporal and physical volatility, waves are treated by scientists and military geographers as physical objects and as architectures in their own right. They are indexed vertically, in strata, from crest to trough, and measured for their "significant wave height" (the vertical distance between crest and trough), "wave length" (the distance between successive peaks or depressions), velocity and "wave period" (the average time it takes for two consecutive wave crests to pass through a fixed point).[32] A separate vocabulary exists to describe their deformations: "swelling", "wave breaking", "white-capping", "bottom friction", "refraction" and "shoaling" are a few of the terms used. As the military geographer John Collins notes, "waves and winds not only make ships surge, sway, heave, roll, pitch, and yaw in heavy seas, but introduce

32 Copernicus, "Ocean surface Waves Indicators for the European Coast for 1977 to 2100 Derived from Climate Projections," cds.climate.copernicus.eu/cdsapp#!/dataset/sis-ocean-wave-indicators?tab=overview'.

great structural stress".[33] Such was the structural stress that caused the bow of the *Göznuru* to break during the towing, and the vessel to capsize. One can only presume that the well-trained coast guard crew were aware of the effects their manoeuvres had on the *Göznuru*.

No matter their provenance, waves in the historically loaded and thickly patrolled Aegean are always some kind of *natureculture*.[34] Or better yet, to use the term coined by the American anthropologist of science Stefan Helmreich to describe "those processes commonly understood to be organic, biological, meteorological, geological, and oceanic that [are] tailored to social projects and endeavours", waves here become a kind of *infranature*.[35] Helmreich indeed describes waves as objects that have long been mutated by human activities. They belong to "an oceanic infrastructure for travel, commerce, or energy exchange"[36] while also functioning as markers of anthropogenic climate change on a planetary scale. In encounters like the one between ΠΛΣ-136 and the Göznuru, waves are merely "sculpted into further infrastructural form".[37] Moulded by the coast-guard, they assume the role of *"architectural materials*, physical processes folded into systems of communication and control",[38] in this case tasked with regulating mobility along the external borders of the EU.

The name of the operation that patrols the Aegean waters leaves little room for doubt. Named after the ancient Greek god of the sea, jointly run by the Greek Coast Guard and assets and personnel deployed from other EU-member as their contribution to FRONTEX,[39] Operation *Poseidon Sea* points to a force that is not simply assembled to patrol and operate on the surface of the sea, but like Poseidon himself, aspires to harness the very matter of the archipelago towards a hybrid project of border defence. This ability to shapeshift between elements and scales, to mutate from culture to nature and back, has now become a key component of mechanisms of border defence at the world's frontiers. As such, operational capacities under *Poseidon* are equally calculated in military assets as they are in winds, currents, temperatures and waves.[40]

Seen in this light, waves are not only physical, but also political objects. If they are understood in their full complexity, "as forces, as vectors, as assemblages of molecules and meanings, as spaces of periodicity, randomness,

33 John M Collins, Military Geography For Professionals and the Public (Washington, D.C.: National Defense University Press, 1998), 60.

34 The term is borrowed from Donna Harraway, who has argued for a disaffiliation from human/non-human manichaeist divisions, and has instead proposed forms of kinship that construct an "artifactual nature", or "natureculture".

35 Stefan Helmreich, "How to Hide an Island," in *New Geographies 8: Island*, eds., Daniel Daou and Pablo Pérez-Ramos, (Cambridge, Massachaussetts : Harvard Graduate School of Design, 2017): 86.

36 Stefan Helmreich, "Waves. An anthropology of scientific things," transcript of the Lewis Henry Morgan Lecture given on, *Hau: Journal of Ethnographic theory* 4 no.3, (October 2014): 265–284.

37 Helmreich, "How to Hide an Island," 84.

38 IBID.

39 FRONTEX, short for frontières extérieures, is the European border and coast guard agency.

40 Critical geographers and authorities in the field of "landscape infrastructures" Pierre Bélanger and Alexander Arroyo make a similar argument of the U.S. Department of Defence in their book *Ecologies of Power,* noting how "it is this cross-scalar capacity and trans-media fluency that distinguishes its multi dimensionality and mutability from any other forms, forces or fields of operations in the world." *Bélanger, Arroyo, Ecologies of Power,* 18.

instability and transformation, and as volumes (depths) and areas (surfaces)—then waves, and the wet ontology they exemplify, may be exceptionally well suited for understanding the politics of our watery planet", as the geographers Philip Steinberg and Kimberley Peters argue.[41] Rearranging the liquid matter of the Aegean, giving it depth, shape, and form, waves here present themselves as unexpected analytical devices; as evidence.

Wakes

On 16 March 2018, between 10:21:02 and 10:40:29 am local time, two small satellites belonging to Planet Labs's fleet of "doves"[42] flew over Agathonisi, and snapped a series of pictures of the island and the sea around it. One of these pictures, taken at 10:22:17, about four hours after the shipwreck, captured three vessels; two of them circling the island and one moving parallel to the border, inside Turkish territorial waters. At a resolution of 3 metres per pixel, the 10 to 20metrelong vessels are hardly visible in the photographs, occupying all but three or four pixels. Instead, it is their movement that registers in the photograph, visible by the waves created by the vessels' disturbance of the water surface.

In fluid dynamics, these waves are called wakes. Like a wave, a wake has its own architecture. It consists of a characteristic wave pattern in the form of a V-shaped region behind the ship, known as the "Kelvin wake",[43] and a "turbulent wake" along the track of the ship. Around and directly behind the ship (what is known as the "local wave disturbance region"), the wake is a complex combination of bow and stern waves, eddies, currents, and foam. At the outer edges of this wedge (called the "cusp line" or "Kelvin arm"), the waves are often highest. From about 3 ship lengths behind the ship (known as the "free wave pattern region"), the Kelvin wake consists of two kinds of waves: "transverse waves" (crests across the ship's track) and "divergent waves" (crests roughly parallel to the ship's track, moving outward). Underneath the water surface, a wake is comprised of an equally complex stratification of internal waves and vortices.[44]

When seen from the point of view of a satellite, this wake architecture becomes an index that allows us to reverse engineer the characteristics of the machine or body that generated it. The shape and opening angle of the wake, for example, may betray the vessel speed and hull shape.[45] Imaged through aerial photography, wakes offer themselves for purposes of maritime surveil-

41 Philip Steinberg and Kimberley Peters, "Wet Ontologies, Fluid Spaces: Giving Depth to Volume through Oceanic Thinking," Environment and Planning D: Society and Space 33, no. 2 (April 2015): 261.

42 Planet Labs is a private earth imaging company. They deploy small satellites which they call "doves".

43 These are named after the British Physicist Lord Kelvin who first explained the physics of ship wakes in 1887.

44 Christian Melsheimer, "Ship Wakes Observed with ERS and SPOT, Centre for Remote Imaging, Sensing and Processing," 2001, crisp.nus.edu.sg/~research/shipwakes/shipwakes.htm (accessed April 2020), and Trond Helge Torsvik et al, "Identification of ship wake structures by a time–frequency method," *Journal of Fluid Mechanics*, 765 (February 2015).

45 Björn Tings et al, "Extension of Ship Wake Detectability Model for Non-Linear Influences of Parameters Using Satellite Based X-Band Synthetic Aperture Radar," *Remote Sens.* 2019, 11 no. 5, (March 2019): 563.

lance, as diverse as military planning, the control of fisheries, or, as is the case here, human rights investigations. When examining cases of shipwrecks in the Aegean, where the precise trajectories, or the very presence of coast guard vessels at sea, are often undisclosed by authorities, wakes can become a ripple on the sea surface through which we can disturb the obscurity that covers these militarised and off-limits waters. They become what Pezzani and Heller have described as a "liquid trace",[46] the inscription of a migrant crossing, or a shipwreck and its aftermath, on the sea's surface.

Scrutinising the satellite photograph from that morning, I attempted a wake taxonomy.[47] Calculating speed, size, and trajectory, and cross-referencing these with later photos capturing the rescue operation that was launched with a day's delay, as well with information from the court files, I tried to identify the vessels visible.

Through this analysis, it was found that the wakes belonged to two vessels of the Greek coast guard, ΠΛΣ-*171* and ΠΛΣ-*612*, and a third, unknown vessel of the Turkish coast guard, all three of which had been deployed to look for the survivors of the sunken vessel. None of the vessels carried AIS[48] tracking data transponders, an omission which is common among coast guards in the Aegean, who prefer to operate in the shadows of optic systems and far from civilian scrutiny. Comparing these wakes to the trajectories the commanders of the Greek vessels had manually plotted with a pencil on a map before the prosecutor showed an inconsistency of almost one nautical mile, prompting questions regarding the veracity of the commanders' claims, as well as the validity of the prosecutor's conclusion which maintained that, had there been a shipwreck on March 16, these vessels would have located it.[49] Analysing the image further in order to look through the clouds that obscured part of the sea surface, longer wakes that were invisible in the raw image, began to surface.[50] A recent history of movement presented itself in the form of waves.

For the American scholar Christina Sharpe, reflecting on the legacies of the Middle Passage to the contemporary existence of black people in the USA, a wake is more than "the track left on the water's surface by a ship; the disturbance caused by a body swimming, or one that is moved, in water; the air currents behind a body in flight; a region of disturbed flow; in the line of sight of

46 Pezzani, "Liquid Traces," 2014.

47 The choice of the term taxonomy is deliberate here, as it captures this double entendre of wakes as physical objects that are created at the intersection of natural and machinic processes. Taxonomy traditionally refers to the categorisation and partition of nature for the purpose of scientific research. As a tool at the disposal of colonial naturalists, taxonomy has historically been deployed to rationalise racism and to create distinctions between the colonisers and the natural environment, as well as colonial subjects. A lesser known use of the term, however, lies in military vernacular, where the term is used as an indexing tool to encompass the domains of weapons, equipment, and tactics. Encompassing both worlds, a wake taxonomy therefore refers to the analysis of physical wave processes with the purpose of indexing and identifying military assets.

48 Automatic Identification System (AIS) is a standard automated tracking system used for vessel navigation.

49 These questions were left unanswered, with the prosecutor dismissing the analysis in my report as 'subjective'.

50 This analysis was undertaken in collaboration with Jamon Van Der Hoek, assistant professor at the school of Earth, Ocean and Atmospheric, Oregon State University, and expert in satellite imagery analysis. The technique used is called Principal Component Analysis (PCA). It is a process that filters the three bands of the image (red, green, blue) and removes any unnecessary noise, like clouds, producing the equivalent of an x-ray of a satellite photograph.

(an observed object); and (something) in the line of recoil of (a gun)".[51] Wakes "are processes; through them we think about the dead and about our relations to them; they are rituals through which to enact grief and memory. Wakes allow those among the living to mourn the passing of the dead through ritual." "In the wake", for Sharpe, "the semiotics of the slave ship continue".

Through encounters like the one between the ΠΛΣ-136 and the *Göznuru*, or non-encounters like the patchy search and rescue operation conducted by ΠΛΣ-171, ΠΛΣ-612 and ΠΛΣ-137, waves (and wakes) emerge as a fundamental component of the larger infrastructure that defines the Aegean carceral archipelago. Following Sharpe, I argue the wakes of the Coast Guard vessels captured in the satellite photo are two dimensional representations of the opaque forces that perform the necropolitical architecture of Fortress Europe. These turbulent inscriptions on the sea's surface churn the situated violent and contested histories of the Aegean with the residue of past colonial regimes and recent military interventions in Africa and Asia. They are, in this sense, part of the imperial legacies that shape the politics of European migration today.

In the context of Aegean crossings, these legacies are manifest in the form of an ever-increasing securitisation of the archipelago, be it through murderous coast guard patrols and push-back operations, modern forms of strategically prolonged incarceration and quarantine in remote islands, or, finally, the externalisation of the very border and its displacement beyond European territory, to the Turkish shore, via the infamous 2016 EU-Turkey deal.[52] The wakes examined here are both ripples of past and present histories of colonial occupation and state violence, and at the same time, they are the building materials of the low intensity warfare that the EU has launched on racialized and illegalised people trying to cross its borders without authorisation. They contain the *longue durée* of state violence in the Aegean.[53]

Pharmakon-nissi

Farmakonisi is a compound place name. The word φάρμακον, or *pharmakon*, in Greek, stands for "remedy", but it can also mean "poison", or "colour". The second component, *-nissi,* stands for "island". According to the legend, Farmakonisi took its original name, *Farmakoussa* - she who holds remedies (or poisons) - from Hippocrates of Kos, the ancient Greek "father of medicine", who used to visit the island to collect herbs. The French philosopher Jacques Derrida, in his text *Plato's Pharmacy*, addresses this double etymology of the word *pharmakon*. "The pharmakon would be a substance", Derrida

51 Christina Sharpe, *In the Wake: on Blackness and Being.* (Durham: Duke University Press, 2016), 21.

52 Under this deal Turkey agreed to implement stricter border controls, in return for money in humanitarian aid and a promise to reopen talks of EU accession. Greece, in turn, was to accommodate the migrants that were stranded in its territory in camps (hotspots), and begin deportations to Turkey, which it thereby would recognise as a "safe third country".

53 The French historian Fernand Braudel used the term *longue durée* to describe an extended historical perspective that includes the broad temporalities of environmental processes. Fernand Braudel, *The Mediterranean and the Mediterranean World in the Age of Philip II*, (Oakland, California: University of California Press 1992).

Χάρτης 18. ΑΓΝΩΣΤΟ ΣΚΑΦΟΣ, Υπολογισμός πορείας_2

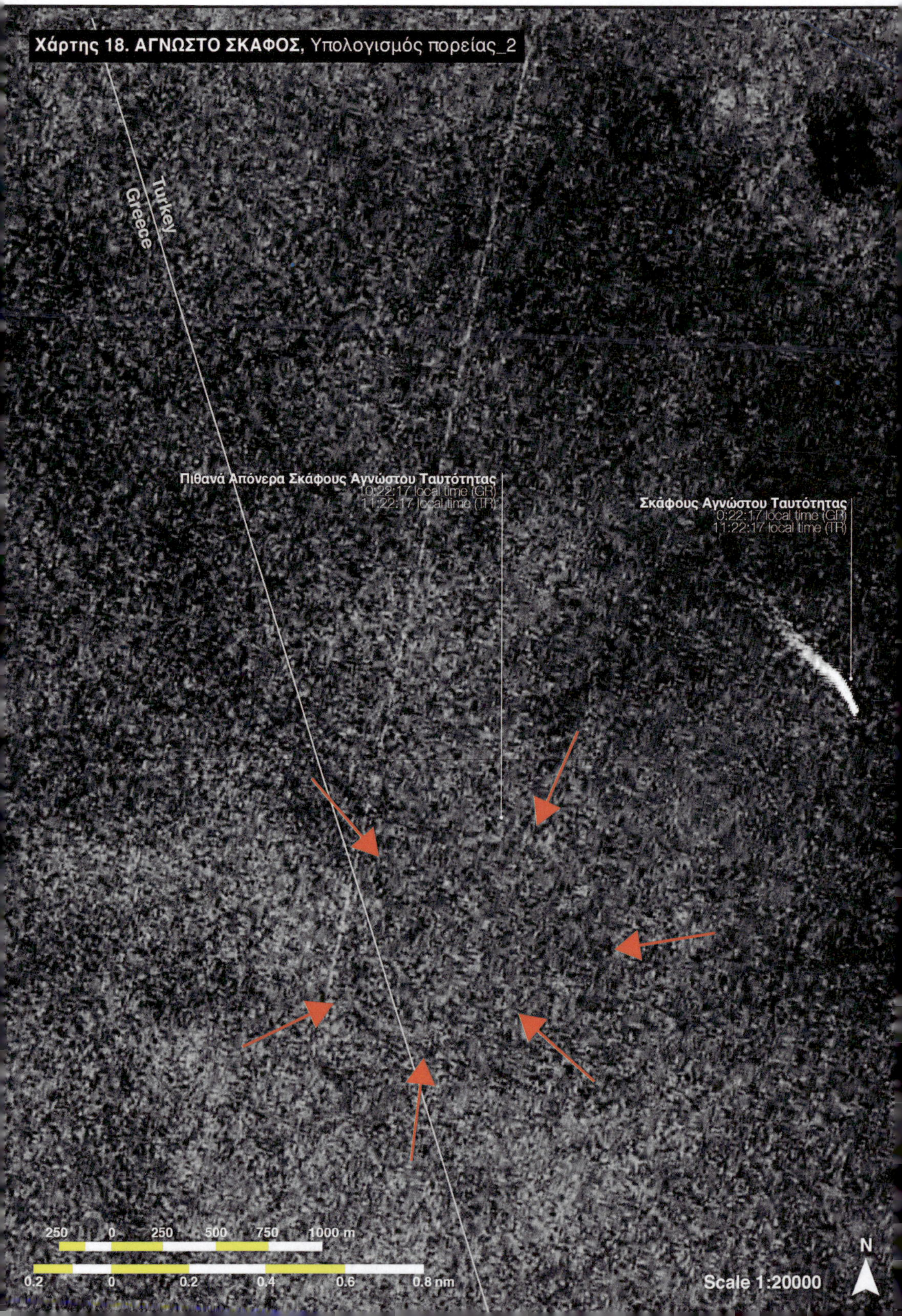

writes, "with all that that word can connote in terms of matter with occult virtues, cryptic depths refusing to submit their ambivalence to analysis".[54] It is in liquid – "the element of the *pharmakon*" - that, for Derrida, "opposites are more easily mixed. [...] And water, pure liquidity, is most easily and dangerously penetrated then corrupted by the *pharmakon*, with which it mixes and immediately unites".[55] Violent histories in the Aegean Sea layer and overlap with the interstitial materialities of the archipelago to produce an uneven geography, where the circulation of both people and information is subject to violent state practices. The two shipwrecks of Farmakonisi and Agathonisi were chosen as paradigmatic objects of study, as folds on the Aegean surface upon which the forces and contestations discussed above crystallise and become legible. Both incidents in turn testify to a deep state continuum that "refuses to submit its ambivalence to analysis".[56]

Occasionally, the surfacing of bodies and boat remains from the "cryptic" Aegean depths disrupts this equilibrium of obfuscation and confronts researchers with non-discursive traces that lend themselves to analysis, as well as with a set of ethical questions to do with one's response to witnessing the routinisation of loss of human life at sea. In order to take up the task of upholding truth claims and calls for accountability in this archipelago we must develop a type of practice– political, theoretical, spatial— that can account for the multiplicity of actants that make up the Aegean border nature, human and non-human alike. An epistemological turn is therefore necessary. When prompted with the right tools, rocks, winds, temperatures, currents and waves can be read against the grain to corroborate or negate human testimony, and can become prisms through which the obscure silences that cover these militarised and off-limits waters can be contested.

I would like to thank Quassim, Fahima, and Darab for entrusting me with their memories, grief, and anger; Spyros Tzouanopoulos, Marianna Tzeferakou, Natassa Strachini and Dimitris Tsouchlis for inviting me to collaborate with them on these two cases; and Jamon Van Der Hoek and Richard Limeburner for enriching my analysis with their expertise. This research was supported by an Onassis Foundation Scholarship.

54 Jacques Derrida, *Dissemination*, trans. Barbara Johnson, (London: Continum, 2004), 150.
55 IBID.
56 Indeed, as I was going through the Agathonisi court files, I stumbled upon a piece of paper, the site of which made me shiver. It was the testimony of one of the high-ranked coast guard officials who were in charge of coordinating the rescue operation from inside the maritime rescue and coordination centre (MRCC) in Piraeus. It was the same person who four years earlier, as the captain of the *PLS-136* had sunk and abandoned the Göznuru in the dark waters off Farmakonisi. Having been found innocent from the maritime court of Piraeus, he had been transferred to the search and rescue coordination centre where he presumably is still stationed.

Principal Component Analysis of a satellite photograph reveals a circular wake cutting across the border. This serves as further proof that this unidentified vessel belonging to the Turkish Coast Guard could have been performing search and rescue. Through further analysis it was found that the vessel was cruising at a speed of 29.02 knots. Source: GIS analysis by author and Jamon Van Der Hoek, satellite photograph by Planet Labs.

Χάρτης 6. Δορυφορικές φωτογραφίες ιδιάζουσας σημασίας, 16/03/2018

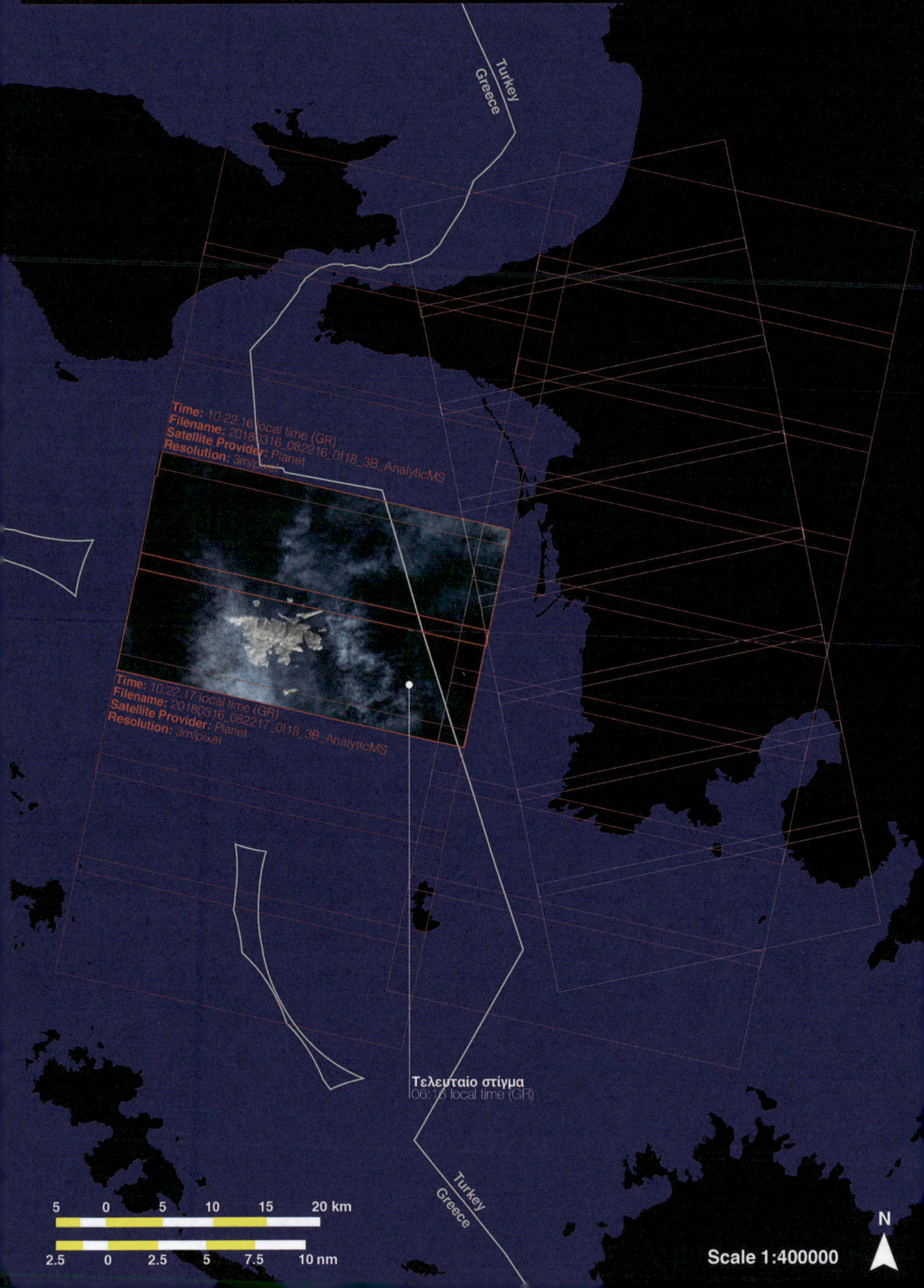

Works cited

Belanger, Pierre and Alexander Arroyo. *Ecologies of Power Countermapping the Logistical Landscapes & Military Geographies of the U.S. Department of Defence.* Cambridge, Massachaussetts: MIT Press, 2016.

Brathwaite, Kamau. *The Arrivants: A New World Trilogy.* Oxford: Oxford University Press, 1981.

Braudel, Fernand. The Mediterranean and the Mediterranean World in the Age of Philip II. Oakland, California: University of California Press, 1992.

Collins, John M. *Military Geography.* Washington, DC: National Defense University Press, 1998.

Derrida, Jacques. Dissemination. Translated by Barbara Johnson. London: Continum, 2004.

Gabrys, Jennifer. "Ocean Sensing and Navigating the End of this World." *e-flux*, June 2019. www.e- flux.com/journal/101/272633/ocean-sensing-and-navigating-the-end-of-this-world/.

Helmreich, Stefan. "How to Hide an Island." In New Geographies 8: Island, edited by Daniel Daou and Pablo Pérez-Ramos. Cambridge, Massachaussetts: Harvard Graduate School of Design, 2017.

Helmreich, Stefan. "Waves. An anthropology of scientific things." *Hau: Journal of Ethnographic theory 4*, no.3 (October 2014): 265-284.

Institute of Migration. "Missing Migrants." Accessed 15 September, 2022. missingmigrants.iom.int/region/mediterranean?migrant_route%5B%5D=1377

Jadidoleslam, Navid et al., "Wave power potential assessment of Aegean Sea with an integrated 15- year data." *Renewable Energy.* 86, (February 2016):1045-1059 .

Lahoud, Adrian. "Floating Bodies." In Forensis: *The Architecture of Public Truth.* Edited by Forensic Architecture. Sternberg Press.

Melsheimer, Christian. "Ship Wakes Observed with ERS and SPOT." Centre for Remote Imaging, Sensing and Processing, 2001, crisp.nus.edu.sg/~research/shipwakes/shipwakes.htm.

Pezzani, Lorenzo. "Liquid Traces." In Forensis: *The Architecture of Public Truth.* Edited by Forensic Architecture. Berlin: Sternberg, 2014.

Schuppli, Susan. *Material Witness: Media, Forensics, Evidence.* Cambridge, Massachaussetts: MIT Press, 2020.

Sharpe, Christina. *In the Wake: on Blackness and Being.* Durham: Duke University Press, 2016.

Steinberg, Philip E., and Kimberley Peters. "Wet ontologies, fluid spaces: Giving depth to volume through oceanic thinking." *Environment and Planning D: Society and Space* 33, no.2 (April 2015): 247 – 264.

Tings, Bjorn, Andrey Pleskachevsky, Domenico Velotto, Sven Jacobsen. "Extension of Ship Wake Detectability Model for Non-Linear Influences of Parameters Using Satellite Based X-Band Synthetic Aperture Radar." *Remote Sensing* 11, no. 5 (March 2019).

Torsvik, Trond Helge et al., "Identification of ship wake structures by a time–frequency method." *Journal of Fluid Mechanics* 765 (February 2015).

Weizman, Eyal. *Forensic Architecture.* New York: Zone Books, 2017.

Death Certificates issued in the island of Leros, 22/01/2014-17/02/2014. Translated from Greek by the author.

Death Certificates issued in the island of Samos, 20/03/2018. Translated from Greek by the author.

Maritime Court of Piraeus, 'Testimony of Bariali Kadiri to Military Judge B." January 30, 2014. Translated from Greek by the author.

Maritime Court of Piraeus, "Testimony of Fahima Malek, with translator." July 18, 2018. Translated from Greek by the author.

Geologic Temporalities and Geopolitical Operations

Juanita Sundberg

The Sonoran Desert tells tumultuous stories that reach deep into the earth and extend up to the sky. In one part of this vast desert—now divided into the United States and México—jagged basalt and granitic rock from multiple geologic eras form narrow mountain ranges. Deceptively impervious, the rocks bely the truth of continuous change, as wind and rain erode mountains, forcing pebbles and fine-grained sediment to accumulate on valley bottoms.

The slow pace of geological change, however, is surpassed by geopolitical temporalities. Since the seventeenth century, European imperial struggles to dispossess Indigenous peoples of their land have prompted dramatic transformations to the Sonoran Desert. This essay focuses on a moment—a blip in geological time—when geopolitical objectives unearthed geological temporalities on the desert floor. The agent of transformation described here is not rifting, wind, or rain, but the United States Border Patrol. When agents patrol the Sonoran Desert in the southwestern state of Arizona, they repeatedly drive over valley bottom soils. Over time, erosion and compaction exposes stratum from previous geological eras; exposed strata with distinct entailments are activated in ways that not only destabilise the very ground on which enforcement activities take place, but also tear at the social fabric of desert life.

Geologic Temporalities and Desert Life

This part of the Sonoran Desert records many of the geologic processes that generated early "continental crust formation and mountain building".[1] Rocks in this region tell stories of tumultuous tectonic activity and volcanic eruptions. Between thirty to twenty-four million years ago, the Earth's crust in this area was stretched east to west as hot magma from the asthenosphere pushed upwards.[2] As the crust thinned and cracked, large north-south trending faults formed, fracturing volcanic rocks into enormous, slanting blocks. Ongoing tectonic and volcanic activity uplifted blocks along these faults to form a series of long narrow mountain ranges with deep valleys between, generating what today is called a Basin and Range landscape.

On desert valley floors, deposits of fine-grained sediment like sand or clay accumulate on subsurface stratum with distinct geologic histories and lithic characteristics. Here, heterogeneous communities of microorgan-

1 John Bezy, James Gutmann, and Gordon Haxel, *A Guide to the geology of Organ Pipe Cactus National Monument and Pinacate Biosphere Reserve* (Tucson: Arizona Geological Survey, 2000), 9.

2 The Earth's lithosphere (composed of the crust and uppermost solid mantle) sits atop the asthenosphere, a zone of extremely hot (1,300 to 3,000 degrees Celsius) and plastic molten rock, which responds to movements deep below.

isms—bacteria, fungi, microbes—interact with lithic materials below, the hydrosphere, and the biosphere above, including plant and animal communities. The ongoing interplay between these beings and processes break down residual matter to orchestrate rich soils that may plunge thousands of feet, and could be just as many years old.

Scanning electron micrograph of cyanobacterial sheath material sticking to sand grains. Source: United States Geological Survey.

A significant portion of valley bottoms are covered by a thin knobby crust, which is formed as Cyanobacteria, one of the planet's oldest forms of life, using its microscopic, filamentous cellular structure to thread together other organisms such as bacteria, lichens, mosses, green algae, or liverwort.[3] Cyanobacteria possess the ability to photosynthesize; they take nitrogen out of the air and provide nutrients to others. Biological soil crusts mediate erosion, increase the absorption of water, and fix nutrients. These "mantles of fertility" make the desert more hospitable to plants and many other living creatures.[4]

Quite literally, soils bequeath worlds to others. "Without soil, the majority of terrestrial creatures – including humans – could not exist".[5] In the Sonoran Desert, soils enact and ground convivial worlds built on interaction and interdependency.[6] Some soils provide stable environments in which plants root and grow. In turn, plants offer a life-line to desert creatures who rely on the nutrients and shade they offer; meanwhile small rodents nourish and aerate soil for plants.

Although pedologists refer to soil with terms like "living body" or "natural bodies", these words mislead. Rather than unified bodies, soils are processes

3 For instance, biological soil crusts on valley bottoms in Cabeza Prieta NWR constitute "somewhat more than one half of the total refuge area, or approximately 192,300 hectares (475,000 acres)." United States Fish & Wildlife Service. *Cabeza Prieta National Wildlife Refuge Comprehensive Conservation Plan, Wilderness Stewardship Plan and Environmental Impact Statement.* (Albuquerque, New Mexico: U.S. F&WS Division of Planning, 2006), 184.

4 Moria L. Nagy, Alejandro Pérez, and Ferran Garcia-Pichel. "The prokaryotic diversity of biological soil crusts in the Sonoran Desert (Organ Pipe Cactus National Monument, AZ)," *FEMS Microbiology Ecology* 54, no. 2 (2005), 234.

5 Daniel Hillel, *Soil in the environment: crucible of terrestrial life* (Boston: Academic Press, 2007), 2.

6 Conviviality can be used in a facile way to convey feasting or making merry together. However, the term also may also be interpreted to mean that living together on earth implies collaboration but also conflict and death; see Given, Michael. "Conviviality and the Life of Soil," Cambridge Archaeological Journal 28, no. 1 (2018): 127-143.

enacted by a multiplicity of organisms interacting over geological temporalities that exceed human timeframes. Soil challenges how humans measure and understand time. Soils also defy— and should not be reduced to— human conceptualisations of the body. Indeed, soil as *process* challenges Western, human-centric imaginaries of agency that are built on assumptions about the individual human subject's capacity for conscious, intentional action. In short, soils have their own origins, rhythms, and purposes. This does not mean soils are unaffected by human actions. Rather, their specific properties in relation to location and subsurface horizons afford soils the capacity to do things that exceed short-term human objectives, such as boundary enforcement.

Geopolitical Temporalities and Transformations

Since time immemorial, this part of the world has been the *jewed* (homeland) of O'odham peoples. For the O'odham, the desert is Mother Earth.[7] In line with their *Him'dag* (way of life), these societies established legal and political orders and built relationships with soil, plant, and animal communities. The O'odham were highly skilled in desert living, including *ak'chin,* farming at the "mouth of the wash" where seasonal rainfall flowed, and *wa'ig*, knowledge of where to get water.[8]

However, in the mid-sixteenth century, the region became a contested frontier of imperial expansion, as European monarchs, and then independent settler colonial states vied for control of Indigenous territories. Throughout the eighteenth century, Spanish colonisers established a tenuous geopolitical and ecological order organised around dispossession, racial hierarchies, and anthropocentrism. When México declared independence from Spain, the region came under the rule of the new settler colonial state. Then, the violence of Manifest Destiny came to this desert land, as the United States sought to expand west and south.[9] In the wake of U.S. imperial aggression and war, México signed the Treaty of Guadalupe Hidalgo (1848), ceding lands to the U.S. The O'odham *jewed* was divided in 1854, when the U.S. negotiated the purchase of 29,670 square miles (76,8000 km) from México. The Gadsden Purchase forced O'odham communities to choose between two settler colonial states, regardless of the ties extending across or beyond the newly established political boundary.[10]

7 Robert Cruz, "In our language is where we will find our liberation," *Berkeley La Raza Law Journal* 22, no. 1 (2012): 97-116.

8 Blake Gentry, Geoffrey Alan Boyce, Jose M. Garcia, and Samuel N. Chambers, "Indigenous survival and settler colonial dispossession on the Mexican frontier: The case of Cedag Wahia and Wo'oson O'odham indigenous communities," *Journal of Latin American Geography* 18, no. 1 (2019): 65-93.

9 Manifest Destiny is an ideological belief in the inevitability and indeed necessity of United States settler expansion westward to spread democracy and freedom. Journalist John L. O'Sullivan coined the term in 1845, giving a name to a widespread belief that Anglo-Saxon expansion was a God-given mission. See Shane Mountjoy, *Manifest Destiny: Westward expansion* (New York: Chelsea House, 2009).

10 Gentry et al., "Indigenous survival;" Christina Leza, *Divided Peoples: Policy, Activism, and Indigenous Identities on the U.S.-Mexico Border* (Tucson: The University of Arizona Press, 2019); Jeffrey M. Schulze, *Are we Not Foreigners here?: Indigenous Nationalism in the U.S.-Mexico Borderlands* (Chapel Hill, North Carolina: University of North Carolina Press, 2018).

In the decades that followed, Anglo-Americans established a white supremacist settler colonial society, built on the massacre and violent displacement of Indigenous communities.[11] Emptied of its people and the sacred duties they performed, parts of the desert were opened to settlers, who dug mining pits, let cattle roam, and hunted animals—some to the point of extermination.[12] The O'odham were forced onto reservations, as with the establishment of the Tohono O'odham Reservation in 1917. Later, the U.S. government would designate some O'odham lands as protected areas, notably Organ Pipe Cactus National Monument in 1937,[13] and Cabeza Prieta National Wildlife Refuge in 1939.[14]

Federal lands, including the Goldwater Range,[15] erase Indigenous territorialities, claims to sovereignty, and modes of sociality. For instance, the first superintendent of Organ Pipe Cactus National Monument (NM) hoped to bring the desert landscape "back to its original state".[16] A press release for the new monument claimed the area was "little changed from…500 million years ago…[at] the borderland between the habitable world and the uninhabitable…a desert country so waterless and formidable that it has rarely been visited by white men".[17] Today, vast portions of Organ Pipe NM and Cabeza Prieta NWR are designated as wilderness, defined as "an area where the earth and its community of life are untrammelled by man, where man himself is a visitor who does not remain".[18] In some areas, Organ Pipe NM has left the architectural remnants of twentieth century cattle ranches and mines; however, all traces of O'odham life have been erased. Ultimately, federal lands in southern Arizona constitute a vast landscape with sporadic and, in some areas, non-existent human infrastructure.

Boundary Enforcement Strategies

Although the Treaty of Guadalupe Hidalgo (1848) established the political boundary, the lines drawn on maps did not become a material reality for decades, especially in the western territories.[19] Nonetheless, both the U.S. and México sought to improve their "ability to manipulate spatial controls

11 Joe Lockard, "Carceral Colonialism in Arizona Territory," *Western American Literature* 55 no. 1 (2020): 131. Roxanne Dunbar-Ortiz, *Not" a Nation of Immigrants": Settler Colonialism, White Supremacy, and a History of Erasure and Exclusion* (Boston: Beacon Press, 2021).

12 Samuel Truett, *Fugitive Landscapes: The Forgotten History of the U.S.-Mexico Borderlands* (New Haven: Yale University Press, 2006).

13 Jessica Piekielek, "Creating a Park, Building a Border: The Establishment of Organ Pipe Cactus National Monument and the Solidification of the US-Mexico Border," *Journal of the Southwest* 58, no. 1 (2016): 1-27.

14 Lisa Meierotto, *Immigration, Environment, and Security on the U.S.-Mexico Border* (New York, NY: Springer International Publishing, 2020).

15 Established in the wake of World War II, the Barry M. Goldwater Range was used was established to train military pilots and crews in live fire and bombing exercises.

16 Cited in Piekielek, "Creating a Park, Building a Border," 4.

17 Cited in Piekielek, "Creating a Park, Building a Border," 4.

18 (Wilderness Act of 1964, Pub. L. No 1964). 88-577, 78 Stat. 890 (1964).

19 Rachel C. St. John, *Line in the sand: The desert border between the United States and Mexico, 1848–1934.* (Princeton: Princeton University Press, 2005).

to reflect state priorities".[20] Indeed, the first boundary enforcement fence was completed between Baja California and California in 1911 to stop the spread of cattle tick fever from México into the U.S.[21] Barbed wire fencing was stretched across the line, while a patrol of mounted officers, called "line riders", sought to prevent the "illegal entry of cattle".[22] Meanwhile, chain link fencing between border towns was erected during World War I and again in World War II. Immigration concerns, however, did not drive such spatial controls until the early twentieth century, and more specifically, the Great Depression.[23]

In the mid-1990s, new spatial strategies, including fences were included in the Southwest Border Enforcement Strategy.[24] The strategy launched a new approach called "prevention through deterrence".[25] To raise the risk of apprehension "to the point that many will consider it futile to continue to attempt illegal entry", enforcement was amplified by deploying more Border Patrol agents and installing new infrastructure and technology at popular urban crossing points.[26]The intention was to push those border crossers who were not deterred into rural areas. [27] There, officials with the U.S. Immigration and Naturalization Service (INS) calculated, "natural barriers" —mountains, deserts, and rivers—"would act as deterrents to illegal entry".[28] Doris Meissner, then Commissioner of the INS, believed "geography would be an ally" to enforcement operations.[29]

Volunteer from 'No More Deaths' inspecting water supplies along a trail.
Source: Photograph by the author.

20 St. John, *Line in the sand,* 6.
21 St. John, *Line in the sand,* 203
22 Joseph Nevins, *Operation Gatekeeper: The rise of the "illegal alien" and the remaking of the US–Mexico boundary* (New York, NY: Routledge, 2002), 26.
23 St. John, *Line in the sand,* 176.
24 Nevins, *Operation Gatekeeper.*
25 U.S. Border Patrol, Border Patrol Strategic Plan, 1994 and Beyond (Washington, DC: Border Patrol, 1994).
26 Border Patrol, *Border Patrol Strategic Plan,* 6. The operation also involved establishing new interior checkpoints to disrupt smuggling operations, and adding more INS inspectors at ports of entry to apprehend those attempting to enter with false documents, see Nevins, *Operation Gatekeeper.*
27 I use the terms border crosser or illegalised migrants to describe those individuals seeking to avoid inspection by entering the U.S. outside official ports of entry.
28 U.S. Government Accountability Office, *INS' Southwest Border Strategy: Resourced and Impact Issues Remain after Seven Years* GAO-01-842 (Washington, DC: GAO, 2001), 24.
29 Cited in Justin Akers Chacón and Mike Davis, *No one is illegal: Fighting violence and state repression on the US-Mexico border* (Chicago : Haymarket Books, 2006), 206.

Prevention through deterrence instrumentalised and weaponised the Sonoran Desert, calculating that the "hostile terrain" would dissuade those wishing to enter the U.S. without inspection.[30] A land manager for Cabeza Prieta National Wildlife Refuge (NWR) summarised his view of the policy:

It's a harsh area. Cabeza, you might say, is the last spot, really the last spot on the border as Border Patrol began cracking down in the urban areas, forcing people into these more hostile environments. And Border Patrol assumed that these hostile environments would act as their own barrier and therefore help contain people. Little did they realise the determination of people to better their lives and the entrepreneurial spirit of drug smugglers.[31]

Instead of deterring, boundary enforcement operations pushed border crossers into desert lands in southwestern Arizona, with mortal consequences.[32] As noted, imperial formations of the past had emptied much of the desert of its people, producing a vast area with little human presence. When prevention through deterrence weaponised this area as a natural barrier, the desert became the graveyard for thousands of illegalized people who lost their lives, dehydrated, overheated, and alone.[33] Now the desert is regularly referred to as a "death trap",[34] "killing fields",[35] and "corridor of death".[36] The actual or even approximate number of deaths remains unknown, as the U.S. Border Patrol does not record complete data on the deaths of border crossers, nor has it addressed limitations in its data collection protocols.[37] However, non-governmental organisations suggest that nearly half of the estimated 8,600 deaths since the mid-1990s have occurred in Arizona.[38]

30 Border Patrol, *Border Patrol Strategic Plan,* 7.

31 Author's interview with a land manager, June 2005.

32 Jason De León, *The land of open graves: Living and dying on the migrant trail* (Oakland, California : University of California Press, 2015).

33 Wayne A. Cornelius, "Death at the border: Efficacy and unintended consequences of U.S. immigration control policy," *Population and development review* 27, no. 4 (2001): 661-685; Geoffrey Alan Boyce, "The rugged border: Surveillance, policing and the dynamic materiality of the U.S./Mexico frontier' *Environment and Planning D: Society and Space* 34, no. 2 (2016): 245-262; Samuel Norton Chambers, Geoffrey Alan Boyce, Sarah Launius, and Alicia Dinsmore, "Mortality, surveillance and the tertiary "funnel effect" on the US-Mexico border: a geospatial modeling of the geography of deterrence," *Journal of Borderlands Studies* 36, no. 3 (2021): 443-468; Joseph Nevins, *Dying to live: A story of U.S. immigration in an age of global apartheid* (City Lights Books, 2008); Jeremy Slack, Daniel E. Martínez, Alison Elizabeth Lee, and Scott Whiteford, "The geography of border militarization: Violence, death and health in Mexico and the United States." *Journal of Latin American Geography* (2016): 7-32. On the experience of crossing the desert, see Margaret Regan, *The death of Josseline: Immigration stories from the Arizona borderlands* (Beacon Press, 2010) and Kathryn Ferguson, Norma A. Price, and Ted Parks, *Crossing with the Virgin: stories from the migrant trail* (Tucson, Arizona: University of Arizona Press, 2010).

34 Bill Ong Hing, *Defining America: through immigration policy* (Temple University Press, 2012), 165.

35 Roxanne Lynn Doty, "Bare life: Border-crossing deaths and spaces of moral alibi," *Environment and Planning D: Society and Space* 29, no. 4 (2011): 608.

36 Thomas Edgar, "Operation Desert Safeguard. National Border, National Park: A History of Organ Pipe Cactus National Monument," accessed September 22, 2022 at https://organpipehistory.com/orpi-a-z/operation-desert-safeguard/.

37 GAO, *Southwest Border: CBP Should Improve Data Collection, Reporting, and Evaluation for the Missing Migrant Program,* GAO-22-105053 (Washington, DC: GAO, 2022).

38 Colibrí Centre for Human Rights, "Frequently Asked Questions," https://colibricenter.org/about/faq/; Colibrí Centre for Human Rights; La Coalición de Derechos Humanos and No More Deaths, Disappeared: *How the U.S. Border Enforcement Agencies are Fueling a Missing Persons Crisis,* http://www.thedisappearedreport.org/reports.html.

Colliding Temporalities

The Sonoran Desert is not simply *the site* of boundary enforcement operations in southwestern Arizona. Rather, the desert-as-presently-configured mediates the daily practices of enforcement.[39] The topographical landscape of today significantly shapes boundary crossing and enforcement.

As a land manager at Cabeza Prieta NWR explained, "We have mountain ranges, but we also have broad valleys, and within that 56 miles [90 kilometres] of border, there's lots of broad valleys that may not have had a road in them, but afford the opportunity for smugglers to move vehicles and to move people up through these valleys".[40] In short, the jagged mountains limit most boundary enforcement activity to slopes and valley bottoms.[41]

Detail of tire drag system used by Border Patrol.
Source: Photograph by the author.

By the early 2000s, hundreds of trucks and cars began crossing from México into these lands in southwestern Arizona to deliver illegalised people and goods north.[42] The Border Patrol followed closely behind. Due to conflicts between federal agencies, multiple agencies signed a Memorandum of Understanding (MOU) in 2006, which indicates the Border Patrol is authorised to drive on "existing public and administrative roads and/or trails".[43] Although

39 Geoffrey Alan Boyce, "The rugged border"; Geoffrey Alan Boyce, "Autonomy, human vulnerability and the volumetric composition of U.S. border policing," in Handbook on the Geographies of Power, ed. Mat Coleman and John Agnew (Edward Elgar Publishing, 2018), 347-361; Juanita Sundberg, "Diabolic Caminos in the Desert & Cat Fights on the Río: A post-humanist political ecology of boundary enforcement in the United States-Mexico borderlands," *Annals of the Association of American Geographers*, 101, no. 2 (2011): 318-336.

40 Interview with a land manager, June 2005.

41 D. C. Whitbeck and J. S. Fehmi, "Variables influencing law enforcement off-road route proliferation on an arid site," *Remote Sensing Applications:* Society and Environment 3 (2016): 45–52.

42 John Annerino, Dead in their tracks: crossing America's desert borderlands (Four Walls Eight Windows, 1999); U.S. Department of the Interior, Forest Service, Environmental Protection Agency, Department of Justice, Report to the House of Representatives Committee on Appropriations on Impacts Caused by Illegal Aliens Crossing Federal Lands in Southeast Arizona (Washington, DC: Committee on Appropriations, 2002).

43 US Department of Homeland Security, U.S. Department of the Interior, and U.S. Department of Agriculture, *Memorandum of Understanding Regarding Cooperative National Security and Counterterrorism Efforts on Federal Lands along the United States' Border* (Washington, DC: 2006), 4. Each Department of Interior agency has its own system of administrative roads. Historically, access to administrative roads was restricted to the land management agency.

agents are not permitted to drive off-road in wilderness areas, except in the case of exigent circumstances or emergency situations involving the life and safety of human beings or threats to national security, what constitutes exigent circumstances is constantly in question.[44]

Despite these regulations and agreements, multiple sources reveal that Border Patrol agents frequently drive off-road creating new tracts on the desert floor, which other agents may see as an authorised road. Agents also drive alongside or around problematic spots in un/authorised roads, thereby extending their width and creating wide turnabouts.[45] "Off road interdiction activities have resulted in a proliferation of roads on the refuge", noted a land manager at Cabeza Prieta NWR.[46] Yet the Border Patrol continues to blame illegal entrants for creating new roads and trails, despite the installation of vehicle barriers at the southern boundary of Organ Pipe Cactus NM in 2006 and Cabeza Prieta NWR 2009, thus limiting vehicle crossings from Mexico.

When heavy vehicles repeatedly drive over organism-rich soils, the convivial fabric of desert life is disturbed. The degree of damage depends on the mode and conditions of exposure—tire tracks breaking soils on slopes or valleys—but also the temporal qualities as a singular event has different outcomes than repeated impacts.[47] For example, repeated vehicle passes over desert soil destroys the living biological crust and compacts the soil. Compaction means the spaces between soil particles, where water is held, are flattened; without water, the particles dry out.

If the substrata is formed of clay, "then you got a mess", said Linda, an ecologist and retired land manager. She explained further:

If you have the surface horizon – a nice sandy loam that absorbs water beautifully – and you expose that sublayer, that water will just sit there, and sit there, because it takes a long time to penetrate that subsurface layer. And then agents drive around it [the sitting water]. And then it dries out, and then agents drive on it again and then it becomes moon dust. Those are, we call them pig pens, because that's what they look like. It's just horrible, horrible to deal with. Really hard to restore an area like that.[48]

When I asked Linda to tell me more about the formation of moon dust, she said, "clay holds water particles tightly", so "when a clay particle dries out, then it's really hard to rehydrate".[49] If Border Patrol agents drive over the area where the clay particles have dried out, the result is a powdery substance, colloquially called moon dust. Moon dust is produced when the social fabric of soil is destroyed through compaction and dehydration.

44 My research, including interviews with land managers and analysis of documents obtained through Freedom of Information requests, suggests that the Border Patrol continuously seeks to redefine exigent circumstances to allow agents unrestricted access to public lands.
45 Meierotto, *Immigration, Environment, and Security;* Defenders of Wildlife, *On the Line: The Impacts of Immigration Policy on Wildlife and Habitat in the Arizona Borderlands* (Washington, DC: Defenders of Wildlife 2005), U.S. Fish & Wildlife Service, Compatibility Determination, Construction of a Communication Tower, (Ajo: Cabeza Prieta National Wildlife Refuge, 2010).
46 US Fish & Wildlife Service, Compatibility Determination, 4.
47 Robert H. Webb, Todd C. Esque, Kenneth E. Nussear, and Mark Sturm, "Disruption rates for one vulnerable soil in Organ Pipe Cactus National Monument, Arizona, USA," Journal of arid environments 95 (2013): 75-83.
48 Author's interview with Linda, (retired land manager), in discussion with the author, July 2015.
49 IBID.

Images from report showing an aerial view of roads and moon-dusted roads. Source: Howard, et al., "Inventory and assessment of unauthorized vehicle routes", 2014.

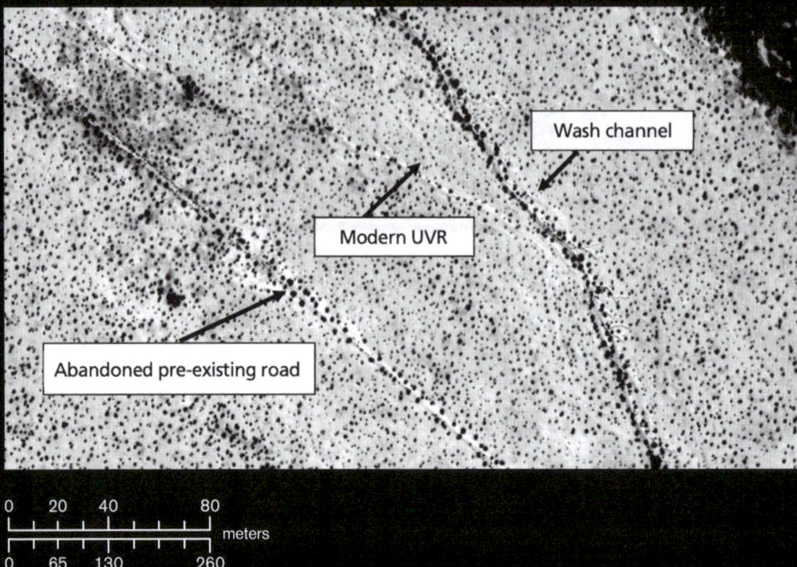

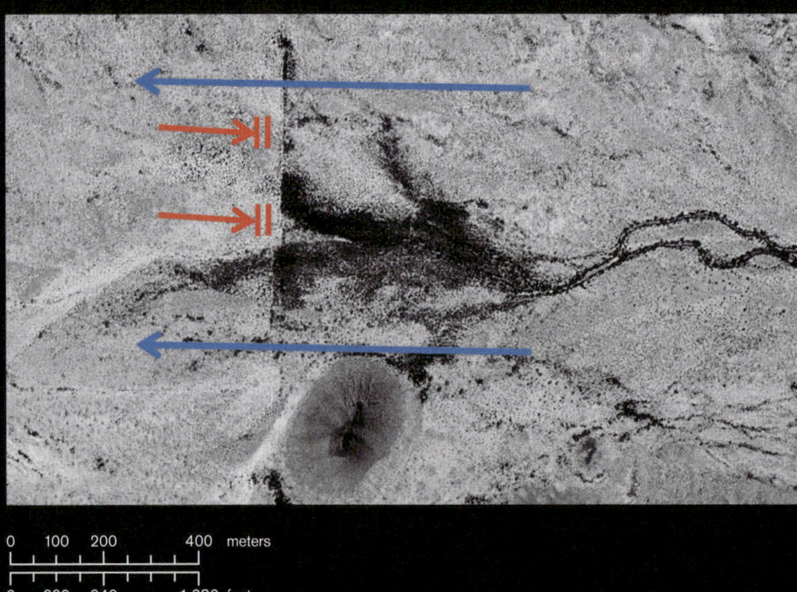

Images from report showing road-induced hydrological changes. Source: Howard, et al., "Inventory and assessment of unauthorized vehicle routes", 2014.

Richard, another land manager, expanded on the outcome of travel on unauthorised roads or off-road:

The very nature of these soils is that the traffic – you can only use these tracks 2 to 3 times before they powder out. So then, the vehicles spread out. So, you get this kind of spider web of roads. In the Growler Valley you cannot walk more than an eighth of a mile without finding [unauthorised] tracks as you walk from east to west or west to east.[50]

In sum, moon dust disrupts the grounding and stabilising function of soil, making roads impassable and challenging the smooth execution of enforcement operations. When vehicles get stuck in moon dust, agents may themselves be at risk. If agents get stuck, and are stranded for long periods of time, they can suffer from dehydration and heat stroke, or face confrontations with so-called smugglers.

Landing mats repurposed by Border Patrol.
Source: Photograph by the author.

Addressing the effects of their operations on desert soils requires the Border Patrol to invest additional time and energy to develop work-arounds.
One strategy has been to place landing mats from the Vietnam war on compacted roadways, highlighting how imperial engagements of the past enable those of the present. Another strategy, one pursued by geopolitical hawks, is to change existing legislation to exempt the Border Patrol from environmental regulations within the border zone.[51] Although this strategy has not yet succeeded, in 2005 Congress authorised the Department of Homeland Security' Secretary to "waive all legal requirements such Secretary, in such Secretary's sole discretion, determines necessary to ensure expeditious construction of the barriers and roads"

50 Author's interview with Richard (land manager), in discussion with the author, July 2005.

51 For instance, Rob Bishop (R-UT) introduced the National Security and Federal Lands Protection Act, H.R. 1505 112th Cong., 2nd sess., which was introduced in the House on April 13, 2011, which would permanently waive 36 laws in public lands situated within the 100-mile border zone. John McCain introduced a similar bill, the Arizona Borderlands Protection and Preservation Act, S. 750, 114th Cong., 1st sess., which was introduced in the Senate on March 17, 2015.

in areas of "high illegal entry".[52] Regardless of future legislation, at present the Border Patrol is rarely held accountable for agents' actions.[53]

Desertification

Federal land managers responsible for managing the ecological systems in border protected areas are gravely concerned about the implications of soil compaction for communities of plants and animals. In the early 2000s, land managers began recording this unfolding story of desert transformation by mapping new vehicle tracks and developing a methodology to assess the scale of soil compaction on unauthorised roads and new tracks.[54] Their studies reveal the detrimental effects of off-road vehicle travel on the desert's hydrology, soils, and vegetation.[55] More difficult to assess are the effects upon wildlife, especially the Sonoran Pronghorn, which is listed as an endangered species. Pronghorns are particularly susceptible to human disturbance and will avoid preferred habitat when experiencing stress. Yet increased vehicle tracks and trails results in more encounters between humans and pronghorns.[56]

In 2006, Cabeza Prieta NWR staff identified approximately 250 miles (400 kilometres) "of illegal roads and trails created by drug and illegal migrant smugglers and the law enforcement actions necessary to deter and interdict the smugglers and illegal migrants and conduct lifesaving search and rescue operations".[57] Three years later, vehicle barriers were installed at the southern boundary of the refuge. By July 2011, refuge staff had mapped 7,968 miles (12,824 kilometres) of vehicle trails; of these, 7,739 miles (12,455 kilometres) were in designated wilderness areas.[58]

52 Blas Nuñez-Neto and Michael John Garcia, *Border Security: The San Diego Fence, CRS Report No. RS22026* (Washington, DC: Congressional Research Service, 2007), 1, 3.

53 US Department of Homeland Security, Final Report of *Customs and Border Protection* Integrity Advisory Panel, (Washington, DC: Homeland Security Advisory Council, 2016); U.S. House of Representatives, *Border Patrol Agents in Secret Facebook Group Faced Few Consequences for Misconduct, Staff Report* (Washington, DC: Committee on Oversight and Reform, 2021). U.S. House of Representatives Committee on Oversight and Reform, *U.S. House of Representatives Oversight and Homeland Security Chairs Request Information from Customs and Border Protection on Potential Misconduct of Specialised Teams* (Washington, D.C.: Committee on Oversight and Reform, 2022).

54 Sue Rutman, 2006, *A foundation for collecting, managing, and integrating information on the U.S./Mexico international border activities, June 2004–September 2005*, Organ Pipe Cactus National Park (Ajo: Organ Pipe National Park, 2006) outlines the methodology. See Todd C. Esque, Rich Inman, Kenneth E. Nussear, R. H. Webb, M. M. Girard, and J. DeGayner, "Comparison of methods to monitor the distribution and impacts of unauthorised travel routes in a border park," *Natural Areas Journal* 36, no. 3 (2016): 248-258; and U.S. Fish & Wildlife Service, Vehicle Trails Associated with Illegal Border Activities on Cabeza Prieta National Wildlife Refuge (Ajo : Cabeza Prieta National Wildlife Refuge, 2011).

55 S. M. S. Howard, S. Rutman, R. Tietjen, and M. Sturm, Inventory and assessment of nauthorised vehicle routes on Department of the Interior lands in the SBInet Ajo-1 project area and vicinity, southwestern Arizona, Natural Resource Technical Report NPS/ORPI/NRTR–2014/900 (Fort Collins: National Park Service, 2014). U.S. Fish & Wildlife Service, Vehicle Trails Associated with Illegal Border Activities, U.S. F&WS 2011; and Webb et al. "Disruption rates for one vulnerable soil".

56 Howard et al., Inventory and assessment of unauthorised vehicle routes, 26.

57 U.S. Fish & Wildlife Service, Cabeza Prieta National Wildlife Refuge Comprehensive Conservation Plan, Wilderness Stewardship Plan and Environmental Impact Statement (Albuquerque: U.S. Fish & Wildlife Service Division of Planning, 2006), 61.

58 U.S. Fish & Wildlife Service, *Vehicle Trails Associated with Illegal Border Activities, page* 2 presents an inventory of off-road travel on the refuge using high resolution aerial photographs from 2008 to 2011.

Of particular concern is the way vehicle tracks on valley bottoms affect the flow of water from summer monsoons, which in turn affects the growth patterns of vegetation crucial to desert creatures.[59] When it rains, water runs off the surface of compacted soil, making it unavailable to plants. If rainfall is "torrential", a land manager explained, "sheet flow from the mountains starts moving down slope;" when captured by vehicle tracks, water is "starve[d]" from areas that would normally "green up".[60] For instance, if water flowing through an existing east-west drainage system hits a newly compacted north-south road, the water will drain into the road because, as Linda said, "water will flow towards the lowest point".[61] If water pools, two things happen. For one, Border Patrol agents will drive around it, which creates new tracks. In addition, if "there is more water than there needs to be, you can get a lot of vegetation" in that particular spot.[62] But, if water is not flowing in the direction it would normally flow, it will not reach established vegetation.

These seemingly small changes to the desert's surface and, therefore, hydrological system can have drastic consequences. A land manager explained: "If there is a lot of rain, these changes may not be a problem because vegetation would be super abundant".[63] But, in dry years, there "would be a little bit of water here, here, here, and here. So, you may not have enough forage for wildlife populations, not just pronghorn but other things".[64]

In sum, plants normally watered by the drainage system will be starved of water and dry out. "Water is being concentrated and desertifying everything around it", Linda said.[65] Linda explained further:

If you haven't run over and killed the plants in the road, you've desertified that surface; you've made it hotter and you've made it drier. If you take plant cover away, if all you did was go out there and cut down the creosote, you would dry out the area because there's more solar radiation hitting the surface and more evaporation going on. And its hotter, it's just hotter, by a couple of degrees, which is a big difference.[66]

Ultimately, Linda is suggesting that the creation of new roads, tracks, and trails is causing desertification in Sonoran Desert protected areas. Climate change will only compound the changes already set in motion by boundary enforcement policies, operations, and infrastructure.

Damage Control

The research and subsequent publication of reports documenting change over time caused tension between the Border Patrol and federal land management agencies. According to Linda, the Border Patrol refuted the research, calling it "unscientific":

59 Howard et al., Inventory and assessment of unauthorised vehicle routes, 33.
60 Author's interview with a land manager, July 2005.
61 Author's interview with Linda, (retired land manager), July 2015.
62 IBID.
63 IBID.
64 IBID.
65 IBID.
66 IBID.

They didn't like the implication that they were causing damage. And also, they didn't care if they were doing damage. They had a job to do and they didn't care about the [land management agency]. They had their mission and they didn't care what the [land management agency's] was.[67]

The installation of vehicle barriers at the southern boundary of Organ Pipe Cactus NM in 2006 and Cabeza Prieta NWR in 2009, blocked most vehicles trying to cross into U.S. territory from México. Yet, off-road travel continued. However, new tracks primarily extend east-west instead of south-north. For instance, a report on Organ Pipe Cactus NM includes a graph (without accompanying explanation) indicating that east-west vehicle tracks doubled in the years immediately after the vehicle barrier was installed.[68] Linda explained what this suggests:
Back when the roads were created by UDAs [Undocumented Aliens], the roads were going north-south. And now, they're every direction and many of 'em east-west, because [Border Patrol] are trying to intercept. And that's one way that we figure out that it's Border Patrol.[69]

Although land managers suspect Border Patrol agents bear responsibility for the vast majority of vehicles now travelling on unauthorised roads or off-road, administrators up the institutional chain have said they are *not* allowed to report this. Even when Linda had witnessed a Border Patrol vehicle off-road, she said her supervisors told her, "'You can't [say that], no".[70]

Due to conflicts with the Border Patrol, reports on the growing web of new vehicle tracks do not mention the agency by name. As Linda told me:
I was writing this [report], and my supervisor [extended pause]. I mean, it was this constant pulling and pushing. In the end, we had to just say 'law enforcement activities.' 'Illegal smuggling and law enforcement activities.[71]

For example, in a 2014 report on unauthorised roads in Organ Pipe Cactus NM, Cabeza Prieta NWR, and Bureau of Land Management (BLM) Ajo Block, the term *undesignated* replaced *unauthorised* to define roads within a given protected area.[72] No explanation is given for the change. Moreover, the Border Patrol is not named in the same 2014 report, except in the list of literature cited. Instead, the report uses the term "law-enforcement interdiction efforts" and more commonly, the compound term "cross-border traffic

67 Author's interview, July 2015.
68 Organ Pipe Cactus National Monument, *Superintendent's 2010 Report on Natural Resource Vital Signs* (Ajo: Organ Pipe Cactus National Monument, 2011), 19.
69 Author's interview with Linda, (retired land manager), in discussion with the author, July 2015.
70 Interview with the author, July 2015
71 IBID.
72 Howard et al. was an outcome of a Biological Opinion on the Border Patrol's Secure Border Initiative (SBI*net* Ajo-1), which called for a study documenting unauthorised roads in the area designated for the installation of surveillance towers. U.S. Fish & Wildlife Service, *Biological Opinion, SBInet Ajo-1 Tower Project*, #22410-F-2009-0089 (Phoenix: Arizona Ecological Services Field Office, 2009). The project area is Sonoran Pronghorn habitat.

Mountains and valleys in Cabeza Prieta National Wildlife Refuge, South-West Arizona. Source: Image courtesy of Michael Hyatt.

Wooden crosses en route to the border. The writing on the centre cross states: "There are more than 2,800. How many more?".

and law-enforcement interdiction efforts".[73] While some academic researchers follow suit, using terms like "law enforcement professionals",[74] others continue to name the agency, as in "Border Patrol interdiction activities".[75]

Soil Memory

According to one study, there were an estimated 9,327 miles (15,010 km) of unauthorised routes in the area designated for the Border Patrol's Secure Border Initiative (SBI*net* Ajo-1).[76] The project area is prime Sonoran Pronghorn habitat in Organ Pipe Cactus NM, Cabeza Prieta NWR, and the BLM's Ajo

73 Howard et al. 2014, Inventory and assessment of unauthorised vehicle routes, 1. U.S. Fish & Wildlife Service uses terms like "illegal border crossings and subsequent interdiction efforts by law enforcement," U.S. Fish & Wildlife Service, *Vehicle Trails Associated with Illegal Border Activities,* 2. In other words, as the report states, "all of the impacts discussed in this document were the result of the illegal smuggling of people and narcotics into the U.S." (U.S. Fish & Wildlife Service, *Vehicle Trails Associated with Illegal Border Activities,*), 11. Neither the U.S. government's immigration policies nor the Border Patrol's strategy are mentioned; rather, the blame is placed on illegalised activities and peoples.

74 Whitbeck and Fehmi, "Variables influencing law enforcement off-road route proliferation.""

75 Esque et al., "Comparison of methods," 248.

76 Howard et al., "Inventory and assessment of unauthorised vehicle routes," ix.

Block. While the majority of routes were "single-use vehicle tracks", the worst were 148.3 feet (45.2 metres) wide.[77] Clearly, the federal government's immigration policies and border enforcement strategies have prompted consequential transformations to the Sonoran Desert, especially on valley bottom soils.

As part of an agreement for SBI*net* Ajo-1, the DHS provided funding for the closure and restoration of unauthorised routes.[78] An initial 300 miles (483 kilometres) were designated for restoration in the project area.[79] Project reports feature photographs showing the erasure of tire tracks, landscape contouring, mulch, transplanted cacti and other vegetation, and the placement of woody debris or wattles to discourage entry.[80]

Although the Border Patrol tries to obfuscate knowledge about the transformations wrought by U.S. immigration policies and border enforcement strategies, soils have their own stories to tell. Indeed, by their very nature, soils have the capacity to store information about their formation and transformation. For this reason, "soil is an in-situ memory of landscape development in time".[81] In addition to recording its own history, soil tells the stories of human presence and "social dynamics".[82] This is also to say that soils in southwestern Arizona are archiving contemporary geopolitical ventures, from foot trails and vehicle tracks to restoration activities. Future generations will be able to read these stories and draw their own conclusions about commitments kept or broken. Soil memory offers a way to hold the Border Patrol accountable for privileging the security of a white supremacist, settler colonial state over the lives of other-than-human desert communities as well as migrants journeying north.

Postscript

In January 2017, President Donald Trump signed an Executive Order mandating the construction of "a physical wall" at the U.S. southern boundary.[83] Against the wishes of land managers at Organ Pipe Cactus NM, Trump ordered vehicle barriers to be replaced with a 30foot high wall of steel bollards; the concrete and steel foundation reaches eight to ten feet down into the desert floor.[84] In addition, contractors used ammonium nitrate-based explosives to

77 Howard et al., "Inventory and assessment of unauthorised vehicle routes," ix.

78 IBID.

79 US Fish & Wildlife Service, *Formal Section 7 Consultation on Implementation of the Ecological Restoration Plan on Organ Pipe Cactus National Monument, Cabeza Prieta National Wildlife Refuge, and Bureau of Land Management Ajo Block, Pima County, Arizona, 02EAAZ00-2014-F-0538* (Phoenix: Arizona Ecological Services Field Office, 2014).

80 US National Park Service, *Restoration of Undesignated Vehicle Routes* (UVRs) (Ajo: National Park Service Internal Report 2015a). U.S. National Park Service, Restoration of Undesignated Vehicle Routes (UVRs) (Ajo, AZ: National Park Service Internal Report, 2015b).

81 V.O. Targulian and S.V. Goryachkin, "Soil memory: types of record, carriers, hierarchy and diversity," Revista Méxicana de Ciencias Geológicas 21, no. 1 (2004): 2.

82 Eva-Maria Swidler, "The social production of soil," *Soil Science* 174, no. 1 (2009): 7.

83 U.S. President. Exec. Order No. 13767, "Border Security and Immigration Enforcement Improvements Executive Order No. 13767 of January 25, 2017, Federal Register 82, no. 18 (January 30 2017): 8793-8797, https://www.federalregister.gov/documents/2017/01/30/2017-02095/border-security-and-immigration-enforcement-improvements

84 Ryan Devereaux, "The Border Patrol invited the press to watch it blow up a national monument," *The Intercept*, February 27 2020, https://theintercept.com/2020/02/27/border-wall-construction-organ-pipe-explosion

blast through Monument Hill to erect the wall on top.[85] Running alongside the wall is an all-weather gravel road, which, already, has begun causing water to pool. Some of this water is inundating nearby saguaro cacti, causing them to rot and die.[86] Other saguaros were removed and relocated, although many died in the process. Saguaro are sacred to the Tohono O'odham.[87] Meanwhile, the construction process destroyed or damaged archaeological sites that record O'odham history.[88] The resulting land and soilscape will forever document the anxieties underpinning the resurgence of white supremacist politics in the early twenty-first century.

85 Devereaux, "The Border Patrol invited the press to watch it blow up a national monument,"

86 I. S. Simonelli, "Unfinished Arizona border barriers harm environment, National Park Service, area ranchers say," *Tucson Weekly*, June 11 2021, https://www.tucsonweekly.com/TheRange/archives/2021/06/11/unfinished-arizona-border-barriers-harm-environment-national-park-service-area-ranchers-say.

87 Carina Dominguez, ''Time honored' harvesting knowledge altered by climate change," Indian Country Today, 8 August 2022, https://indiancountrytoday.com/news/time-honored-harvesting-knowledge-altered-by-climate-change.

88 V. Jose, "Border wall construction disrupts Native traditions and violates spiritual freedom," *Indian Country Today*, 12 June 2020, https://indiancountrytoday.com/opinion/border-wall-construction-disrupts-native-traditions-and-violates-spiritual-freedom.

Works cited

Akers Chacón, Justin and Mike Davis. *No one is illegal: Fighting violence and state repression on the US-Mexico border.* Chicago: Haymarket Books, 2006.

Annerino, John. *Dead in their tracks: crossing America's desert borderlands.* New York: Four Walls Eight Windows, 1999.

Bezy, John, James Gutmann, and Gordon Haxel. *A Guide to the geology of Organ Pipe Cactus National Monument and Pinacate Biosphere Reserve.* Tucson: Arizona Geological Survey, 2000.

The Binational Migration Institute. *Migrant Deaths in Southern Arizona: Recovered Undocumented Border Crosser Remains Investigated by the Pima County Office of the Medical Examiner, 1990 – 2020.* Tucson : University of Arizona, 2021.

Boyce, Geoffrey Alan. "The rugged border: Surveillance, policing and the dynamic materiality of the US/Mexico frontier." *Environment and Planning D: Society and Space* 34, no. 2 (2016): 245-262.

Boyce, Geoffrey Alan. "Autonomy, human vulnerability and the volumetric composition of U.S. border policing." In *Handbook on the Geographies of Power*, edited by Mat Coleman and John Agnew, 347-361. Cheltenham: Edward Elgar Publishing, 2018.

Chambers, Samuel N., Geoffrey Alan Boyce, Sarah Launius, and Alicia Dinsmore. "Mortality, surveillance and the tertiary "funnel effect" on the US-Mexico border: a geospatial modeling of the geography of deterrence." *Journal of Borderlands Studies* 36, no. 3 (2021): 443-468.

Colibrí Centre for Human Rights. Frequently Asked Questions. Accessed 14 June, 2022. https://colibricenter.org/about/faq/

Cornelius, Wayne A. "Death at the border: Efficacy and unintended consequences of U.S. immigration control policy." *Population and development review* 27, no. 4 (2001): 661-685.

Cruz, Robert. "In our language is where we will find our liberation." *Berkeley La Raza Law Journal* 22, no. 1 (2012): 97-116.

De León, Jason. *The land of open graves: Living and dying on the migrant trail.* Berkeley: University of California Press, 2015.

Defenders of Wildlife. 2006. *On the Line: The Impacts of Immigration Policy on Wildlife and Habitat in the Arizona Borderlands.* Washington, DC: Defenders of Wildlife. Accessed 21 June, 2022. https://grist.org/wp-content/uploads/2007/10/on_the_line_report.pdf

Devereaux, Ryan. The Border Patrol invited the press to watch it blow up a national monument. *The Intercept.* 27 February, 2020 . Accessed 20 June, 2022. https://theintercept.com/2020/02/27/border-wall-construction-organ-pipe-explosion/

Doty, Roxanne Lynn. "Bare life: Border-crossing deaths and spaces of moral alibi." *Environment and Planning D: Society and Space* 29, no. 4 (2011): 599-612

Dunbar-Ortiz, Roxanne. *Not "a Nation of Immigrants": Settler Colonialism, White Supremacy, and a History of Erasure and Exclusion.* Boston: Beacon Press, 2021.

Edgar, Thomas. "Operation Desert Safeguard." National Border, National Park: A History of Organ Pipe Cactus National Monument. Accessed 20 June, 2022. https://organpipehistory.com/orpi-a-z/operation-desert-safeguard/

Esque, Todd C., Rich Inman, Kenneth E. Nussear, R. H. Webb, M. M. Girard, and J. DeGayner. "Comparison of methods to monitor the distribution and impacts of unauthorised travel routes in a border park." *Natural Areas Journal* 36, no. 3 (2016): 248-258.

Ferguson, Kathryn, Norma A. Price, and Ted Parks. *Crossing with the Virgin: stories from the migrant trail.* Tucson: University of Arizona Press, 2010.

Gentry, Blake, Geoffrey Alan Boyce, Jose M. Garcia, and Samuel N. Chambers. "Indigenous survival and settler colonial dispossession on the Mexican frontier: The case of Cedag Wahia and Wo'oson O'odham indigenous communities," *Journal of Latin American Geography* 18, no. 1 (2019): 65-93.

Given, Michael. "Conviviality and the Life of Soil," *Cambridge Archaeological Journal* 28, no. 1 (2018): 127-143.

Hillel, Daniel. *Soil in the environment: crucible of terrestrial life.* Amsterdam: Elsevier, 2007.

Hing, Bill Ong. *Defining America: through immigration policy.* Philadelphia: Temple University Press, 2012.

Howard, S. M. S., S. Rutman, R. Tietien, and M. Sturm. "Inventory and assessment of unauthorised vehicle routes on Department of the Interior lands in the SBInet Ajo-1 project area and vicinity, southwestern Arizona." 2014. Natural Resource Technical Report NPS/ORPI/NRTR–2014/900. National Park Service, Fort Collins, Colorado. Accessed 20 June, 2022. https://irma.nps.gov/DataStore/Reference/Profile/2214834

Jose, V.. Border wall construction disrupts Native traditions and violates spiritual freedom. *Indian Country Today*, 12 June, 2020. Accessed 20 June, 2022 at https://indiancountrytoday.com/opinion/border-wall-construction-disrupts-native-traditions-and-violates-spiritual-freedom?redir=1

La Coalición de Derechos Humanos and No More Deaths. *Disappeared: How the U.S. Border Enforcement Agencies are Fueling a Missing Persons Crisis.* Accessed 14 June, 2022. http://www.thedisappearedreport.org/reports.html

Leza, Christina. *Divided Peoples: Policy, Activism, and Indigenous Identities on the U.S.-Mexico Border.* Tucson: The University of Arizona Press, 2019.

Meierotto, Lisa. "The blame game on the border: perceptions of environmental degradation on the United States-Mexico border," *Human Organisation* 71, no. 1 (2012): 11-21.

---. *Immigration, Environment, and Security on the U.S.-Mexico Border.* Cham: Springer International Publishing, 2020.

Nagy, Moria L., Alejandro Pérez, and Ferran Garcia-Pichel. "The prokaryotic diversity of biological soil crusts in the Sonoran Desert (Organ Pipe Cactus National Monument, AZ)." *FEMS Microbiology Ecology* 54, no. 2 (2005): 233-245.

Nevins, Joseph. *Dying to live: A story of U.S. immigration in an age of global apartheid.* San Francisco: City Lights Books, 2008.

Nevins, Joseph. *Operation Gatekeeper: The rise of the "illegal alien" and the remaking of the US–Mexico boundary.* New York: Routledge, 2001.

Nuñez-Neto, Blas and Michael John Garcia. "Border Security: The San Diego Fence." RS22026. Washington, DC: Congressional Research Service, 2007. Accessed 14 June, 2022. https://sgp.fas.org/crs/homesec/RS22026.pdf.

Piekielek, Jessica. "Creating a Park, Building a Border: The Establishment of Organ Pipe Cactus National Monument and the Solidification of the US-Mexico Border," *Journal of the Southwest* (2016): 1-27.

Regan, Margaret. *The death of Josseline: Immigration stories from the Arizona borderlands.* Boston: Beacon Press, 2010.

Rutman, Sue. "A foundation for collecting, managing, and integrating information on the U.S./Mexico international border activities, June 2004–September 2005, Organ Pipe Cactus National Park." Ajo: Organ Pipe National Park, 2006.

Schulze, Jeffrey M.. *Are we Not Foreigners here?: Indigenous Nationalism in the U.S.-Mexico Borderlands.* Chapel Hill: University of North Carolina Press, 2018.

Simonelli, I. S.. Unfinished Arizona border barriers harm environment, National Park Service, area ranchers say. *Tucson Weekly,* 11 June, 2021. Accessed 20 June, 2022. https://www.tucsonweekly.com/TheRange/archives/2021/06/11/unfinished-arizona-border-barriers-harm-environment-national-park-service-area-ranchers-say

Slack, Jeremy, Daniel E. Martínez, Alison Elizabeth Lee, and Scott Whiteford. "The geography of border militarization: Violence, death and health in Mexico and the United States," *Journal of Latin American Geography* (2016): 7-32.

St. John, Rachel C. *Line in the sand: The desert border between the United States and Mexico, 1848–1934.* Stanford University, 2005.

Sundberg, Juanita. "Diabolic Caminos in the Desert & Cat Fights on the Río: A post-humanist political ecology of boundary enforcement in the United States-Mexico borderlands," *Annals of the Association of American Geographers* 101 no. 2 (2011): 318-336.

Swidler, Eva-Maria. "The social production of soil." *Soil Science* 174, no. 1 (2009): 2-8.

Targulian, V.O., S.V. Goryachkin. "Soil memory: types of record, carriers, hierarchy and diversity," Revista Mexicana de Ciencias GeolSóogilcamse 21, no. 1 (2004): 1–8.

Truett, Samuel. *Fugitive Landscapes: The Forgotten History of the U.S.-Mexico Borderlands.* New Haven: Yale University Press, 2006.

US Border Patrol. *Border Patrol Strategic Plan, 1994 and Beyond,* 1994. Accessed 21 June, 2022.
https://www.hsdl.org/?search=&searchfield=title&all=Border+Patrol+Strategic+Plan%2C+1994+and+Beyond&collection=public&submitted=Search

US Department of Homeland Security. *Final Report of CBP Integrity Advisory Panel.* Washington, D.C.: Homeland Security Advisory Council, 2016.
https://www.dhs.gov/sites/default/files/publications/HSAC%20CBP%20IAP_Final%20Report_FINAL%20(accessible)_0.pdf.

US DHS, U.S. DOI,.and U.S. DOA. *MOU Regarding Cooperative National Security and Counterterrorism Efforts on Federal Lands along the United States' Border, 2006.* Accessed 21 June, 2022. https://winapps.umt.edu/winapps/media2/wilderness/NWPS/documents/Border%20Patrol%20MOU.pdf

US Department of the Interior, U S Forest Service, U S Environmental Protection Agency, U S Department of Justice. *Report to the House of Representatives Committee on Appropriations on Impacts Caused by Illegal Aliens Crossing Federal Lands in Southeast Arizona,* Washington, D.C.: Committee on Appropriations, 2002. Accessed 17 June, 2022. https://www.hsdl.org/?abstract&did=19156.

US Fish & Wildlife Service. *Cabeza Prieta National Wildlife Refuge Comprehensive Conservation Plan, Wilderness Stewardship Plan and Environmental Impact Statement.* Albuquerque: U.S. F&WS Division of Planning, 2006. Accessed 17 June, 2022.
https://www.sciencebase.gov/catalog/item/57e1a214e4b0908250033af5.

US Fish & Wildlife Service. *Biological Opinion, SBInet Ajo-1 Tower Project.* #22410-F-2009-0089. Phoenix, AZ: Arizona Ecological Services Field Office, 2009.

US Fish & Wildlife Service. *Compatibility Determination, Construction of a Communication Tower,* Ajo: Cabeza Prieta National Wildlife Refuge, 2010. Accessed 17 June, 2022. https://wildernesswatch.org/pdf/USFWS_DRAFT-CompatDet_Tower189.1.2010.pdf.

US Fish & Wildlife Service. *Vehicle Trails Associated with Illegal Border Activities on Cabeza Prieta National Wildlife Refuge,* Ajo: Cabeza Prieta National Wildlife Refuge, 2011. Accessed 17 June, 2022. https://rewilding.org/wp-content/uploads/2012/04/Cabeza-Prieta-Vehicle-Trails_2011July.pdf

US Fish & Wildlife Service. *Formal Section 7 Consultation on Implementation of the Ecological Restoration Plan on Organ Pipe Cactus National Monument, Cabeza Prieta National Wildlife Refuge, and Bureau of Land Management Ajo Block, Pima County, Arizona. 02EAAZ00-2014-F-0538.* Phoenix: Arizona Ecological Services Field Office, 2014.

US Government Accountability Office. *Illegal Immigration. Status of Southwest Border Strategy Implementation.* GAO/GGD-99-44. Washington, DC: GAO, 1999. Accessed 17 June, 2022.
https://www.gao.gov/products/ggd-98-21.

---. *INS' Southwest Border Strategy: Resourced and Impact Issues Remain after Seven Years.* GAO-01-842. Washington, DC: GAO, 2001. Accessed 22 June, 2022. https://www.gao.gov/products/gao-01-842

---. Southwest Border: CBP Should Improve Data Collection, Reporting, and Evaluation for the Missing Migrant Program. GAO-22-105053. Washington, DC: GAO, 2022. Accessed 17 June, 2022. https://www.gao.gov/assets/730/720137.pdf.

U.S. House of Representatives Border Patrol Agents in Secret Facebook Group Faced Few Consequences for Misconduct. Staff Report. Washington, D.C.: Committee on Oversight and Reform. 2021.Accessed 17 June, 2022. https://oversight.house.gov/cbp-report.

U.S. House of Representatives Oversight and Homeland Security Chairs Request Information from Customs and Border Protection on Potential Misconduct of Specialized Teams. Washington, D.C.: Committee on Oversight and Reform, 2022. Accessed 15 June, 2022. https://oversight.house.gov/news/press-releases/oversight-and-homeland-security-chairs-request-information-from-customs.

US NPS. *Restoration of Undesignated Vehicle Routes (UVRs).* Ajo: National Park Service Internal Report, 2015a. Accessed 21 June, 2022. https://www.nps.gov/orpi/upload/restoration-may1.pdf.

---. *Restoration of Undesignated Vehicle Routes (UVRs).* Ajo: National Park Service Internal Report, 2015b. Accessed 21 June, 2022. https://www.nps.gov/orpi/upload/restoration-7.pdf

---. *Organ Pipe Cactus National Monument: Superintendent's 2010 Report on Natural Resource Vital Signs.* Ajo, Arizona: Organ Pipe Cactus National Monument, 2011. Accessed 15 June, 2022. https://www.nps.gov/orpi/learn/nature/upload/orpi_vitalsigns2010.pdf

Veech, A. *Archaeological Survey of 18.2 kilometers (11.3 miles) of the U.S.-Mexico International Border, Organ Pipe Cactus National Monument, Pima County, Arizona.* Intermountain Regional Archaeology Program, 2019. Accessed 20 June, 2022. https://gamescdn.washingtonpost.com/notes/prod/default/documents/cbd7ef6a-3b5b-4608-9913-4d488464823b/note/7a429f63-9e46-41fa-afeb-c8e238fcd8bb.pdf.

Webb, Robert H., Todd C. Esque, Kenneth E. Nussear, and Mark Sturm. "Disruption rates for one vulnerable soil in Organ Pipe Cactus National Monument, Arizona, USA," *Journal of arid environments* 95 (2013): 75-83.

Wilderness Act. 1964. Washington, DC: U.S. Congress, Public Law 88-577. Accessed 20 June, 2022. https://wilderness.net/learn-about-wilderness/key-laws/wilderness-act/default.php

Shifting Borderlands of Kutch

Ishita Sharma

I do not know any English word exactly corresponding to Rann. It is neither exclusively a swamp, nor a fen, nor a desert, nor a salt marsh, but a compound of all. The Indo-Pakistan Western Boundary Case Award, quoting Captain GL Jacob, one of the earliest travellers to the Rann in 1844, 24

It is 23 December 2020 and I am sitting with Sadiq,[1] a friend and acquaintance in Kutch. He says "sab uthal puthal ho gaya", indicating that everything turned upside down after the earthquake of 2001. He wasn't referring to the impacts of the earthquake but what followed; the quick industrialisation of the region in the guise of reconstruction.

Once an independent political kingdom, Kutch was governed since 1819 by the British empire and ceded to the Indian state with independence. In the 1960s, Kutch became an administrative district in the more prosperous, as well as linguistically and culturally distinct, state of Gujarat.[2] Seen as a frontier state by the British, and subsequently peripheral by the Indian state, Kutch has been drawn into a plan of port-led logistical development and militarisation since 2001. As Sadiq described, the earthquake accelerated processes already in motion, ushering in a new economic and political regime.[3] Its tremors were felt before in the 90s, as coastal land was demarcated for industrial use.[4] Local politics began to be controlled by industrial houses and power was concentrated outside of Kutchi communities. Since then, occupations of fishing, agriculture and pastoralism are being side-lined, with the dispossession of local communities who are negotiating new hierarchies of labour, security and property. With increasing maritime security, the coastal zones are increasingly coming under surveillance, with the presence of Muslim communities at the border determined a threat.[5]

Reading through British archival works pertaining to Kutch, I found that a similar tectonic moment had occurred with the earthquake of 1819. James

1 Names changed for anonymity.

2 The relationship of Kutch with Sindh, Gujarat and Rajasthan has been fluid, with the region ruled by competing dynasties with political affiliations from as far as Afghanistan and Iran. Its nomadic inhabitants have had limited relationships of patronage with ruling dynasties (Ibrahim 2008; Kothari 2013).

3 Edward Simpson writes, "In Gujarat, change has run deep. The different scales and types of policies co-opted to restructure the region have allowed for the formation of new kinds of citizens and consumers, as well as religious and cultural subjects. A phoenix of industrial sprawl has risen from the desert". Edward Simpson, *The political biography of an earthquake: aftermath and amnesia in Gujarat, India*. (London : Hurst Publishers, 2013), 4.

4 In the historic port city of Mundra, 3000 hectares of coastal land was given to Adani and the conglomerate Cargill for salt production. India was on the cusp of liberalisation, and after protests halted direct foreign investment by international companies, Cargill was forced to withdraw. Coastal land demarcated for salt production transformed into a private port. It is currently the largest notified port and is spread over 13,500 hectares. Land was given at Rs.1 to RS.32 per square metre. (Rs. 1 is £0.010). Multiple cases of environmental violation have been filed against the Port and SEZ and a strong resistance movement of fishing, pastoral and agricultural communities exist.

5 Kutch is spelt differently at different historic moments. The current official spelling is Kachchh. I chose to use the simpler Kutch across the text, except in direct quotes.

Two sides of the same road at Jakhau: mangroves on the left and salt pans on the right. As Dolly Kikon writes, "all these activities involved crossing some kind of border. In sites ranging from a tea plantation boundary to a barricaded oil rig, to a coal mining village, the activities and movements here constituted the political drama of resource extraction and its effect on daily life". Source: Dolly Kikon, *Living with Oil and Coal: Resource politics and militarization in Northeast India* (Seattle: University of Washington Press, 2019 & Delhi: Yoda Press, 2020)

Burnes, the political representative of the British Empire in Kutch wrote,[6]
The tyranny and injustice of Rao Bharmuljee had scarcely been crushed, and a new and better order of things introduced through the means of the British government, when the hand of providence seemed to join in depriving Cutch of some of the instruments of cruelty. A violent shock of an earthquake, levelled with the dust nearly all the walled towns in the country, and anticipated an intention, which had often been conceived, of dismantling some of these nests of discontent and treason. The desolation which ensued can scarcely be imagined.[7]

Reflecting upon the ways that tectonic geological shifts act as an impetus for larger changes, this essay attempts to trace a partial but alternative pathway from the mainstream political and environmental history of Kutch. As Dr.

6 The treaty of suzerainty between the British and the King of Kutch, against local opposition, was signed 2 months before and James Burnes, the political agent at Kutch, suggests that the seismic shock aided the British control of the territory.

7 James Burns, *A Sketch of the History of Cutch* (New Delhi: Gyan Publishing House, 2020), 6.

Thakkar, Head of the Department of Earth and Environmental Science at the KSKV Kachchh University, pointed out to me tectonic shifts are both slow and sudden.[8] While earthquakes remain in our collective memories and cause unimaginable destruction, the ground itself is constantly in motion, a consequence of the interaction between climate and water.[9] As a result of the geological nature of the region, such structural features of the geological timescale spanning 200 years are evident in Kutch. This attention to temporality and the ground resonates with my interactions with the Wagher fishing community and the Fakirani Jat, a pastoral community that herds cattle, including Kharai camels that feed on mangroves. Researching alongside these communities inhabiting the coastal regions of Kutch made me attentive to the materiality of the ground as an *amphibious geography* that is constituted by the mixing of fresh and salt water in combination with interactions with subterranean rock. This condition forms mangrove and intertidal systems that host fish breeding grounds and nourish saline plants that cattle, particularly the Kharai camels, feed on. But with the increasing industrialisation of the coastline, these coastal habitations are being dredged, reclaimed and transformed into industrial and real-estate property. These material changes manifest deeply in the lives of the communities I work with. The framing of amphibiousness here, allows me to rethink connections between subterranean and surface histories, by anchoring the same in the geological and environmental history of the region.[10]

Rather than taking the ground as an a priori condition, I investigate the myriad ways in which narratives of the ground become a site of political claims.[11] I trace how these led to the creation of a border regime that makes possible particular logistical futures and forms of development which in turn are determined by the territorial logic of nation states. I approach archival work as a kind of speculative and interpretive practice—as such, there is no one privileged historical narrative. I read to find mentions of communities that I work with and to find speculative trajectories or "lines of flight" that go against current extractive and neoliberal practices that permeate the region and are trying to define, regulate and curtail people's lives.[12] In the absence of contemporary narratives or access to the Rann, I've looked to archives in order to find the shifting and relational nature of the landscape as well as see how it has been fixed in place.

I begin by following materials and documentation around seismic activities to unearth and highlight routes, movements and a continuously shifting landscape. I then read these archives as used in the Indo-Pak Tribunal of 1965

8 Author's interview with Dr.Thakkar (Head of the Department of Earth and Environmental Science at the KSKV Kachchh University), in discussion with the author, 7 October, 2021.

9 Climate refers to weather or atmospheric patterns across long periods of time that work upon and influence water systems and rock formations. For example, it is one factor in determining how much sand is carried by a river to form intertidal zones or sandy beaches.

10 I use it not as a definitive description but a conceptual tool that allows space for alternative histories, valuation and forms of life.

11 Ayesha Omer writes, "This paper takes up the ground not as an a priori condition but as a political substrate that produces the very shapes and inflections of global infrastructural networks". Ayesha Omer, 'Coal ground', *Cultural Studies* 35, no. 4-5 (March 2021): 920-945, 923.

12 Gilles Deleuze and Félix Guattari, *A Thousand Plateaus: Capitalism and Schizophrenia* (Minneapolis: University of Minnesota Press, 1987).

against the grain to find how this movement of the ground is incorporated into fixed landed border histories .[13] The Tribunal of 1965 demarcated the border in the Rann—acting as a bridge between the colonial past and compromised post-colonial futures. I end with reflecting on how vocabularies that emerged during my fieldwork enable a reading of relational geographies that are reflective of the actual movements of people, cattle, and fish across the landscape.[14]

G catching crabs within the territories of the Kandla Port and SEZ. The port is built on intertidal lands that have historically been inhabited by fishing communities, now living within these logistical infrastructures. Source: Image by Varun Kurtkoti during research with the author.

Slow Seismicity

The first shock was the most violence, continuing for around two minutes 'shaking every house from the Prince's palace to the paupers grass - hut to its centre; nor were the places of the dead exempt from the devastation produced by this mighty convulsion of nature.[15]

Large masses of rock and soil were detached from the precipice of hills, and vast clouds of dust were seen to ascend from all their summits.[16]

The Memoir on the Geology of Kutch explains that although the region of Kutch was long-known as earthquake prone, the earthquake of 16 June 1819 was one the largest quakes in recorded history.[17] Multiple correspondences

13 Ranajit Guha, *Elementary aspects of peasant insurgency in colonial India* (Delhi: Oxford University Press, 2002).

14 I use English language archives to explore how a reading of environmental, administrative and geological records in a specific historical and political context constructed the post-colonial future. These determine how power flows, in whose hands it is retained, how development takes place, what modernisation comes to mean, and how places are classified and mined – setting up trajectories that determine the lives of people who call such landscapes home.

15 A.B.Wynne and F. Fedden, 'Memoir on the Geology of Kutch, to accompany the map compiled by A B Wynne and F Fedden during the season 1867–1868, 1868–1869'; *Geol. Surv. India Memoir* 19(2) 1–269 (1872),6 .

16 IBID. The memoirs also quote a report by James MacMurdo, political agent of the British at Kutch.

17 Kutch was drawn into colonial forms of knowledge production due to its geography and geopolitical location. The rise of geology as a scientific discipline and the need for administration resulted in geological studies and administrative reports forming one of the first English language sources that describe its geography and inhibition.

from British agents stationed in different parts of western India record the moment of the earthquake and its aftermath.[18] Tracing geological and seismic information generated by the British shows that alongside short term impacts, the earthquake led to long lasting changes in topography. Water levels and routes varied across time and season. For example, Kori creek (also spelt as Khori and Cori), a main estuary of the Indus near Lakhpat fort, could be crossed on foot, but increased to 5.4 meters at low tide after the earthquake. Soundings carried out by British political agents and administrators show that it kept fluctuating at least until 1829.[19] Land and levels and water varied and fluctuated; the earthquake depressed a portion of the Rann lying north of Lakhpat and its neighbouring areas. The fort of Sindree, where the Kutch kingdom levied customs to those crossing from and towards Sindh was swept over by ocean waters and was converted into an inland lake. A scarp was thrown up across the channel at Kori creek, stopping the flow of the Nara river. This mound was given the name of Allah Bund,[20] a bandh or dam thrown up by God, running East to West between the Rann. Alexander Burnes describes Allah Bund as composed of "soft clay with shells elevated about 10 feet from the surface of the water, and cut through like a canal with vertical banks on either side. The channel was about 35 yards broad and three fathoms deep; and a body of the freshwater of the Indus rolled down it into the lake".[21] 25 years after the earthquake, the reputed geologist and seismologist, Richard Dixon Oldham, described the shifting landscape once more,

Ten years later, the ruins of the fort were seen still standing out of a waste of waters, and twenty-five years later, in 1844, a careful survey was made and levels taken, and this survey revealed a remarkable condition of things. From the north the surface of the delta sloped southwards, at about eight to ten inches in the mile, to within six miles from the crest of the Allah Bund, when a reverse slope was met, and the surface gradually rose to nearly 20 feet above the level of the continuation of the southerly slope, or the level at which it presumably stood before the earthquake. Thence there was a steep slope downwards, to the water of the Sindri lake. On the south the original reports mention a depth of twelve feet of water close to the shore, immediately after the earthquake, and, as the original surface level must have been a few feet above that of the sea, we have a depression of some fifteen feet, which gradually died out in a distance of some six miles to the southward. From these facts it is clear that there was no appreciable change of level at a distance of about six miles on either side of the line of the Allah Bund, but that along that line the ground on the north was upraised by some twenty feet and on the south depressed by some fifteen at the time of the earthquake.[22]

18 S Dasgupta, and Basab Mukhopadhyay, 'Historiography and commentary on the 16 June 1819 Kutch Earthquake, Gujarat, India.' *Indian Journal of Geosciences* 68 (2014): 57-126.

19 Lieutenant Alex, 'Memoir on the Eastern Branch of the River Indus, Giving an Account of the Alterations Produced on It by an Earthquake, Also a Theory of the Formation of the Runn, and Some Conjectures on the Route of Alexander the Great; Drawn up in the Years 1827-1828'. *Transactions of the Royal Asiatic Society of Great Britain and Ireland* 3, no. 3 (1834): 550–588.

20 Please see diagram on page 75. CP Rajendran describes the Allah bund as a scrap - a linear mound, "60-70 km, long, 16 km wide and between 2-4 m off the ground, stretching in the east to west direction on the plains of the Rann".

21 Wynne and Fedden, 'Memoirs of Geology', 54 and Lieutenant Alex, 'Memoirs on the Eastern Branch of the River Indus,' 35.

22 Richard Oldham,'The Character and Cause of Earthquakes,' *Nature* III (1923), 432–434: 432.

Images from Kandla port and trust (now renamed Deendayal port trust) showing the range of activities carried out in the port and the infrastructure surrounding the the Juna Kandla village.

Source: Images by Varun Kurtkoti during research with author.

What was the significance of the earthquake and why does it occupy an important place in the theories of geologists who are considered today some of the key figures in the discipline? As Oldham wrote in 1923, and as my interviews with geologists suggest, the 1819 earthquake indicated for the first time that interior continents can also produce tectonic movements. A geological condition expressed by similar earthquakes that took place in Madrid (1811) and California (1906). These occurrences validated the "elastic rebound theory of earthquakes", feeding into Lyell's larger theory which suggested that the earth is created through sedimented movements that are continuous rather than only through sudden shocks.[23]

Reading about the changes to the landscape in memoirs and reports, I found numerous mentions of riverine and land routes that were adapting to the changing geological conditions. This becomes particularly important when it comes to imagining the fluid and navigable nature of the region, which mainstream narrations do not describe, instead creating a conception of the Rann only as a barren, inhospitable and dangerous territory. As recounted in the geological survey, "the latter route is now disused in consequence of the dangerous state of the Runn, quicksand occurring on that side of the Sindree basin, and a more circuitous one has been adopted".[24]

Reports from 1826 and 1829 mention other changes. They detail that the coastal routes between Lakhpat, Sando (a few miles away from Lakhpat) and towards Sindree—the inland lake created by the earthquake—were once again navigable as the Indus burst, overflowing all-man made dams towards Sindh and cutting through the Allah Bund. Water was brackish at Sando and sweet at Sindree. They also mention water communication and the trade of Ghee (clarified butter) between Lakhpat, Wunga Bazaar and Umercote (now in Sindh).[25] The Allah bund blocked the course of the river Nara, a tributary of the Indus that used to flow through the Rann of Kutch, and was used as a waterway to conduct trade between inland and coastal areas of the Indus. Commenting on this, CP Rajendran, a seismologist, writes that "it was the first large historically known earthquake that impacted flourishing human settlements and their corresponding infrastructure, including waterways and tax-collection centres".[26]

If the event of the earthquake sheds light on the ways that the movement of water and ground behave differently and even change course to impact surface economies, documentation indicates that changes were a constant and some were just more visible. Prior and subsequent accounts show that multiple smaller earthquakes took place after 1918.[27] Other records indicate that tectonic movements as well as shifts in weather conditions, monsoons and rainfall patterns have changed river courses, altered routes of travel and trade, and shifted human settlements.

23 Charles Lyell, *Principles of Geology.* (Germany:Verlag Von J. Cramer; S-H Service Agency, 1970).
24 Wynne and Fedden, 'Memoirs of Geology', 34.
25 Wynne and Fedden, 'Memoirs of Geology', 35, and Lieutenant Alex, 'Memoirs on the Eastern Branch of the River Indus'.
26 C.P Rajendran, 'The Significance of the 1819 Allah Bund Earthquake, 200 Years on', *The Wire,* June 5, 2019, https://thewire.in/the-sciences/the-significance-of-the-1819-allah-bund-earthquake-200-years-on.
27 See Wynne and Fedden, 'Memoirs of Geology', 2014.

Dr. Thakkar narrated to me his own visit to the Allah Bund in the early 2000s. As he recounted, processes of wind and water remain constant and slowly wear away even the most solid of materials and startling of events. The Allah bund is slowly eroding as a network of miniature ravines and valleys are carving a new topography on it. These regions of Allah Bund and the Nara riverbed are now part of the border apparatus, accessible through geological expeditions with approval and surveillance of the Border Security Forces (BSF) or through records such as those described above. Thresholds of access exist—local pastoral and fishing communities can no longer utilise the mangrove and routes to Sindh that sustained their livelihoods. In the face of this changing landscape and human movement, how does a border come to be?

Fixing Territory Cum Grano Salis

To separate the coast from the rights that appertain to it and what lies beyond the coast in the horizontal plane, is like separating the ground from the rights that appertain to it in the atmosphere which extends above it in the vertical plane. The same principle is operating and I submit that in neither case, neither in the horizontal plane nor in the vertical plane, can that which appertains to that ground be separated from that ground.[28]

One of the ways in which archival materials were utilised to produce stable terrestrial histories is via instruments such as the Indo-Pakistan Western Boundary Case Tribunal, instituted in 1965, and awarded in 1968.[29] The tribunal determined the border between India and Pakistan in the Rann of Kutch and was one of the first instances of international arbitration in the period after the Second World War. Tribunal members consisted of Nasrollah Entezam and Ales Bebler, with Gunnar Lagergen nominated as chairman by the United Nations. The tribunal took the nature of colonial occupation for granted, defining territorial rights through the prism of Sindh and Kutch as occupied territories, governed by forms of law that were based on the British exercise of jurisdiction. The award was based on documentary and archival evidence consisting of official communications between the Kingdom of Kutch, Kingdom of Sindh, imperial maps, boundary disputes, administrative reports and acts of governmental authority in the region, corresponding to the period of 1870 to 1947.

I've returned to this tribunal award to read it as a *book of records*. I'm not reading it in order to determine its veracity, but to understand how the tribunal assessed and demarcated the region, producing it as a border territory that contrasted with some of the above descriptions I have found in different archival

28 Counsel for Pakistan, Verbatim records, tribunal Award, 417.

29 The Indo-Pakistan Western Boundary Rann of Kutch) Case Tribunal between India and Pakistan (India, Pakistan), February 1968, United Nations, 2006. Submissions to the tribunal by India and Pakistan are classified and this analysis is based on an extensive 900 page document that includes the discussions that took place in the tribunal as well as three separate notes and opinions by the three jury members. Presented here is a partial reading of the same, as the award is rich and extremely complex. I have not mentioned multiple boundary disputes that took place between smaller kingdoms bordering the east part of the Rann (now Rajasthan), and in the Gulf of Kutch in the south.

India and Adjacent Countries, Sheet No. 40 Hyderabad (Sindh), 2nd Revised Edition, 1926, prepared under Surveyor General of India. I share this map to give a sense of the kind of maps the tribunal was looking at and representations of symbols, boundaries and colours. Source: Maharashtra State Archives.

Border Security Forces (BSF) signage in Lakhpat near pastoral villages. The text says that we are on the western most road of India and that permission is necessary to enter the village. Source: Photograph by the author.

documents.[30] Here, inadvertently, the tribunal becomes a moment when British instruments and practices of imperial rule are interrogated, highlighting the ways that archival materials submitted to the tribunal, representing administrative actions on ecological and political demarcation, function as claims rather than as authoritative truths. While a reading of the award exposes the fragmentary nature of colonial rule, it also reaffirms and re-establishes its authority.

No geographical or geological description is neutral. Geography became a site of political claims; Pakistan argued that the Rann was a marine feature, a depression below sea level. India claimed it as a vast expanse of land consisting of salt waste, with sea water covering the western portion of the Rann from May onwards. The tribunal found that historical administrative and travel records deploy similar descriptions but differ in their use of terms. It was decided that the geographical description of the Rann was not pertinent to the demarcation of the border—the only important point to be clarified was the true nature of the Rann.[31] But the shifting nature of the landscape and political control did not allow for any easy resolution. Acknowledging the impossibility in defining the true or singular character of the Rann, the focus of the Tribunal shifted towards two key issues. Firstly, the accuracy of maps prepared by the British and secondly, whether the exercise of jurisdiction constitutes an acceptable form of sovereignty. These debates shape the ways in which the nature of the ground and movements based on them were erased from contemporary understandings of the region. They point to what forms of belonging and utilisation were deemed to hold value.

The map introduced as key evidence by India was at the centre of the debates.[32] Firstly, disagreement existed on how the Rann was represented

30 Elden writes, "understanding territory as a political technology is not to define territory once and for all; rather it is to indicate the issues at stake in grasping how it was understood in different historical and geographical contexts". In Stuart Elden, 'Land, Terrain, Territory.' *Progress in Human Geography* 34, no. 6 (December 2010): 799–817, 812.

31 Tribunal Award, 22-30.

32 Survey maps under consideration included the survey of Sindh and survey of Kutch by the survey department of the Government of India. These included maps from 1855 to 1928. Boundaries depicted are changing over time, and the discussion includes smaller disputes and resolutions on parts of the territory. Not all maps were available to the tribunal. The fuzziness and uncertainty in the making of maps is quite evident in the discussions and representations.

and whether it was signified as a water body or a marsh. The second issue pertained to whether the boundaries on the maps were actually boundary lines agreed upon by the British. To gauge this, the tribunal recounted communications by the Government of India; communications between local administrators, surveyors and the higher authorities of the Government of India that showed that maps were produced via negotiations.

Local officials from Kutch and Sindh and British officials had different ideas regarding where boundaries between Kutch and Sindh lay and whether the maps even attempted to represent them in a definitive manner. These communications, when read in detail, indicated the differential experiences involved in experiencing and classifying the Rann, leading the tribunal to conclude that existing boundary lines could not be seen as definitive. These were never dealt with as a political question (as per the tribunal), and so they decided that the accuracy of maps then must be taken *cum grano sali* (with a grain of salt).[33] As the Award notes,

When however, the true extension of sovereignty over a territory became the subject of investigation and enquiry, and specially of an exhaustive judicial enquiry, the evidentiary value of the maps was lessened as far as the relevant boundaries were concerned, and they were made to yield to evidence of superior weight, particularly evidence of the exercise of jurisdiction. [34]

The debate shifted to the nature of jurisdiction and sovereignty; submissions made by India and Pakistan reveal that forms of sovereignty varied in British occupied India and existed in a multitude of combinations. In the case of the Rann, particular forms of sanctioned usage were recognised as constituting claims on jurisdiction. The tribunal gave a limited importance to grazing patterns and fishing rights, while emphasising expressions of British authority and control—namely, criminal jurisprudence in the areas and patrolling via British troops, police work and surveillance. The question of sovereignty was tied into the exercise of jurisdiction, and the proof of jurisdiction was considered as a form of control over inhabitation. But a shifting landscape exceeds colonial law. Sovereignty, while resting on the exercise of (limited) jurisdiction, was tied into the question of topography. This forms the crux of the matter in many ways. What recognisable forms of jurisdiction and ownership exist in such shifting geographies? How is jurisdiction exercised in differently inhabited landscapes?[35] I see this debate as one between different forms of inhabitation, and the inability or political decision of the tribunal to grasp the same.

Rather than address this amphibious condition, the tribunal discounted the shifting and changing nature of the landscape and the pathways of movement and nomadic practices of inhabitation that existed. The tribunal conceived of the Rann only as a static and ecologically unique border territory in which complexity was laid to rest, as far as the legal regime was concerned. Colonial narratives of changing geographies and topographies, read with the agenda of demarcating a fixed border were subsumed into the legal framework

33 A trace of humour perhaps, considering the Rann is defined as a salt desert?

34 Tribunal Award, 566.

35 It was suggested that neither Sindh nor Kutch gave enough evidence to establish that either had continuous or effective jurisdiction over the whole Great Rann.

Charri Dhand Wetland conservation reserve situated between the banni grasslands and salt marshes of the Rann of Kutch, Charri Hand is lowland that forms a sanctuary and grazing ground for pastoralists in Kutch. Source: Photograph by the author.

Inland mangroves of Guneri situated in Lakhpat, near the border between India and Pakistan, these inland mangroves are remains of the sea and an indication of shifting landscapes, sustained by underground streams of salt water and nurtured by villagers of Guneri village. Source: Photograph by the author.

of the tribunal, functioning as scientific evidence that have resonance even today. The border once demarcated, did not come up at once but accreted slowly, swallowing up the region and its connection with the Rann. The tribunal noted while awarding the final decision, "Because of the imprecise topographical features in the region and the *impossibility* of exactly *delimiting* many acts of state authority, the boundary must sometimes be represented by approximate straight lines". [36]

Conclusion

On the coast of Mohadi is a village called New Nimdivandh. The original NNimdivandh was on a bet (island) and moved inland after the cyclone of 1991. Near Nimdivandh live fishworkers displaced from Jakhau, around 40 kilometres away by road.[37] The fishers, also Fakirani jat, moved here after salt pan factories destroyed the mangrove systems that formed their fish breeding and grazing grounds. Such movements are common across the coast. People and villages move because of changes in topography and water levels, changing patterns of monsoon, drying river creeks and mangrove systems caused by climate and disaster, both natural and increasingly human-made. Such a shifting landscape repeats itself in the archives. For example, references to Sayra, which are found strewn across multiple reports and the Tribunal award, point to how human-made and climatic changes are entangled. A river fed by the Indus flowed into the mouth of the Kori Creek (now a disputed maritime border between India and Pakistan) till the 1700s. But because of the construction of barrages upstream on the Indus and the ever-changing course of the tributaries of the Indus , the waters dried up and Sayra was deserted, eventually becoming part of the Rann.

Reading Kutch through the histories and current practices of the ground reveal complex amphibious geographies comprised of both land and water. Kutch was once underwater, and its geomorphology consists of four main upwellings or islands that compose the islands of Bela, Paccham, Khadir and the mainland. The region emerged from the sea and its river systems are connected to each other through the Great Rann and the Little Rann. Rather than dry and water deficit, as Kutch is typically described, different forms of water percolate Kutch. To think through the lens of land or surface is to restrict these hydrological and subterranean connections. Water exits the landscape in degrees and in relation as salt water, runoff, fresh water, in creeks, streams and non-perennial rivers, as rain, and as evaporation.[38]

As the anthropologist Andreas Ballestros in her study of the aquifer writes that "moments of conceptual confusion in making the aquifer legible challenge the seamless separation between aquifer as figure and the subsurface

36 Tribunal Award, 570.

37 The straight path is through mudflats and streams and is approximately 10-12 km.

38 I draw upon the following theoretical works: Dilip da Cunha, *The invention of rivers: Alexander's eye and Ganga's descent* (Philadelphia:University of Pennsylvania Press, 2018), Anuradha Mathur, and Dilip da Cunha, *Soak: Mumbai in an estuary* (New Delhi: Rupa & Co, 2009), Layla Mehta, "The Manufacture of Popular Perceptions of Scarcity: Dams and Water-Related Narratives in Gujarat, India', *World Development* 29, no 12 (2001), K. Lahiri – Dutt. 'Beyond the water-land binary in geography: Water/Lands of Bengal re-visioning hybridity,' *ACME: An International Journal for Critical Geographies* 13, no3, (2014): 505-529.

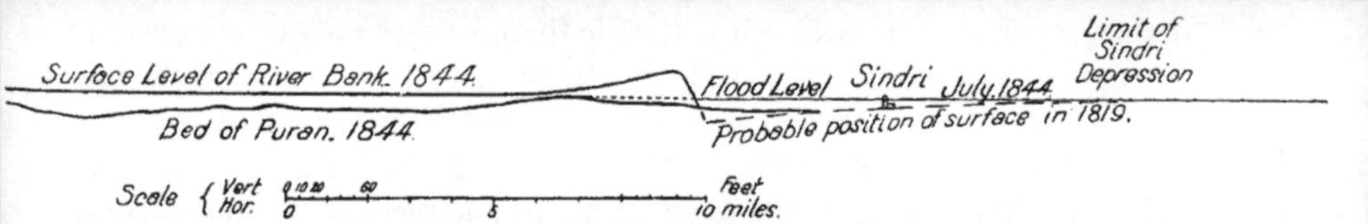

FIG. 1.—Section across the Allah Bund and Sindri depression of June 16, 1819.

Section across the Allah bund and Sindri depressions of 16 June 1819.
Source: Oldham, "The Character and Cause of Earthquakes".

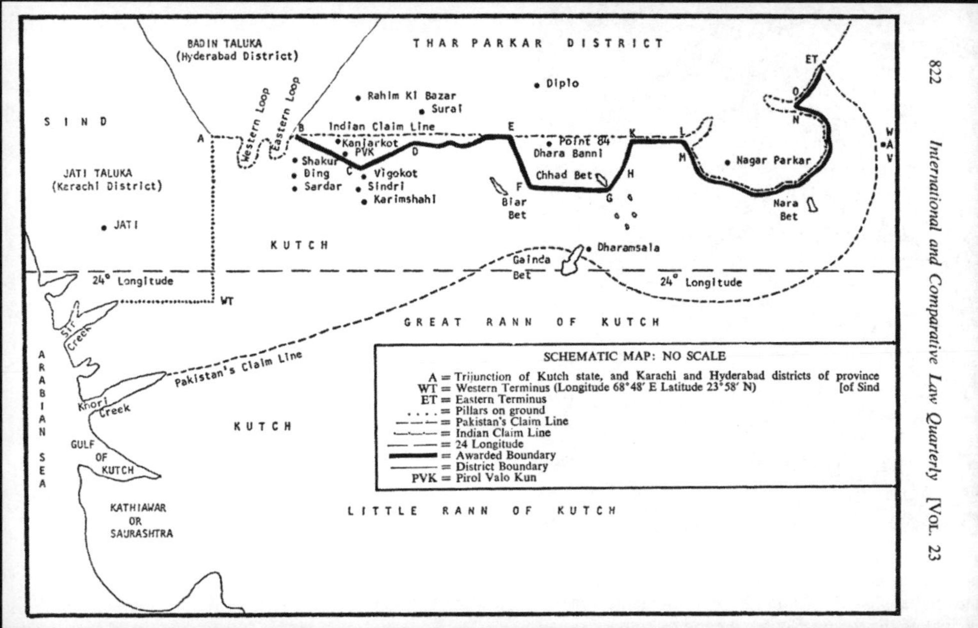

Final Award of the tribunal demarcating the border between India and Pakistan in the Great Rann. Boundaries claimed by India and Pakistan are also represented in this image. Schematic map, no scale, Source: Untawale, "The Kutch-Sindh Dispute".

as its ground. They remind us of the arbitrary, yet inevitable cuts we make as we single out an infrastructure as a figure and invite us to attend more carefully to the alternate possibilities inscribed in those cuts".[39] In Kutch, different forms of the ground and water as well as the life that they sustain are demarcated through infrastructural cuts, producing them as discrete objects: as the Great and Little Rann, as mangroves, as desert, as wasteland, as property with defined geographic and conceptual limits. The nature of geographic claims are political, indicating that geography acts as an epistemic and meaning making system.[40]

The Rann when filled with water abounds with different fish, some of which are peculiar to it I believe, and are exceedingly delicious.[41]

This is a speculative Van Dyke image. The process utilised soil and through this I try to think through the relationship of soil and salt–both elements that constitute the region. Source: Image by author.

While the Rann itself is perhaps impossible to define, it exists today as a discrete and stable environmental or ecological object, despite its histories of constant transformations. The archival materials and narratives I've explored point to how histories of relational affinities between ecosystems and a continuously changing topography have been disappeared from view. This has made possible the demarcation of the border as a more or less straight line and of Kutch as an administrative territory. But in fact, vocabularies of the region hold these

39 Andrea Ballestero, 'The Underground as Infrastructure?: Water, Figure/Ground Reversals, and Dissolution in Sardinal.' In *Infrastructure, Environment, and Life in the Anthropocene*, edited by Kregg Hetherington(Durham, North Carolina: Duke University Press, 2019), 25.

40 Irit Rogoff, *Terra infirma: geography's visual culture* (London: Routledge, 2000).

41 Tribunal Award, quoting Captain MacMurdo, 25.

relations together. Whereas the Rann refers in existing written works to the Salt Rann consisting of the Great and Little Rann of Kutch, during fieldwork, pastoral communities referred to wetland systems across the coast as Rann as well. This became a moment of conceptual confusion that questioned my own understanding. They point to how the Rann is a shifting, shared and relational ecology, held together, not by its geographical limits and surface resources of salt and minerals, but rather through subterranean and river systems that cut through the region. In local vocabularies, the usage of the word 'rann' for different geographies points to how alluvium and alluvial landscapes hold different degrees and forms of soil and salt, yet are part of continuous amphibious landscapes, now divided by the border as well as geological and environmental discourses that determine our understanding of the world.[42] These relations map onto the routes of grazing and fishing, inhabited geographies that are made visible by the movement of these communities.

A focus on the materiality of the ground illustrates how interpretations of it determine current forms of development and bordering practices. If tectonic events such as earthquakes of 1819 and 2001 led to a consolidation of political acts that define and shape the region, local vocabularies and a re-reading of the archives reveal a slower movement of the ground, unearthing the shifting and relational nature of alternative geographical-political imaginations.

42 Increasingly, it seems as though there is a new emphasis in environmental discourses on the rann and coastal ecologies as wetlands relates more closely to local identifications of the region.

Works cited

Ballestero, Andrea. 'The Underground as Infrastructure?: Water, Figure/Ground Reversals, and Dissolution in Sardinal.' In *Infrastructure, Environment, and Life in the Anthropocene*, edited by Kregg Hetherington. Durham, North Carolina: Duke University Press, 2019.

Burns, James. *A Sketch of the History of Cutch.* 1839; reis., New Delhi : Gyan Publishing House, 2020.

da Cunha, Dilip. *The invention of rivers: Alexander's eye and Ganga's descent*, Philadelphia: University of Pennsylvania Press, 2018.

Dasgupta, S. and Basab Mukhopadhyay, 'Historiography and commentary on the 16 June 1819 Kutch Earthquake, Gujarat, India.' *Indian Journal of Geosciences* 68 (2014): 57-126.

Deleuze, Gilles and Félix Guattari. *A Thousand Plateaus: Capitalism and Schizophrenia*. Minneapolis: University of Minnesota Press, 1987.

Elden, Stuart. 'Land, Terrain, Territory.' Progress in Human Geography 34, no. 6 (December 2010): 799–817.

Guha, Ranajit. 2002. *Elementary aspects of peasant insurgency in colonial India.* Delhi: Oxford University. Press, 2002.

Lahiri–Dutt, K..'Beyond the water-land binary in geography: Water/Lands of Bengal re-visioning hybridity,' *ACME: An International Journal for Critical Geographies* 13, no. 3, (2014).

Lyell, Charles. *Principles of Geology.* Germany: Verlag Von J. Cramer, S-H Service Agency, 1970.

Mathur, Anuradha and Dilip da Cunha. *Soak: Mumbai in an estuary.*New Delhi: Rupa & Co, 2009.

Mehta, Layla. 'The Manufacture of Popular Perceptions of Scarcity: Dams and Water-Related Narratives in Gujarat, India', *World Development* 29, no 12 (2001).

Oldham, Richard. 'The Character and Cause of Earthquakes,'*Nature* III, (1923): 432–434.

Omer, Ayesha. 'Coal ground', *Cultural Studies* 35, no. 4-5 (March 2021).

Rajendran, C.P.. "'The Significance of the 1819 Allah Bund Earthquake, 200 Years on"', *The Wire,* June 5, 2019, https://thewire.in/the-sciences/the-significance-of-the-1819-allah-bund-earthquake-200-years-on.

Rogoff, Irit. *Terra infirma: geography's visual culture.* London: Routledge, 2000.

Simpson, Edward. *The political biography of an earthquake: aftermath and amnesia in Gujarat, India.* London : Hurst Publishers, 2013.

Wynne, A. B and F. Fedden. 'Memoir on the Geology of Kutch, to accompany the map compiled by A. B. Wynne and F. Fedden during the season 1867–1868, 1868–1869.' *Geol. Surv. India Memoir* 19(2) 1–269 (1872).

Lieutenant Alex. 'Memoir on the Eastern Branch of the River Indus, Giving an Account of the Alterations Produced on It by an Earthquake, Also a Theory of the Formation of the Runn, and Some Conjectures on the Route of Alexander the Great; Drawn up in the Years 1827-1828.' *Transactions of the Royal Asiatic Society of Great Britain and Ireland* 3, no. 3 (1834).

Hypothermic Tactics

Susan Schuppli

If they talked too loudly, or if children were crying, the guards would threaten to turn the air temperature down further. Kimberly Martinez, a Honduran migrant who spent time in a Customs and Border Protection (CBP) facility in the Rio Grande Valley, Texas speaking on condition of anonymity to Guardian journalist Andrew Gumbel in 2018.[1]

Deterrence and Punishment

Migrants trying to cross the Italian border into France via the icy verticality of the Alps or the watery expanse of the Evros river delta between Turkey and Greece, both of which form 'natural' borders between their respective nation states, have become a frequent occurrence in recent years. The consequences of undertaking such perilous journeys has resulted in numerous cases of hypothermia and at times, even death. In these and other migrant crossings, temperature—specifically exposure to cold—has played a critical role in European border management as a 'natural' agent with potentially lethal force. While exposure to cold temperatures is not in and of itself always consequential given the many protective measures that we can take to maintain our well-being and safety in even the most adverse of conditions, it is rather the differential experiences of temperature that put migrant bodies at risk in such geographies. The alps or a river system are not necessarily hostile to all bodies, as is evidenced by the many leisure activities that take place within such environments. Yet when temperatures drop, they can prove deadly to bodies that are not adequately equipped or in sufficiently good health (anxious, exhausted by extended journeys and in need of proper nourishment) to deal with such localised climatic conditions. As Fortress Europe battens down, migrants have had no choice but to seek alternate and ever-more treacherous trajectories in their search for sanctuary. Yet, authorities rely on bad weather and dangerous routes to force migrants back, enlisting the environment as an unwitting but strategic accomplice in their efforts at deterrence, while simultaneously insisting that they have no control over weather fronts and other natural hazards and thus bear no responsibility when people succumb to hypothermia or perish. The implicit role of temperature in facilitating these bordering practices must be understood as an integral part of the complex assemblage of racialised violence inflicted directly upon bodies and cannot be dismissed as an incidental feature of such crossings.[2]

1 Kimberly Martinez is not her real name. See Andrew Gumbel, "'They Were Laughing at Us': Immigrants Tell of Cruelty, Illness and Filth in U.S. Detention," *The Guardian*, 12 September.

2 While temperature doesn't feature in EU migration documents, it is acknowledged as an factor that can aid in deterring migration in U.S. policy. "Temperatures ranging from sub-zero along the northern border to the searing heat of the southern border affect illegal entry traffic as well as enforcement efforts. Illegal entrants crossing through remote, uninhabited expanses of land and sea along the border can find themselves in mortal danger." See U.S. Border Patrol, *Border Patrol Strategic Plan 1994 and Beyond.*

When guards threaten to turn down the thermostat in a migrant detention facility in the Rio Grande Valley near the U.S. Mexico border, it is clear that cold is being used explicitly as a form of deliberate punishment by law enforcement against migrant bodies. Thermostatic modulation in this carceral context becomes a regulatory mechanism for exerting biopolitical control over bodies that have been rendered illegal and are thus out-of-place. As has been recounted by investigative journalists, migrants in these temporary holding cells, also referred to as "hieleras" in Spanish, or iceboxes, often have their long-sleeve clothing and jackets removed because they allegedly pose a suicide risk, whereas guards are fully outfitted with warm jackets, vests, and boots.[3] Temperature in these CBP detention facilities is not an external ambient characteristic of a natural phenomenon—the scorching day-time heat and night-time chill that emanates from the desert ecologies that span the U.S.-Mexico border—but is engineered into the architecture of incarceration in the form of "air conditioning" and "climate control" systems which can be instrumentalised with the flick of a switch. Most of us have likely adjusted the thermostats in our living spaces, a seemingly banal and ordinary gesture, yet one, which in another situation, could be considered abusive and in violation of human rights.[4] The different thermostatic regimes that operate across the contexts of cross-border migration from open-air movement through arid deserts, alpine geographies, and watery deltas into the air conditioned spaces of detention along the U.S.-Mexico border highlight the degree to which environmental factors have increasingly been incorporated into the tactics and practices of law enforcement as tools for managing and policing racialised bodies. Alongside these developments, we also witness a shift in the ways in which temperature has been instrumentalised from an opportune mode of deterrence to a designed means of punishment.

Temperature Ethics

Today, the consequences of changing temperature are central to the climate crisis, so it may seem somewhat surprising that little public attention has been paid to the ways in which temperature has been used to inflict harm in other circumstances. Cold, in particular, rarely features in general discussions of climate change (except by those denying warming trends) nor in debates around civilian policing. Yet, even when media forums focus on the cryosphere or frozen geographies of our planet, the emphasis is primarily on warming resulting from greenhouse gas emissions. These are discussions in which anthropogenic activities are demonstrably causal with respect to how rising temperatures are responsible for glacial recession, sea ice retreat, and the fracturing of the polar ice sheets. While the impacts of such dramatic material changes have direct consequences for all planetary life forms, few considerations reflect upon the ways that the thermal properties of environmental systems are enlisted as indirect

3 Gumbel, "'They Were Laughing at Us': Immigrants Tell of Cruelty, Illness and Filth in U.S. Detention."

4 For example: the right to life, the right to health, freedom of movement, right to asylum, freedom from arbitrary detention, the rights of those most affected by climate change, etc. as entrenched in the articles of the Universal Declaration of Human Rights.

weapons against people, although there are endless examples in which 'we' have simply 'let' compromised 'nature' run its course with devastating effect on human as well as more-than-human ecologies. When the changing material conditions of cold, expressed by permafrost thaw, sea ice retreat, glacial recession, and the collapse of the Antarctic ice shelves, does enter the political sphere, it is often deliberated within the framework of sovereignty disputes and security concerns that threaten to re-organise territorial relations between states. This has been the case in the Circumpolar region for decades. As sea ice liquifies, access to oil and gas reserves along with new transportation arteries and logistical networks are opened up to new political actors with competing territorial claims.[5]

Cold politics demands an engagement with a climatic sense of justice, rather than a partitioning of rights to states and treaty signatories. Yet for affected communities in the North who have been dealing with the ravages of global warming, especially Indigenous peoples, the "right to be cold" has become a potent political demand that underscores our very inseparability from the environments in which we are all enfolded.[6] Although this legal claim was dismissed by the Inter-American Commission on Human Rights in 2005 (when Inuk activist Sheila Watt-Cloutier first filed a petition "Seeking Relief From Violations Resulting from Global Warming Caused By Acts and Omissions of the United States" on behalf of herself and sixty-two Inuit people living in the Arctic regions of Canada and the USA), the transformation of a thermostatic condition into an ethical claim for cold rights has never been more urgent.[7] The "right to be cold" is not a call to be subjected to harsh or inhospitable conditions, but is a provocation which recognises that the material integrity of environments upon which cryospheric communities depend are thermostatically interdependent. It is thus a plea for an "ethics of temperature" that is relational and committed to life's flourishing—the right to exist within a stable temperature regime that sustains rather than destroys life worlds.

Experiencing Temperature

Although temperature is defined quantitatively by a series of gradient degrees that are indicative of thermal intensity, the actual lived experience of temperature is always qualitative and dependent upon a wide-range of input variables that combine to produce a feeling of either cold or heat. Each person experiences the same thermal conditions differently depending on their gender, body type, health, fitness, clothing etc. In a conversation with Mike Tipton, Professor of Human & Applied Physiology who runs the Extreme Environments Laboratory, School of Sport, Health & Exercise Science at the University of Portsmouth, he explained the biological differences: *The ideal office temperature for men in suits is about 21 degrees Celsius, and because men in suits deter-*

5 With the melting of the Arctic ice sheets, extant national borders with their established 200 nautical mile limit are actively being redrawn. The agreements that created circumpolar sovereignties have consequently come under considerable pressure to be re-drafted, with some states like Canada refusing to relinquish land that has now become water.

6 Sheila Watt-Cloutier, *The Right to Be Cold: One Woman's Story of Protecting Her Culture, the Arctic, and the Whole Planet* (Toronto: Allen Lane, 2015).

7 IBID.

mined all the regulations – the optimal room temperature is set at 21. Whereas if you're female, it's 24, which is why lots of women feel uncomfortable in offices that men have designed. Females are more sensitive to cold than males, particularly in their extremities. So when you cool a room females shut down more profoundly, and it takes more heat to open up the blood flow control to their hands and feet again. The relevant point is that the temperature of the extremities is a really big determinant of overall thermal comfort so you could have quite normal chest or back temperature. But if you've got cold hands or feet, it'll feel really uncomfortable. So if you're standing on a cold floor, and you're a female it will feel much colder than for a male.[8]

All building materials have a thermal mass, which refers to their ability to absorb, store, and release heat. The rate at which materials discharge absorbed heat is known as thermal lag. Poured concrete flooring, the kind found in CBP detention facilities, has a high thermal mass and a long thermal lag, meaning its capacity to release its stored heat is slow. This is why concrete floors feel very cold to bare feet, and why so many detainees spoke of their extreme cold when forced to sit and sleep on the floor for days and even weeks, despite the illegality of such extended detention in what is supposed to be a temporary holding and processing facility.

CCTV footage inside CBP detention facility, Tucson, Arizona, 2015. Source: Still from *Icebox Detention along the US-Mexico Border*, dir. Susan Schuppli, HD video, 14:18 mins. 2021-22.

We were completely soaked from crossing the river. We'd waded in the water up to our waists. The place they held us was really cold. They only gave us a paper blanket. That's all we had to keep us warm. We were sitting on the cement floor, completely freezing. In the end, I had to sleep seated upright, with my son in my lap, because I couldn't let him lay down on the cement floor. He would have been much too cold. - Alejandra J., a 24-year-old Salvadoran woman, held in a temporary Customs Border Protection (CBP) detention center near Eagle Pass, Texas, with her young son, Noah, in August 2015.[9]

8 Author's interview with Mike Tipton (Professor of Human & Applied Physiology who runs the Extreme Environments Laboratory, School of Sport, Health & Exercise Science at the University of Portsmouth) in discussion with the author, 6 August 2021.

9 Alejandra J., a 24-year-old Salvadoran woman, held in a temporary Customs Border Protection detention centre near Eagle Pass, Texas, with her young son, Noah, in August 2015. See *In the Freezer: Abusive Conditions for Women and Children in U.S. Immigration Holding Cells* (London: Human Rights Watch, 2018).

Consequently, the experiential impacts of temperature can never be reduced to an isolated property of a complex system, but are aggregate and mutable, expressing themselves differently across contexts and bodies. When hundreds of protestors opposing the Dakota Access Pipeline were doused with water hoses by the Morton County Sheriff in sub-zero temperatures during the night of 20 November, 2016 at Standing Rock, North Dakota, the water from the hoses was not deliberately made cold. Rather, it was the combination of air temperature interacting with bodies whose clothing was completely soaked that exacerbated heat loss and intensified the experience of cold, a situation which resulted in over 300 reported cases of hypothermia.[10] This COLD CASE, alongside two other related documentaries to which I will now turn, concern what might appear to be incidental or seemingly random uses of cold temperatures by authorities against 'problematic' bodies, a distinction that the project aims to problematise.

Cold Cases

Through the analysis of a series of contemporary as well as historic "cold cases", I set out to explore the strategic role of temperature and speculate about the emergence of a thermo-politics defined by cold. Each of the three documentary videos I produced exposes the degree to which temperature is a register of violence that includes the legacies of climate colonialism, longstanding socio-economic inequalities, and ongoing structural racism. Moreover, the response of authorities and police to many of the cases discussed in the project has been wilfully negligent and largely indifferent. Accountability for their acts of hypothermic harm remains painfully elusive. The dual meaning of the term "cold case" invoked by the project's title thus refers both to events of temperature-induced violence, but also to police files that are no longer under active investigation. Exploring the politics of cold through these cases invites viewers to reflect upon an ethics of temperature guided by a conception of 'cold rights' and by extension, the evidential valence of cold as it both interacts with and is instrumentalised by institutions, bodies, materials, and environments.[11]

Freezing Deaths and Police Abandonment Across Canada

In June 2003, Russell Sabo, Chief of the Saskatoon Police Service, admitted that an officer was disciplined in 1976 for abandoning a woman who was eight-

10 It is worth noting that the role of cold water in the production of harm by states and their shadowy subcontractors has a long history if we include the use of cold-water showers as forms of torture against military prisoners, insurgents, and political dissidents throughout the twentieth century or more recently by the CIA as part of their "enhanced interrogation techniques". In these situations, the property of cold was intentionally mobilised as part of an arsenal of state sanctioned tools of torture, and thus also dubiously justified as a legitimate and even legal form of coercive power. See Darius M. Rejali, *Torture and Democracy* (Princeton: Princeton University Press, 2007).

11 The project COLD CASES emerged out of my multi-year artistic research project *Learning from Ice*. https://learning-from-ice.org.

months pregnant on the outskirts of the city.[12] During the night, three people, all First Nations, were taken into custody by Constable Ken King, and driven to an isolated area. There, they were dropped off and forced to walk back in cold night-time temperatures. King reportedly drove them outside the city limits as punishment for "having liquor in a place other than a dwelling" rather than lay charges.[13] Paperwork would have necessitated bringing the three people into police facilities, where they would have spent the remainder of the night. King was eventually charged with discreditable conduct and neglect of duty—charges he repudiated. On October 15, Constable King was fined $200. This clandestine practice is known as taking someone on a "starlight tour". A shadow system of racist policing in Canada aimed at evading the justice system; one that would repeat itself over decades to come.[14] With only the stories of survivors and limited police record-keeping, the true number of people taken into custody and abandoned is still not known. Twenty-five years after the first reported case, Amnesty International's 2001 summary of global human rights violations, detailed a pattern of police abuse in Canada highlighting the practice of starlight tours: "There were reports that members of Saskatoon City Police had for a number of years had an unofficial policy of abandoning intoxicated or 'troublesome' members of the Indigenous community away from the population centre of Saskatoon, thereby placing them at great risk of dying of hypothermia during the winter months".[15]

The ten cases that I analysed map a pattern of abuse in which temperature, in particular cold, would come to play a strategic role in the violence perpetrated against indigenous bodies. As each case unfolds, we (myself and Forensic Architecture) tracked the journey taken through the city using historic temperature data, which is synced along the route. The point of interception by police and subsequent abandonment of those taken into custody, usually in remote areas of the city, is highlighted. As daytime temperatures drop under the cover of darkness, wind-chill and precipitation would combine, with often deadly consequences. The timeline produced for each case expands and contracts, focusing on minute details leading up to the period when indigenous people were apprehended by police, threatened and abused, eventually deserted and even left to die. It also maps the protracted institutional responses to the practice of starlight tours, in which years of apathy would rarely see any form of justice done.

When racialised people, especially First Nations, come into the custodial 'care' of authorities—police, prisons, and schools—harm, abuse, and violence is a frequent outcome. Admission to freezing deaths and abandonment as an informal operation of policing has been vigorously denied, and disciplinary action and accountability remains infrequent and are ,at best, significantly delayed. Yet the pattern and practice of "starlight tours" have unfolded

12 "Saskatoon Police Chief Says Drop-Offs Happened 'More Than Once'," *CBC*, June 9, 2003. https://www.cbc.ca/news/canada/saskatoon-police-chief-says-drop-offs-happened-more-than-once-1.380299.

13 IBID.

14 Tasha Hubbard's film documents the response of local community and family members in Saskatoon to freezing deaths and their struggles with the Police Service. Two Worlds Colliding, directed by Tasha Hubbard (National Film Board of Canada, 2004), 49 mins. https://www.nfb.ca/film/two_worlds_colliding/.

15 Amnesty, *Amnesty International Report 2001* (London: Amnesty International, 2001), 66, https://www.amnesty.org/en/documents/pol10/0001/2001/en/.

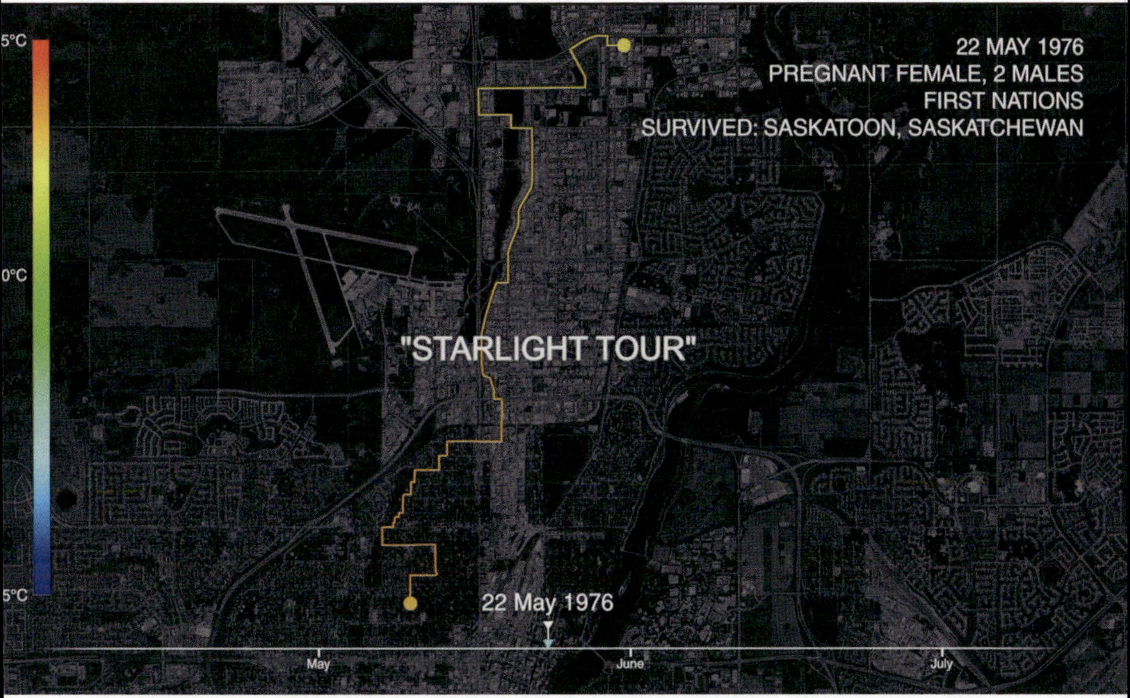

In 2003 evidence emerged that a Starlight Tour had occurred in 1976. Source: Still from *Freezing Deaths and Abandonment Across Canada*, dir. Susan Schuppli, HD video, 31:55 mins. 2021-22.

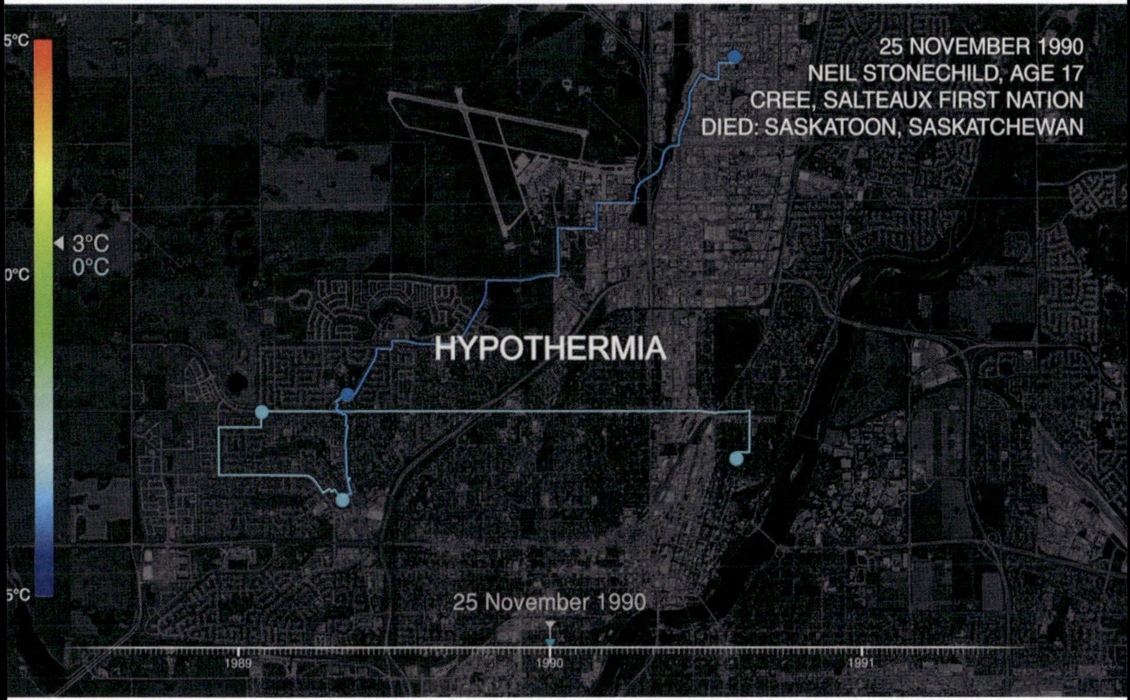

The frozen body of Neil Stonechild was found by two construction workers in north Saskatoon in 1990. Source: Still from *Freezing Deaths and Abandonment Across Canada*.

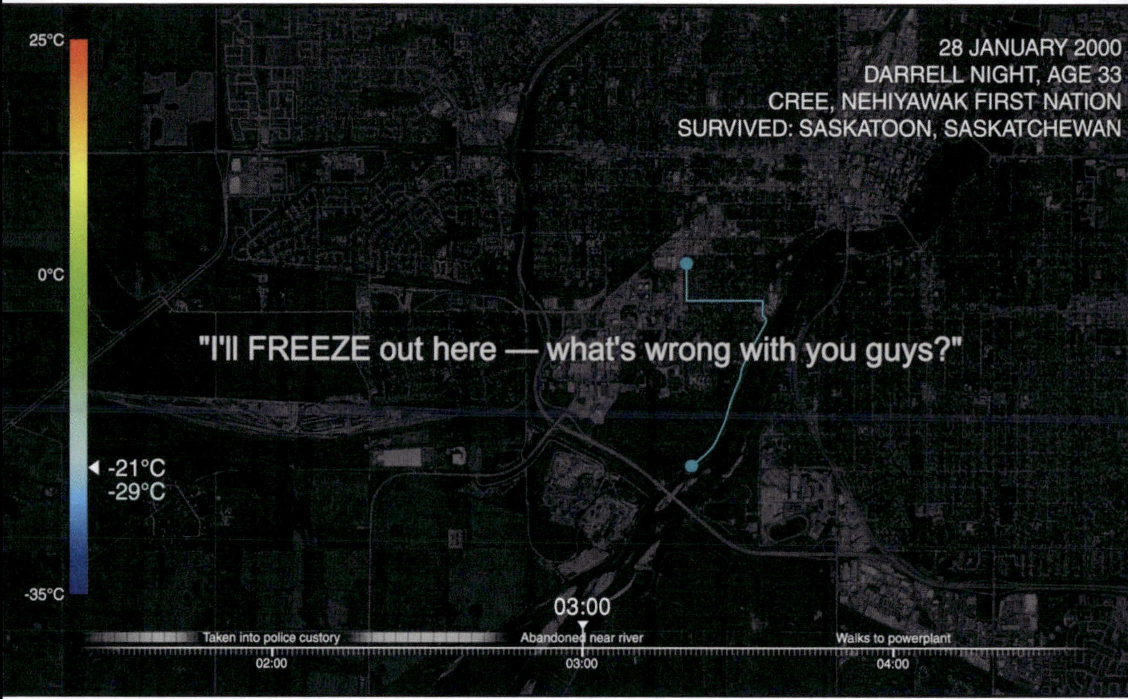

Darrell Night was threatened with a Starlight Tour in 2000 by police who had taken him into their custody. Source: Still from *Freezing Deaths and Abandonment Across Canada*.

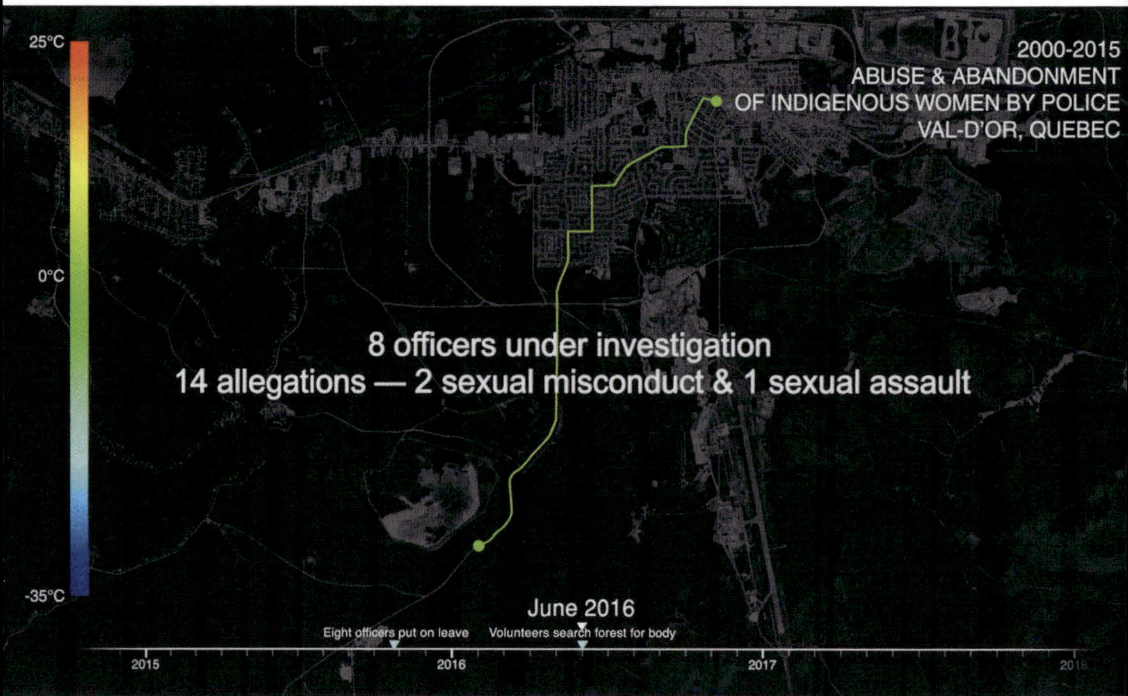

In 2015, allegations dating back over a decade were brought against police officers in Val-d'Or, Québec accused of sexual abuse and abandonment of Indigenous women. According to victims, officers would pick up women drive them out of town and leave them to walk home. Sindy Ruperthouse, a 44-year-old woman from the Pikogan community was last seen on April 23rd, 2014 at the hospital in Val-d'Or. Her parents have accused the Sûreté du Québec of failing to take her disappearance seriously. Source: Still from *Freezing Deaths and Abandonment Across Canada*.

across cities and rural communities in Canada for decades. When authorities were forced to confront the outcomes of inquiries and commissions, denial and indifference on the part of those implicated was the norm. Dropping temperatures and environmental conditions became lethal weapons and tools of force for managing and abusing racialised people. Yet, findings of exposure and hypothermia in autopsy reports could not prove that the weather was used deliberately on the part of those authorities who took people into their custody, nor indeed would any coroner's inquest establish the actual cause of death; namely structural racism and settler colonialism.

No death certificate will ever disclose the real reasons that Neil Stonechild, Frank Joseph Paul, Lloyd Joseph Dustyhorn, Rodney Naistus, and Lawrence Kim Wegner perished, nor the hundreds of others who have disappeared or died through wilful neglect and abandonment.

Weaponising Water Against Water Protectors at Standing Rock, N. Dakota

On 27 October, 2016, hundreds of law enforcement officers descended upon the Oceti Sakowin 1851 Treaty Camp just north of the Standing Rock Sioux Reservation to disband its Indigenous activists, international observers, and allies. This camp stood in the immediate path of the Dakota Access Pipeline and was the site of much direct action and resistance.[16] A day after the October raid, police installed a military-style blockade; chaining burnout-out trucks to concrete barricades on Highway 1806 at Backwater Bridge, just north of the frontline camp; hampering access to the site and obstructing potential exit routes. On 18 November, the Morton County Sheriff of North Dakota released a cold weather warning detailing the many consequences of exposure to the elements. It was specifically directed towards Water Protectors and other protestors involved in the #NODAPL movement.

Two days later, despite sub-zero temperatures and a wind chill of 14 degrees Fahrenheit (-10 degrees Celsius), the Morton County Sheriff began a 12-hour assault against Water Protectors at Backwater Bridge, Standing Rock Indian Reservation. The assault involved the use of tear gas, concussion grenades, less lethal shotgun rounds and in particular the use of water, drenching protestors throughout the night. As the core temperatures of bodies fell into the danger zone, the campfires that were being used to generate warmth were also targeted by police. Over 200 peaceful protestors were injured that night, with twenty-six needing immediate hospitalisation. Over 300 cases of hypothermia were reported.

A forensic examination of the extensive archive of thermal aerial footage obtained through a FOIA request by the non-profit media collective Unicorn Riot details the differential regimes of temperature operating over the course of the night. It also clearly proves that water was sprayed indiscriminately against protestors, chilling them to bone. Using photogrammetry software, we were able to calibrate the drone footage obtained by Unicorn Riot. This allowed us to build a precise model of the area around the blockade and

16 "Oceti Sakowin," *Stand with Standing Rock*, https://standwithstandingrock.net/oceti-sakowin/.

Correct caption: Water hoses are deliberately sprayed at protestors. Source: Still from *Weaponizing Water Against Water Protectors at Standing Rock, N. Dakota*, dir. Susan Schuppli, HD video, 18:34 mins. 2021-22.

Icicles on barbed wire provide evidence of sub-zero temperatures. Source: Still from *Weaponizing Water Against Water Protectors at Standing Rock, N. Dakota.*

locate people, vehicles, and objects within the site. Although the temperature of the water when first fired was not freezing, winter conditions dramatically exacerbated heat loss through processes of evaporation and conduction. The body loses about 2% of its overall heat through air conduction. Water causes even greater heat loss than air, because heat dissipates extremely quickly when clothing becomes wet. Bodies become critically hypothermic when core temperature drops a mere two degrees: from 37 to 35 degrees Celsius. Given the advance warning the Morton County Sheriff posted as to the dangers of frostbite and hypothermia, they were clearly aware of the significant repercussions their hypothermal tactics posed that night.

On 28 November 2016, The Water Protector Legal Collective filed suit in U.S. District Court against Morton County and other law enforcement agencies for using excessive force against peaceful Water Protectors. On 10 September 2020, in a long-awaited ruling, United States District Court Judge Daniel Traynor allowed a lawsuit challenging law enforcement's 2016 use of water hoses and munitions against Water Protectors opposing the Dakota Access Pipeline to move forward with discovery. The case had been stalled for more than two years after Morton County and other defendants filed a motion asking the court to dismiss the case.

Overhead shot of protestors trapped on the highway. Source: Still from *Weaponizing Water Against Water Protectors at Standing Rock, N. Dakota.*

Forensic Architecture model detailing the site of the blockade on Highway 806 at Backwater Bridge. Source: Still from *Weaponizing Water Against Water Protectors at Standing Rock, N. Dakota.*

Forensic Architecture model detailing use of water hoses against protestors as well as to extinguish the campfires keeping them warm. Source: Still from *Weaponizing Water Against Water Protectors at Standing Rock, N. Dakota.*

Ice Box Detention Along the U.S.–Mexico Border

All along the U.S.-Mexico border, a desert landscape emanates with intense heat by day. Located within this increasingly militarised geography are a series of icebox detention centres: carceral spaces derived from the cold calculations of U.S. Homeland Security. When the U.S. Homeland Security Act came into effect in November 2002, it dramatically transformed all areas of government tasked with anti-terrorism, border control, immigration, and detention. A key agency to emerge out of the newly formed Department of Homeland Security was U.S. Immigration and Customs Enforcement. ICE currently runs more than 200 permanent detention centres across the United States. In 2003, U.S. Customs and Border Protection was created as a parallel mechanism for detaining non-citizens, including children, apprehended along the US-Mexico border and at ports of entry in temporary, short-term holding facilities with the express aim of deterrence and deportation.

CBP detention facilities are subject to National Standards that specify that "[e]very effort must be made to hold detainees for the least amount of time required for their processing, transfer, release, or repatriation as appropriate and as operationally feasible," and that individuals "should generally not be held for longer than 72 hours".[17] Yet, as is well-documented by human rights organisations, prolonged detention for up to four weeks has

17 R. Gil Kerlikowske, "National Standards on Transport, Escort, Detention, and Search," ed. U.S. Customs and Border Protection (Washington, D.C.: U.S. Department of Homeland Security, 2015), 4, 14.

been going on for many years.[18] Testimonies from former "ice box" detainees and even guards, corroborate accounts of the dire conditions experienced in these cells—all emphasising how frigid it gets with air conditioning blasting throughout the facilities.[19] Despite numerous investigative reports exposing these inhumane conditions and even allegations that CBP is violating both its own policies and that of the U.S. constitution, "ice box" detention continues unabated.

According to regulations, temperatures in the temporary CBP holding cells must be maintained at between 69-76 degrees Fahrenheit (20.5-24.4 degrees Celsius).[20] In order to better understand the ways in which the experience of temperature is conditioned by a complex set of dynamic interactions between entities over time, we modelled the architecture, materials, bodies, and air of a typical holding cell based on visual evidence revealed during a 2015 class action lawsuit filed in federal district court, Tucson, Arizona.[21] This legal proceeding accused the border patrol of holding migrants in dirt and crowded cells at stations in south-eastern Arizona after they were caught illegally entering the United States. Still images from surveillance video captured at the facilities offer a glimpse inside these cells.

Plausible deniability—"we didn't realise it would get so cold or we have no control over the weather"—featured in many of the responses to allegations around the lethal consequences of temperature in the clandestine practice of "starlight tours", as well as when confronted with the hypothermic chill that resulted when winter weather compounded the violent impacts of water hoses directed towards Water Protectors at Standing Rock. In the operations of "ice box" detention, temperature is formally inscribed within its regulatory framework and thus functions as a strategic weapon of law enforcement and so can't be attributed to external causalities. The role of temperature in facilitating in all of these practices of policing and border management must be confronted as an integral part of the complex assemblage of racialised violence inflicted directly upon bodies and cannot be dismissed as an incidental feature of such activities. Together, these videos make the "case" that the continued use and abuse of temperature is itself a crime.

18 Emily Butera and Katharina Obser, *Prison for Survivors: The Detention of Women Seeking Asylum in the United States* (Washington, D.C.: Women's Refugee Commission, 2017).

19 *In the Freezer: Abusive Conditions for Women and Children in U.S. Immigration Holding Cells*, 13.

20 According to the National Institute of Corrections, "anything in a range of 69–76 degrees could be acceptable in terms of thermal comfort depending on levels of humidity (and factoring in ambient conditions in summer or winter)." See "What Is the Appropriate Temperature for Jail/Prison Housing Units?", National Institute of Corrections (February 9, 2022), https://nicic.gov/what-appropriate-temperature-jailprison-housing-unit. In Doe v.Kelly, District Court Judge Bury ordered CBP to maintain temperatures from 71 to 74 degrees Fahrenheit in his preliminary injunction order. Doe, 878 F.3d, 716. (9th Cir. 2017). According to CBP guidelines "Temperature Controls" :"When it is within CBP control, officers/agents should maintain hold room temperature within a reasonable and comfortable range for both detainees and officers/agents. Under no circumstances will officers/agents use temperature controls in a punitive manner". R.Gil Kerlikowske, *National Standards on Transport, Escort, Detention, and Search.* (Washington, D.C.: U.S. Department of Homeland Security, 2015), 16.

21 Case 4:15-cv-00250-DCB Document, filed June 8, 2015.

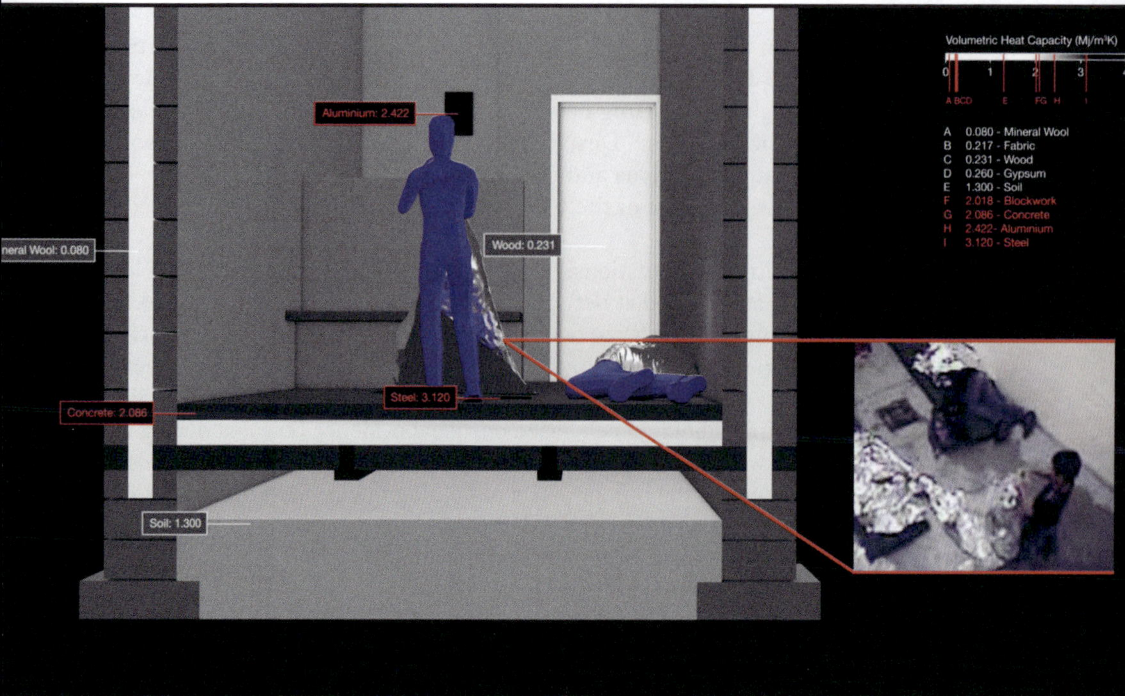

Forensic Architecture model of holding CBP cell. Source: Still from *Icebox Detention along the US-Mexico Border.*

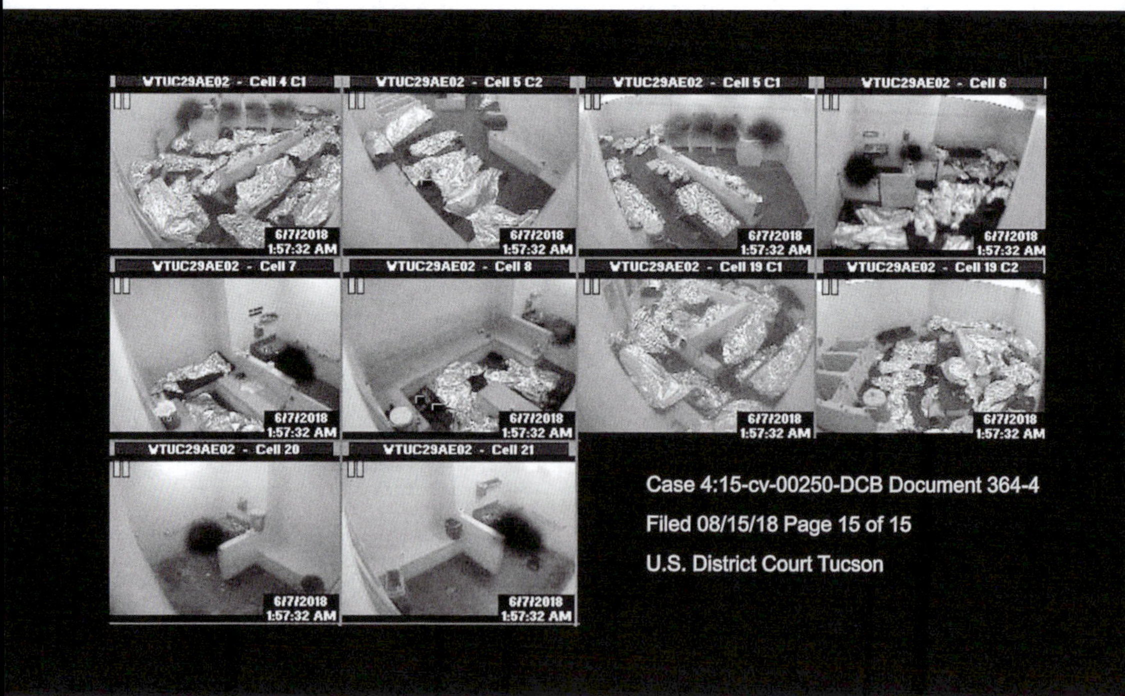

CCTV footage inside CBP detention facility, Tucson, Arizona, 2015. Source: Still from *Icebox Detention along the US-Mexico Border.*

Works cited

Amnesty International Report 2001. London: Amnesty International, 2001.

Butera, Emily, and Katharina Obser. *Prison for Survivors: The Detention of Women Seeking Asylum in the United States.* Washington, D.C.: Women's Refugee Commission, 2017.

Gumbel, Andrew. "'They Were Laughing at Us': Immigrants Tell of Cruelty, Illness and Filth in U.S. Detention." *The Guardian*, 12 September 2018.

Hubbard, Tasha. *Two Worlds Colliding.* 49 minutes. Canada: National Film Board of Canada, 2004.

In the Freezer: Abusive Conditions for Women and Children in U.S. Immigration Holding Cells. London: Human Rights Watch, 2018.

Kerlikowske, R. Gil. *National Standards on Transport, Escort, Detention, and Search.* Edited by U.S. Customs and Border Protection, Washington, D.C.: U.S. Department of Homeland Security, 2015.

U.S. Border Patrol. *Border Patrol Strategic Plan 1994 and Beyond.* Washington D.C.: Department of Immigration and Naturalization Service, 1994.

Rejali, Darius M. *Torture and Democracy.* Princeton: Princeton University Press, 2007.

"Saskatoon Police Chief Says Drop-Offs Happened 'More Than Once'." *CBC*, 9 June 2003.

Watt-Cloutier, Sheila. *The Right to Be Cold: One Woman's Story of Protecting Her Culture, the Arctic, and the Whole Planet.* Toronto: Allen Lane, 2015.

UNITED FAMILIES AND FRIENDS CAMPAIGN
NO MORE DEATHS IN CUSTODY
UNITED FAMILIES AND FRIENDS
JUSTICE FOR KINGSLEY BURRELL
COVER UP
UNITED WE STAND DIVIDED WE FALL
WHY?
WHY?
JUSTICE FOR SEAN RIGG
No more deaths in police custody

Race, Law, and the Air we Breathe

Nadine El-Enany

Breathlessness is not a momentary condition. We could have told you that an airway is not obstructed merely from the moment it is physically blocked, it begins when you are expected to breathe in a world which denies you access to air.
Suhaiymah Manzoor-Khan, 'Breathlessness is not a momentary condition'.

Here I examine the racialised effects of air pollution and argue that the state's failure to limit the harmful, often fatal consequences of air pollution amounts to racial state violence. Drawing on the literature on racialised custodial deaths and families' struggles for justice for their loved ones, I question whether the law can be relied on to account for racialised deaths pursuant to air pollution. If the law cannot deliver truth, justice and accountability in cases of clearly identifiable racist state violence, its capacity to do so is even more limited in instances where such violence is harder to identify or detect. The climate catastrophe and its racialised effects are a less visible but no less brutal form of racial state violence than racialised police killings. I explore modes of resistance to such violence and ask whether it is possible to locate justice for victims of racial state violence and their families beyond the legal system.

Violence Sudden and Slow

I have spent time talking to the families of racialised death in custody victims about their experiences of grief and how it might be affected by racism as a causal factor in the death of their loved one. Custody deaths are at the sharp end of racial state violence. The stories we hear, and see captured in film, that involve police shootings of unarmed black people bring home the reality that racialised people are disproportionately at risk of the most brutal forms of state violence as they move through white spaces. In Britain, inquest juries have yielded conclusions (formerly known as verdicts) of unlawful killing in 12 death in custody cases.[1] Yet, even in these cases, the officers involved have not been held criminally responsible.

In my work on deaths in custody, I ask what it means for questions of justice and strategies towards it when racial state violence is both illegible to and produced by the legal system.[2] Custodial deaths are at the sharp end of such violence. Even cases which involve extreme levels of police brutality, racial abuse, and which are caught on film and so available for public viewing, do not yield justice and accountability outcomes in any traditional sense. If the law cannot account for such deaths, how can it be relied on in instances where racial state violence is even harder to detect?

1 Harmit Athwal and Jenny Bourne, (eds.), *Dying For Justice* (Institute for Race Relations, 2015), 2.
2 Nadine El-Enany, "From Love to Justice: Families' Interrogation of Racial State Violence," *Social & Legal Studies* (2022).

There are a number of intersections between the topic of race and environmental harm and my work on custodial deaths. Here, I focus on the limitations of law in addressing violence, whether sudden or slow, which has its roots in structural causes. Climate change and its racialised effects are a subtle but no less brutal form of racial violence than racialised police killings. Yet, it is more difficult to identify than the sudden violent spectacle. Still, it is a kind of violence affecting people living at the edge, in borderlands, in the marginalised parts of urban landscapes.

I concentrate on one instance of slow violence, that of the introduction of poisonous substances into the air we breathe. If the effects of air pollution are racialised, then the state's sanctioning of air pollution and its failure to act to limit its fatal consequences amounts to racial state violence. In this context, I explore challenges for a family justice campaign for a racialised victim of air pollution in light of the law's role in producing and sustaining racial violence.

"I can't breathe"

The taking of breath is the taking of life. Eric Garner's last words as he was restrained by police officers in NYC in 2014 were, "I can't breathe". In 2010, Jimmy Mubenga's final words as he was restrained by G4S guards contracted by the Home Office to deport him to Angola were, "I can't breathe". Ella Kissi-Debrah also couldn't breathe. Ella was 9 years old when she died following an asthma attack in February 2013. She lived in London, in Lewisham, 25 metres from the South Circular Road. Before she died, she had suffered three years of seizures brought on by asthma attacks, which resulted in 27 visits to hospital.[3]

While more research is needed to understand the link between asthma and social deprivation, it is known that asthma is caused by a number of factors, including those that are genetic and environmental. Its symptoms are triggered by various behavioural and environmental factors.[4] Long-term exposure to high concentrations of air pollution is a cause of asthma among children and adults. Babies who are exposed to high levels of air pollution at the pre-natal stage are at higher risk of developing asthma. Children living in highly polluted areas are more likely to have reduced lung function as adults. Air pollution is a significant trigger of the symptoms of asthma.[5] Although air pollution affects us all, respiratory diseases in particular have been linked to social deprivation.[6] The racialised effects of air pollution are stark when looked at in global terms. In 2018, the World Health Organisation reported that ninety-three per cent of people under the age of 15 across the world 'are breathing unsafe levels of pollutants on a daily

3 Sandra Laville, "Mother wins right to seek new inquest into girl's death linked to air pollution," *The Guardian*, 11 January 2019, https://www.theguardian.com/environment/2019/jan/11/ella-kissi-debrah-mother-wins-right-seek-new-inquest-high-court-air-pollution.

4 Asthma UK, "On the edge: How inequality affects people with asthma," 2018, https://www.asthma.org.uk/globalassets/get-involved/external-affairs-campaigns/publications/health-inequality/auk-health-inequalities-final.pdf.

5 Asthma UK, "Air pollution and asthma," https://www.asthma.org.uk/advice/triggers/pollution/.

6 Matthew King, "Air pollution is destroying our health and we can't just hold our breath and hope for action," *The Independent,* 29 October 2018, https://www.independent.co.uk/news/health/air-pollution-health-effects-harm-lung-disease-who-greenpeace-a8607741.html.

basis'.[7] Racialised nations in the Global South are disproportionately affected.[8]

Health inequalities are defined as the "preventable differences in health outcomes between groups when separated by factors such as geography, socio-economic status or race".[9] Despite the British government's legal obligations under the National Health Service Act 2006 as amended by the Health and Social Care Act 2012 to reduce health inequalities,[10] they are on the rise.[11] According to the British Lung Foundation, in 2012 "incidence rates of asthma were 36% higher in the most deprived communities than in the least deprived".[12] Fifty percent "of people of African descent live in poverty" and "overall, two-fifths of ethnic minorities live in a household earning below average income".[13] There are markedly higher rates of asthma among the racialised poor in England and Wales. Racialised people born in Britain have a higher incidence of asthma than racialised people living in Britain but born elsewhere. Research thus suggests that children of racialised migrants are particularly at risk of experiencing high rates of asthma incidence.[14] This tells us something about the conditions in which the racialised poor live in Britain—conditions which make them vulnerable to harm and premature death.[15]

Ruth Wilson Gilmore describes racism as "the state-sanctioned and/or extra-legal production and exploitation of group-differentiated vulnerability to premature death".[16] Dean Spade has observed how Gilmore's definition of racism aids us in understanding how "systems of meaning and control", such as law, "distribute chances at life and death".[17] Gilmore highlights the importance of recognising that racism is structurally produced. This is of particular help when applied to the legal field. It enables us to depart from traditional discrimination law frameworks that require the locating of an individual who can be shown to have intentionally discriminated against an individual on the basis of a protected characteristic such as race.[18] Instead, we can alter our focus, drawing attention to how harmful conditions are experienced across populations that are targeted for abandonment by the state.[19]

In considering the reasons for the over-representation of racialised people among lower income households, and in under-resourced spaces we

7 WHO, "Air pollution and child health: prescribing clean air," 2018, https://www.who.int/ceh/publications/air-pollution-child-health/en/.
8 IBID.
9 Asthma UK, note 4 above.
10 United Kingdom, UK Parliament, *National Health Service Act 2006 (as amended by the Health and Social Care Act 2012), c.41, Section 1C,* https://www.legislation.gov.uk/ukpga/2006/41/section/1C.
11 See Asthma UK, note 4 above.
12 British Lung Foundation, "The battle for breath," (2016) cited in IBID.
13 Dawn Foster, "Would a White British Community have burned in Grenfell Tower," *New York Times,* 20 June 2017, https://www.nytimes.com/2017/06/20/opinion/london-tower-grenfell-fire.html.
14 Gopalakrishnan Netuveli, Brian Hurwitz, and Aziz Sheikh, "Ethnic variations in incidence of asthma episodes in England & Wales: national study of 502,482 patients in primary care," *Respiratory Research* 6 (2005). Accessed at https://respiratory-research.biomedcentral.com/articles/10.1186/1465-9921-6-120, 4.
15 Ruth Wilson Gilmore, *Golden Gulag: Prisons, Surplus, Crisis, and Opposition in Globalizing California* (Oakland, California: University of California Press, 2006), 28.
16 IBID.
17 Dean Spade, *Normal Life: Administrative Violence, Critical Trans Politics and the Limits of the Law* (New York City: South End Press, 2011), 46.
18 IBID.
19 IBID.

can turn to Britain's imperial history. In my work on the colonial origins of British immigration law, I show how in the course of changes to British immigration and nationality law in the 1960s, 70s and 80s, as Britain transitioned from an empire to a nation-state, effectively creating itself as a post-imperial, principally white nation state, the entitlement of racialised people to enter and remain in Britain was halted. As colonial populations fought the British from their territories, British lawmakers abandoned the myth of imperial unity and equality and moved to introduce controls targeted at racialised colonial subjects and Commonwealth citizens.[20]

This legislation culminated in the 1981 British Nationality Act, which had the effect of conjuring Britain as post-imperial, territorially defined and circumscribed entity. It cut Britain off from the rest of its colonies and Commonwealth, announcing it as a notionally white and geographically distinct nation space. Through the concept of patriality, which had been invented for the purposes of the 1971 Immigration Act, whiteness was made intrinsic to British identity. Patrials were defined as people born in Britain or with a parent born in Britain, and only they had a right of abode, and thus a right of entry and stay in Britain.[21] In 1971, a person born in Britain was 98% likely to be white.[22] The patriality provision was drafted so as to ensure that white Australians, Canadians and New Zealanders would retain the right to enter Britain, whilst non-white Commonwealth citizens would not.

The concept of British citizenship later introduced in the 1981 British Nationality Act continued this process of racial exclusion. British citizenship was made to rest on the foundation of the 1971 Act's concept of patriality, tethering it to the right of entry and abode.[23] This had significant material and symbolic consequences. Britain was to be considered spatially distinct and now had a concept of citizenship that made Britishness commensurate with whiteness. Not only were non-white colony and Commonwealth citizens to be prevented from entering and residing in Britain, but the presence of those already in Britain was questioned through institutionalised practices of racial control and exclusion.[24] This occurred at the external borders and internally, with racialised people being confined to spaces of extreme deprivation, predominantly in the inner cities. These spaces and their residents were brutally policed, with officers performing the role of enforcing Britain's white nationalist borders.[25] Contemporary racial state violence, whether in the form of racialised deaths in custody, or disproportionate exposure to air pollution and corresponding vulnerability to ill health and premature death, must be understood as latent expressions of empire.

Sherene Razack, in her work on state-sponsorship of spatially unjust zones in Canadian cities, writes that, "the presence of the racial Other in

20 Nadine El-Enany, *(B)ordering Britain: law, race and empire* (Manchester: Manchester University Press, 2020).
21 Section 2(6) Immigration Act 1971. See IBID.
22 The racialised population in Britain in 1971 is estimated to have been 1.3 million of a total population of 55 million. See David Owen, "Ethnic minorities in Great Britain: Patterns of population change, 1981-91," (Centre for Research in Ethnic Relations, National Ethnic Minatory Data Archive, 1991 Census Statistical Paper No. 10. December 1995).
23 Rieko Karatani, Defining British Citizenship: Empire, Commonwealth and Modern Britain (London: Routledge, 2003), 185.
24 See El-Enany, note 20 above.
25 Paul Gilroy, *There Ain't No Black in the Union Jack* (London: Routledge, 1987).

white space gives rise to a careful management of boundaries within the urban space".[26] Razack has shown how the effect of the transition from the colonial era and urbanisation policies of segregation in the 1950s and 60s was to replicate colonial spatial zones whereby "slum administration replaces colonial administration".[27] Such practices are recognisable in post-imperial Britain. Colonial subjects and Commonwealth citizens who came to Britain in the 1950s and 60s were denied help by the British government. Ministers refused to introduce legislation making racial discrimination illegal.[28] The Cabinet Committee on Commonwealth Immigration feared that providing housing and other support and advice services to new arrivals would encourage more racialised people to travel to Britain. This is the reason the Committee refused to provide the necessary funds to housing trusts to improve accommodation problems in places such as Notting Hill,[29] a stone's throw away from where Grenfell Tower was to be built a decade later as part of slum clearing operation.

The Grenfell Tower fire of 14 June 2017 is a terrifying example of how the confinement of the racialised poor to dangerous and under-resourced buildings makes them acutely vulnerable to harm and premature death. Spatially unjust zones are produced and maintained through processes of deregulation that have the effect of legitimising and de-politicising the disastrous consequences for racialised people.[30] Similarly, the racialised poor are at greater risk of exposure to air pollution in part because they are more likely to live in zones in the city where emissions are particularly high. Rosenblatt and Wallace have shown how in the U.S. "[r]acism leads directly or indirectly to greater poverty, a less healthful environment, poorer health, fewer physician visits, poorer pregnancy care, poorer nutrition, and poorer access to health care".[31] Along with racism that occurs in medical institutions and industrial environments, they demonstrate that "[d]irect experiences of racism and such indirect effects of racism as housing deficiencies, lack of jobs, poverty may so stress the cardiovascular system, the immune system, and other bodily systems as to jeopardise health [...] Toxic waste dumps and chemical plants that emit hazardous chemicals into the air and the water table are located in places where a relatively high percentage of the people living in the nearby danger zone are African American".[32]

Like the vulnerability that flows from being in police detention and the inability to escape targeted abuse, the racialised poor find themselves disproportionately trapped in parts of the city where the air they breathe makes them vulnerable to harm and premature death. Unlike people from high income households, they do not have access to the financial resources which makes it possible to retreat to parts of the city where the air is cleaner.

26 Sherene Razack, *Dying from Improvement: Inquests and Inquiries into Indigenous Deaths In Custody* (Toronto: University of Toronto Press, 2002), 129.
27 IBID.
28 Dennis Dean, "The Conservative government and the 1961 Commonwealth Immigrants Act: The inside story," *Race and Class* 35 (2) (1993), 58.
29 IBID.
30 Nadine El-Enany, "Before Grenfell," in Dan Bulley, Jenny Edkins and Nadine El-Enany (eds.) *After Grenfell: violence, resistance and response* (London: Pluto Press, 2019).
31 Paul C. Rosenblatt and Beverly, R. Wallace, *African American Grief* (London: Routledge, 2005), 8.
32 IBID.

What Caused Ella Kissi-Debrah's Death?

Article 2 of the European Convention on Human Rights (ECHR) protects the right to life. This places both positive and negative obligations on states. They must not intentionally take life, and must take positive measures to protect life. Article 2 also requires that where a state has failed to take reasonable steps to protect life, such deaths must be investigated. In the UK, an Article 2 inquest takes place in circumstances where it is arguable that the state has breached its Convention obligation to protect the right to life.

An inquest into Ella Kissi-Debrah's death at Southwark Coroner's Court in 2014 concluded that her death was caused by acute respiratory failure, a severe asthma attack followed by a seizure, possibly caused by an allergic reaction to something in the air.[33] However, the exact cause of her death was not identified. After a long campaign, Ella's mother, Rosamund Kissi-Debrah, was granted a new inquest by the High Court. The Attorney General was persuaded to quash the previous inquest findings after being presented with new evidence which linked Ella's death with spikes in air pollution near her home in Lewisham, South London. In the High Court, Judge Mark Lucraft KC stated that "in our judgement, the discovery of new evidence makes it necessary in the interests of justice that a fresh inquest be held".[34]

Professor Stephen Holgate, an expert in asthma and air pollution, was commissioned to write a report into Ella's death by her mother. Prof. Holgate found a "striking association" between the times Ella was admitted to hospital and "recorded spikes in nitrogen dioxide and PM10s, the most noxious pollutants, near her home".[35] He stated that there was a "real prospect that without unlawful levels of air pollution, Ella would not have died".[36] Holgate also considered that Ella's death certificate should be amended to reflect the fact that air pollution was a contributory factor in her death.[37] In the past, the government was found to be in breach of its obligations under European Union law to reduce the public's exposure to air pollution and putting in place plans to reduce air pollution.[38] Rosamund Kissi-Debrah argued that the government's failure to act to reduce air pollution from diesel traffic was a breach of her daughter's right to life under Article 2 of the ECHR. Ella's mother hoped at the time that "a new inquest [would] make those in power realise that our children are dying as a result of the air that they breathe".[39]

In December 2020, the new inquest took place. The coroner found that Ella Kissi-Debrah's death was caused by acute respiratory failure, severe asthma and air pollution exposure. He said she was exposed to nitrogen dioxide and particulate matter (PM) pollution in excess of World Health

33 Rosamund Kissi-Debrah, "Air pollution killed my daughter – and now I can prove it," *The Guardian,* 31 August 2018, https://www.theguardian.com/commentisfree/2018/aug/31/proof-air-pollution-killed-my-daughter-ella-new-inquest.

34 "Ella Kissi-Debrah: New Inquest into girl's 'pollution' death" *BBC News,* 2 May 2019, https://www.bbc.co.uk/news/uk-england-london-48132490.

35 See Sandra Laville, note 3 above.

36 IBID.

37 IBID.

38 Sandra Laville, "Child's asthma death linked to illegal levels of air pollution," *The Guardian,* 4 July 2018, https://www.theguardian.com/environment/2018/jul/04/report-links-childs-asthma-death-to-illegal-levels-of-air-pollution.

39 See Sandra Laville, note 3 above.

Organization guidelines, the main source of which were traffic emissions. He considered that the failure to reduce pollution levels to legal limits possibly contributed to Ella's death, as did the failure to provide her mother with information about the potential for air pollution to exacerbate asthma. What the new inquest did not address is the question of whether Ella's racialisation made her particularly vulnerable to the fatal effects of air pollution. It is important to make clear that I am in no way questioning the strategy adopted by Rosamund Kissi-Debrah. There is no doubt that a new inquest finding that air pollution contributed to the cause of Ella's death has provided the clarity Ella's family needs, drawn attention to the consequences of breaches in air pollution regulations and rightly implicated the government in her death. As Rosamund Kissi-Debrah has said, "this is the first time that air pollution has ever been cited on a UK death certificate".[40] She has also said that, "Ella deserves to have the real cause of her death on her death certificate, to reflect all that suffering, the intensive care, the tubes, the fear, and to show the government that they have to act".[41]

While the new inquest has found that air pollution was a contributory cause of Ella's death, it is unlikely to lead to the sort of outcomes that would be required to reduce health inequalities. Rosamund Kissi-Debrah has said that "Ella always wanted to know what was making her so ill – she asked all of the many doctors who treated her but it was a mystery for so long".[42] A new inquest has told her mother that air pollution, and by implication, the government's failure to do anything about it, was what was making Ella so ill. What it hasn't told her, what it can't tell us, is that race and class, as structures of oppression and exclusion, are what made Ella particularly and disproportionately vulnerable to breathing poisonous air, to suffering in her short life and to a premature death.

Research carried out in 2017 showed that black British and other racialised groups (other than Asian British) were more likely to be exposed to exceedances of the EU legal limit on air pollutants. White and Asian British were the only racialised groups whose proportion of the total population of London was greater than the proportion of people exposed to exceedances of the legal limit.[43] The following maps, included in the 2017 study, are helpful in visualising the variation in air pollution exposure for sections of the London population and correspondence with locations of deprivation.

The first map shows that there are relatively few geographical areas in London where both the proportion of the white population and deprivation are high. These areas are generally located in the outskirts of London where air quality limits are not exceeded. The grey area is where air pollution was above the legal limit in 2017 and the green area is the location of the 30% most deprived areas in London with the highest proportion of white people.

40 See Sandra Laville, "In the days around Ella's death, there were big spikes of air pollution," *The Guardian* 7 July 2018, https://www.theguardian.com/environment/2018/jul/07/in-the-days-around-ellas-death-there-were-big-spikes-in-air-pollution.

41 IBID.

42 IBID.

43 Rosie Brook and Katie King, "Updated Analysis of Air Pollution Exposure in London: Report to Greater London Authority," 2017, accessed 13 September, 2022. https://www.london.gov.uk/sites/default/files/aether_updated_london_air_pollution_exposure_final_20-2-17.pdf.

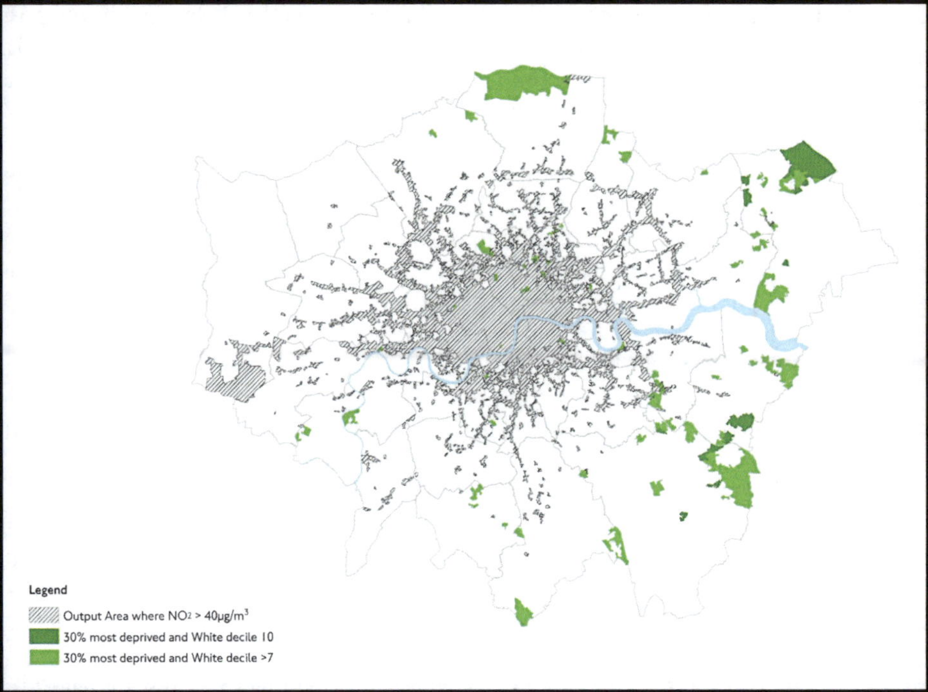

Source: Rosie Brook and Katie King, "Updated Analysis of Air Pollution Exposure in London: Report to Greater London Authority." 2017: 25.

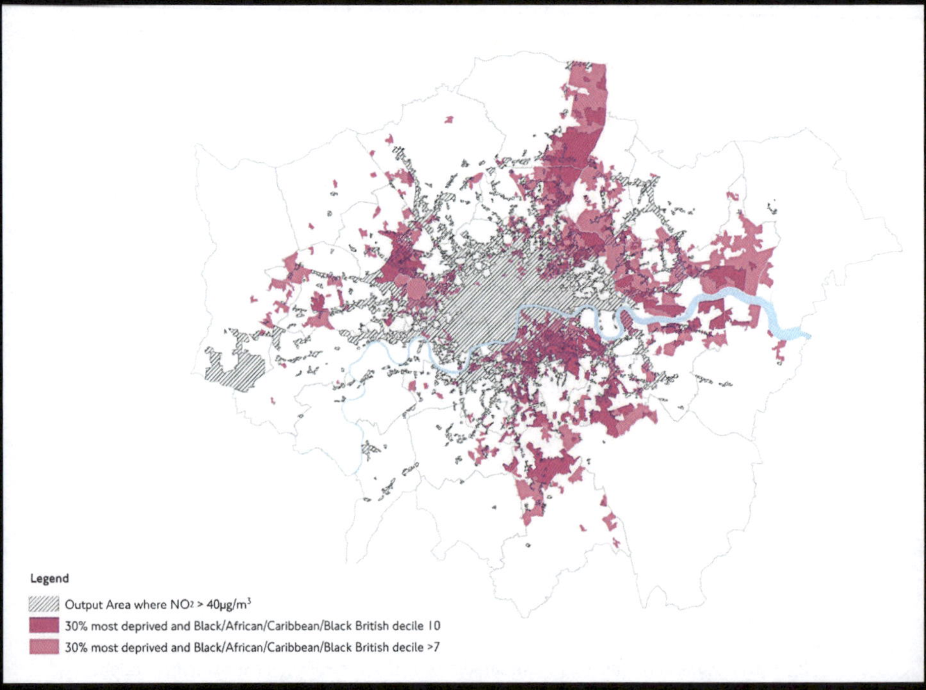

Source: Rosie Brook and Katie King, "Updated Analysis of Air Pollution Exposure in London: Report to Greater London Authority." 2017: 27.

was a higher concentration of areas where pollution exceeds the legal limit. This correlates most strongly to Black, mixed and other racialised groups. Again, the grey area shows where air pollution was above the legal limit and the purple area is the location of the 30% most deprived areas in London with the highest proportion of black people.

Lewisham, where Ella Kissi-Debrah lived, is an area in which air pollution exceeded the legal limit.

The 2019 updated report on air pollution and inequalities in London confirms this variation in the distribution of both NO2 and PM2.5. Between 31 and 35% of areas with the highest proportion of black and mixed/multiple racialised groups coincide with areas with higher levels of air pollution (top 25%). In comparison, the figures drop to 15 to 18% for areas with the majority of people from Asian racialised groups, and 4-5% for white groups. The report states, "looking at the exposure across the populations, white ethnic groups are more likely to be exposed to lower levels of air pollution and are the only group whose average exposure is lower than the overall London average".[44]

A 2021 study by Environmental Defence Fund Europe found that nitrogen dioxide (NO2) is 24-31% higher in areas of London where people from black, Asian or minority backgrounds are most likely to live. Additionally, it found that the most deprived Londoners are more than six times more likely to live in areas with higher pollution than the least deprived.[45] The campaign organisation, Choked Up, a group of black and brown teenagers from South London, one of whom went to primary school with Ella Kissi-Debrah, put up 'hacked' road signs across London to highlight the disproportionate impact of toxic air on people of colour. The signs read 'pollution zones' and 'breathing kills'.[46]

The inquest system, and the legal system more broadly, has proved itself unable to identify state racism as a cause of death even in the clearest cases. In relation to the public inquiry into the Grenfell Tower fire, official documentation was provided in Arabic and Farsi as well as English. This is an indication of the racialisation of the majority of the victims. Yet, racial discrimination was not an issue under investigation. This is despite the fact that understanding the causes of the fire and preventing a similar atrocity happening again requires confronting the institutional racism faced by residents of the tower. Although they had repeatedly demanded that their homes be made safe before the fire, they were ignored and treated as being undeserving of living in North Kensington.[47] Sherene Razack has written about how at inquests into custodial deaths of racialised people, we encounter stories of addiction, "alcoholism and dysfunction rather than the interrogation of the violence…committed by state actors".[48]

44 Logika Noise Air Quality Consultants, "Air Pollution and Inequalities in London: 2019 Update," October 2021, accessed 3 October 2022, https://www.london.gov.uk/sites/default/files/air_pollution_and_inequalities_in_london_2019_update_0.pdf, 24.

45 Cambridge Environmental Research Consultants, "Breathe London Project: D.91 final report," 22 January 2021. https://globalcleanair.org/files/2021/02/BL-CERC-Final-Report.pdf.

46 Matthew Taylor, "London teenagers' road signs highlight effect of toxic air on people of colour," *The Guardian,* 11 March 2021, https://www.theguardian.com/environment/2021/mar/11/london-teenagers-road-signs-highlight-effect-of-toxic-air-on-people-of-colour.

47 Nadine El-Enany "Before Grenfell," in D. Bulley, J. Edkins and N. El-Enany (eds.), *After Grenfell: Violence Resistance and Response* (London: Pluto Press, 2019).

48 Sherene Razack, note 26 above, 4.

Anti-pollution road sign in London by Choked Up activist group.
Source: Photograph by Martin Godwin.

The legal system is uninterested in the causes of death that lie beyond the immediate. As Razack writes, inquests "are structured to have little time for the past".[49] In colonial contexts such as Canada and Britain, where colonial legacies of racism mean that personhood is daily denied, racial state violence is part of the work of the state. In turn, this violence is illegible to the legal system.[50]

For Ella, simply breathing was a struggle. She died following an asthma attack, but she could not breathe because she lived, in the words of Christina Sharpe, "in the wake" of the violence of colonialism and slavery.[51] While Ella's breath mattered to the individual health professionals with whom she regularly came into contact, the reasons for her difficulty breathing cannot come to the surface in a context in which Britain's colonial history and its legacies are deemed irrelevant. Sherene Razack has described legal processes as being "in the first instance pedagogical".[52] The inquest system teaches us that victims of racial state violence have died of natural causes, whether 'excited delirium', a medical condition conveniently invented to explain apparently unprovoked custodial deaths or, in the case of Ella-Kissi-Debrah, an asthma attack.

In view of this, it is to somewhere other than the legal system that we must look to learn about the intersections between race, class and air pollution. For Judith Butler, "we make a mistake if we take the definitions of who we are, legally, to be adequate descriptions of what we are about".[53] Butler encourages us to "do justice to passion and grief and rage, all of which tear us from ourselves, bind us to others, transport us, undo us, implicate us in lives that are not our own, irreversibly, if not fatally".[54] In my work on custodial deaths, I pay attention to justice, passion, grief and rage, centring understandings of love, grief and solidarity in families' struggles for justice.[55] I identify moments and modes of anti-racist and anti-colonial resistance to racial state violence which occur externally to the legal system. For example, the United Families

49 Sherene Razack, IBID, 6.
50 See Nadine El-Enany, note 2 above.
51 Christina Sharpe, *In the Wake: On Blackness and Being,* (Durham, North Carolina: Duke University Press, 2016).
52 Sherene Razack, note 26 above, 9.
53 Judith Butler, *Precarious Lives: The Powers of Mourning and Violence* (London: Verso, 2006), 25.
54 IBID.
55 See Nadine El-Enany, note 2 above.

and Friends Campaign (UFFC) is a coalition of those affected by deaths in police, prison and psychiatric custody. Marcia Rigg, whose brother Sean Rigg died in Brixton police station in August 2008, describes the purpose of the collective as being to support families "so that they can meet other families, share their stories, share their pain, and have somebody else to talk to that understands what they've been going through".[56] UFFC, and its gathering of families across Britain affected by custodial deaths, focuses our attention on the prevalence of racial state violence, which is otherwise misconstrued as being exceptional. UFFC works to allow for collective expressions of grief and memorialisation that embody a defiance of the state's treatment of black deaths as "ungrievable".[57] UFFC organises an annual memorial procession in remembrance of those who have died in custody. Marcia Rigg describes the occasion as one "where families can give an account of their pain and tell their stories".[58] The procession is powerful because it marks, in Butler's words, "relations that cannot be honoured, cannot be publicly grieved" and that "involve persons who are also restricted in the very act of grieving, who are denied the power to confer legitimacy on loss".[59] These bold public expressions of grief are at the same time demands for truth, justice and accountability.[60]

Perhaps one place to start thinking about mobilising against climate catastrophe and its racialised effects in productive ways which "tear us from ourselves and bind us to others" in modes that show solidarity and recognise privilege is to look to an action like that of the Stansted 15. In March 2017, 15 activists stopped a chartered deportation flight to Nigeria and Ghana from taking off.[61] Although the immediate political demand of the activists was to end deportations, the action indirectly drew attention to how risks are differentially allocated in a world still colonially structured. While air travel is predominantly a privilege of white people, it is used as a means of racial exclusion in the form of deportation. Poor racialised people denied visas have to make dangerous and often fatal journeys across deserts and seas to find safety. Meanwhile, air travel's harmful by-products, air pollution and climate disaster, disproportionately impact the racialised poor, exacerbating conditions that are colonial legacies, of displacement, poor health and vulnerability to premature death.

In recent years we have seen how the Covid-19 pandemic has disproportionately affected racialised populations. The so-called underlying conditions that mean racialised people are more likely to die from Covid-19 are in the pre-existing structural conditions that make them more vulnerable to all risks, not just that of the virus. A UK government report confirmed that the pandemic has reproduced existing health inequalities. It showed that the risk of dying of the virus was higher among people living in more deprived areas and higher still among black, Asian, and minority racialised people living in these areas. Members of the Bangladeshi population were overall

56 Marcia Rigg, https://uffcampaign.org.
57 See Nadine El-Enany, note 2 above.
58 Marcia Rigg, https://uffcampaign.org.
59 Butler, note 51 above, 79.
60 See Nadine El-Enany, note 2 above.
61 Nadine El-Enany, "Deportation is a forced racial exclusion: why the charges against the Stansted 15 must be dropped," *Media Diversified,* March 19 2018, https://mediadiversified.org/2018/03/19/deportation-is-forced-racial-exclusion-why-charges-against-the-stansted-15-must-be-dropped/.

"I can't breathe", people protest on the one-year anniversary of the killing of Eric Garner on 17 July 2015 in New York City. Source: Photograph by Spencer Platt.

The Stansted 15, a group of non-violent human rights activists, entered London Stansted Airport to block the Titan Airways Boeing 767 that the UK Home Office chartered to deport 60 migrants to Ghana, Nigeria, and Sierra Leone, 28 March 2017.

twice as likely to die of the virus as white people. There was a particularly high increase in deaths from all causes during the pandemic among people born outside the UK, as well as among nursing and care workers, transport and security staff, and people working in construction and processing plants. Black, Asian, and minority racialised people died disproportionately in these sectors. In London, more than a quarter of transport workers driving tube trains and buses are racialised.[62]

62 "Beyond the data: Understanding the impact of Covid 19 on BAME groups," Public Health England , 2020, https://assets.publishing.service.gov.uk/government/uploads/system/uploads/attachment_data/file/892376/COVID_stakeholder_engagement_synthesis_beyond_the_data.pdf.

Conclusion

Ella Kissi-Debrah couldn't breathe under the weight of centuries of colonial and racial violence. The same violence is embodied in the actions of the police officers who physically weighed down Eric Garner and the G4S guards who restrained Jimmy Mubenga, making it impossible for them to breathe. It is difficult not to feel rage when thinking about these lives cut short. Grief studies have shown that in cases of preventable deaths, especially those caused by racism, grief is particularly intense and includes feelings of anger and rage.[63] And of course, in the words of rboylorn, "the pain we feel in solidarity is only a measure of [their loved ones'] loss".[64]

James Baldwin's character, Ida, a black woman living in New York in the 1950s whose brother, Rufus, dies after throwing himself from a bridge, describes her grief to Rufus's white friend, Vivaldo as follows:

[W]ouldn't you hate all white people if they kept you in prison here?...Kept you here, and stunted you and starved you, and made you watch your mother and father and sister and lover and brother and son and daughter die or go mad or go under, before your very eyes? And not in a hurry, like from one day to the next, but, every day, for years, for generations? Shit. They keep you here because you're black, while they go around jerking themselves off with all the jazz about the land of the free and the home of the brave.[65]

Ida captures the weight of centuries of oppression, the slow, protracted way of colonial violence. In my work I try to acknowledge this rage and look to its expressions as a mode of anti-colonial resistance. These expressions need not be orderly, nor quiet, nor legal. They can be riotous, discordant and sometimes seem to fail. For Gabriela Jimenez, systemic injustice requires listening "to and for" the "elsewhere in the voices performing decolonial efforts" in the course of resistance movements.[66] She writes that "shouting" or "chanting is another way of breathing elsewhere into existence".[67] This is of course not to say that we shouldn't seek to rely on the law for progressive ends, and protect it as an avenue for justice for the marginalised. We must, just as Rosamund Kissi-Debrah and the families of death in custody victims are doing. But we must also keep in mind that the law renders racialised victims nonentities insofar as it cannot account for what makes them acutely vulnerable to harm and premature death, fatal forces of which it is one.

63 See Paul C. Rosenblatt and Beverly, R. Wallace, note 31 above; Nadine El-Enany, note 2 above.

64 rboylorn, "The Forgotten Ones (For Those Who Survive Black Death)," Crunk Feminist Collective, July 8 2016.

65 James Baldwin, Another Country (New York: Dial Press, 1962), 343-344.

66 Gabriela Jimenez, "Christina Sharpe". Accessed 13 September 2022. https://soundstudiesblog.com/tag/christina-sharpe/.

67 IBID.

Works cited

Asthma UK. "On the edge: How inequality affects people with asthma." Accessed 13 September, 2022. https://www.asthma.org.uk/globalassets/get-involved/external-affairs-campaigns/publications/health-inequality/auk-health-inequalities-final.pdf

Asthma UK. "Air pollution and asthma." Accessed 13 September, 2022. https://www.asthma.org.uk/advice/triggers/pollution/

Athwal, Harmit. and Jenny Bourne. (eds.) *Dying For Justice*. Institute for Race Relations, 2015.

Baldwin, James. Another Country. New York: Dial Press, 1962.

BBC News. "Ella Kissi-Debrah: New Inquest into girl's 'pollution' death." 2 May 2019. https://www.bbc.co.uk/news/uk-england-london-48132490

British Lung Foundation. "The battle for breath." (2016). https://www.blf.org.uk/policy/the-battle-for-breath-2016.

Brook, Rosie and Katie King. "Updated Analysis of Air Pollution Exposure in London: Report to Greater London Authority." (London : Aether, City Hall, 2017). Accessed 13 September, 2022. https://www.london.gov.uk/sites/default/files/aether_updated_london_air_pollution_exposure_final_20-2-17.pdf.

Butler, Judith. Precarious Lives: The Powers of Mourning and Violence. London, New York: Verso, 2006.

Cambridge Environmental Research Consultants, "Breathe London Project: D.91 final report." 22 January 2021. https://globalcleanair.org/files/2021/02/BL-CERC-Final-Report.pdf.

El-Enany, Nadine. "Deportation is a forced racial exclusion: why the charges against the Stansted 15 must be dropped." Media Diversified, 19 March 2018. https://mediadiversified.org/2018/03/19/deportation-is-forced-racial-exclusion-why-charges-against-the-stansted-15-must-be-dropped/

El-Enany, Nadine. "Before Grenfell." In Dan Bulley, Jenny Edkins, and Nadine El-Enany (eds.) *After Grenfell: violence, resistance and response* (Pluto, 2019).

El-Enany, Nadine. (B)ordering Britain: Law, race and empire. Manchester: Manchester University Press, 2020.

El-Enany, Nadine. "From Love to Justice: Families' Interrogation of Racial State Violence." Social and Legal Studies (2022).

Foster, Dawn. "Would a White British Community have burned in Grenfell Tower." New York Times, 20 June 2017. https://www.nytimes.com/2017/06/20/opinion/london-tower-grenfell-fire.html

Dean, Dennis. "The Conservative government and the 1961 Commonwealth Immigrants Act: The inside story." Race and Class 35, no.2 (1993).

Gilmore, Ruth Wilson. Golden Gulag: Prisons, Surplus, Crisis, and Opposition in Globalizing California. California: University of California Press, 2006.

Gilroy, Paul. There Ain't No Black in the Union Jack. London: Routledge, 1987.

Jimenez, Gabriela "Christina Sharpe". Accessed 13 September 2022. https://soundstudiesblog.com/tag/christina-sharpe/

Karatani, Rieko. Defining British Citizenship: Empire, Commonwealth and Modern Britain. London: Routledge, 2003.

King, Matthew. "Air pollution is destroying our health and we can't just hold our breath and hope for action." The Independent, 29 October, 2018. https://www.independent.co.uk/news/health/air-pollution-health-effects-harm-lung-disease-who-greenpeace-a8607741.html

Kissi-Debrah, Rosamund. "Air pollution killed my daughter – and now I can prove it." The Guardian, 31 August 2018. https://www.theguardian.com/commentisfree/2018/aug/31/proof-air-pollution-killed-my-daughter-ella-new-inquest

Laville, Sandra. "In the days around Ella's death, there were big spikes of air pollution." The Guardian 7 July 2018. https://www.theguardian.com/environment/2018/jul/07/in-the-days-around-ellas-death-there-were-big-spikes-in-air-pollution

Laville, Sandra. "Mother wins right to seek new inquest into girl's death linked to air pollution." The Guardian, 11 January 2019. https://www.theguardian.com/environment/2019/jan/11/ella-kissi-debrah-mother-wins-right-seek-new-inquest-high-court-air-pollution.

Laville, Sandra. "Child's asthma death linked to illegal levels of air pollution." The Guardian, 4 July 2018. https://www.theguardian.com/environment/2018/jul/04/report-links-childs-asthma-death-to-illegal-levels-of-air-pollution

United Kingdom. UK Parliament. National Health Service Act 2006 (as amended by the Health and Social Care Act 2012), c.41, Section 1C, https://www.legislation.gov.uk/ukpga/2006/41/section/1C.

Netuveli, Gopalakrishnan, Brian Hurwitz, and Aziz Sheikh. "Ethnic variations in incidence of asthma episodes in England & Wales: national study of 502,482 patients in primary care." Respiratory Research 6 (2005).

Owen, David. "Ethnic minorities in Great Britain: Patterns of population change, 1981-91." Centre for Research in Ethnic Relations, National Ethnic Minatory Data Archive, 1991 Census Statistical Paper no. 10. December 1995.

Public Health England. "Beyond the data: Understanding the impact of Covid 19 on BAME groups." 2020. https://assets.publishing.service.gov.uk/government/uploads/system/uploads/attachment_data/file/892376/COVID_stakeholder_engagement_synthesis_beyond_the_data.pdf

Razack, Sherene. *Dying from Improvement: Inquests and Inquiries into Indigenous Deaths In Custody*. Toronto: University of Toronto Press, 2002.

Rigg, Marcia. Accessed 13 September 2022. https://uff-campaign.org, rboylorn, "The Forgotten Ones (For Those Who Survive Black Death)." Crunk Feminist Collective, July 8, 2016.

Sharpe, Christina. *In the Wake: On Blackness and Being*. Durham, North Carolina: Duke University Press, 2016.

Spade, Dean. *Normal Life: Administrative Violence, Critical Trans Politics and the Limits of the Law*. South End Press, Brooklyn, New York, 2011.

Taylor, Matthew. "London teenagers' road signs highlight effect of toxic air on people of colour." *The Guardian*, 11 March 2021.

WHO, Air pollution and child health: prescribing clean air (2018), https://www.who.int/ceh/publications/air-pollution-child-health/en/.

This text is a lightly edited transcript of a discussion that took place in response Nadine El-Enany's lecture 'Race, Law and the Air we Breathe' delivered on 13 May 2022 in the context of the Border Environments event at Goldsmiths, University of London. Organised by the Centre for Research Architecture in collaboration with Het Nieuwe Instituut, Rotterdam.

Lorenzo Pezzani Nadine, in your talk you are describing an encounter between the violence of the "everyday" and racialised people in specific contexts. One of the things that research about bordering practices in Britain today have really brought to the fore has been this idea of how the border has infiltrated everyday lives in a very pervasive way, in terms of bureaucracy and paperwork, etc. But of course, when you look at this from an environmental perspective, that metaphorical encounter becomes very physical and very real, and the interpenetration and pervasiveness takes another scale and becomes micro, operating at the levels of your lungs and of the respiratory system.

I wanted to ask you what forms of resistance and activism, might arise from such stories, when you realise that forms of bordering and of racialised violence are deeply embedded with environmental violence? What new spaces and opportunities for struggle and protest might arise there beyond, of course, those that already exists?

Nadine El-Enany I think we have seen over several years more creative or joined up thinking in terms of direct action protest I was talking about, like the Stansted 15, for example, where it does feel like there's real depth and sensitive thinking around the implications of what is being protested and how it's being protested. On the other hand, there's been other kinds of direct-action protests, for instance Extinction Rebellion, that have taken place specifically around the environment that have sometimes been quite insensitive to questions of race and borders.

I feel like there is awareness, momentum and a space opening up for much more connected struggle. I think with the Police, Crime, Sentencing and Courts Act 2022, by seeking to prevent, in particular, direct-action protests through the introduction of new offenses [we can see that] the authorities know how successful and effective these strategies can be. So, I think that the attempts the government is making to crush, prevent or pre-empt, are a sign of how it is aware of the spaces that are opening up. For instance, useful connections have been drawn during the Black Lives Matter protests, particularly between the immediacy of racial violence, like police killings, and the Grenfell Tower fire. I think that the ability to join the dots and recognise the connections between struggles that have distant origins in history was, for me, one of the most fruitful and hopeful moment in the Black Lives Matter protest. I feel like there is space opening up for joining, for thinking through and for strategizing.

I know that lots of people that are involved are also involved in activism are trying to think theoretically, practically, and strategically how to both engage with the law, and how to resist it.

Lorenzo Pezzani I feel that, besides tactics of direct action, which are obviously very important and relevant, there are moments of conflict within social movements, that open up interesting spaces. I'm thinking of the open letter to Extinction Rebellion with which the Wretched of the Earth collective exposed the witness the environmental movement and its inability to think through questions of race and colonialism, etc. It's clear that their letter was not an act of closure, but, instead, something that can open up other spaces of intervention.

Susan Schuppli Nadine, I really appreciate the ways in which you're working through different registers. That is why I'd be interested to hear your thoughts on something slightly outside the specific context you ad dressed today. I was wondering about the emergence within legal scholarship of the necessity for a jurisprudence specifically oriented toward environmental violations, such as the attempts codify a legal conception of 'ecocide' vis-à-vis 'genocide'. What are your views on trying to introduce a specific legal category to address environmental violations when your work so clearly demonstrates that these things are inextricably intertwined and interpenetrate each other?

Nadine El-Enany I always appreciate the attention paid to articulating the gaps in protection and the turn towards the law to fill those gaps. Although, I struggle to think of an example where we've seen the results we wanted from a new legal intervention. We know that the idea that the law will save us is simply not true. If you think of international criminal justice, we have all the laws, we have all the institutions, we have the courts, but we still have genocide, we still have mass murder, we still have mass violence. We have a refugee convention, but people are still drowning at sea, they are still sent back to harm.

I think that there's also a way in which legal categorisation actually shuts off the kind of connected, joined up understandings that we need, which I think is what you were hinting at. I think we close off avenues for resistance when we're thinking too specifically about forms of violence that are interconnected. Like I said, it's not to say paying attention to gaps in protection and harm is not important, but I suppose I grew weary of the turn to law because, throughout history, you can see how legal categorisation and the siphoning off of particular forms of harm from others or particular groups from others has had an impact. The obvious example in my own work is the categorisation of the refugee versus the migrant and how granting protection to one particular group [has had the effect of dehumanising the other].

Ghalya Saadawi Regarding the reticence to resorting to the legal infrastructure, I was thinking about the difference, say, between antisemitism and anti-Zionism and the keeping of that distinction as that which can permit certain forms of resistance, boycott, sanctions, etc. to take place and how it's quite key to make distinctions, within the legal apparatus, in order to permit certain avenues of understanding and action. You brought up Ruth Wilson Gilmore in thinking about the differences between the ways in which the law understands or translates race and racism versus thinking about racism structurally in the way that you did in your presentation, say. So, I wonder whether there would be a way to integrate the two, to have legal avenues for integrating a structural understanding, or definition of race? What would be that legal avenue for integrating this structural understanding of racism?

Nadine El-Enany This is great for me because my mind just keeps trying to imagine the courtroom scene and what the terms of the legislation would be, and who would be in the dock. Because with law, it is always about: How are you going to implement this? How are we going to find the perpetrators of this structural offense? I'm curious to think with you about this. What I find difficult is the legal principles that must be in place, like the presumption of innocence or the test of causality. For instance, how can you demonstrate accountability with structural causes? I really don't think lawyers would agree that it would either meet the standard for criminal responsibility or civil, neither a balance of probabilities nor beyond reasonable doubt.

Ghalya Saadawi Let's take Grenfell Tower as an example to think about organised negligence in terms of race and class. That would be one avenue of thinking about the fire in exponential terms, historically, as something that happens over time. I am sure this is not the way the legal framework would make sense of the event, although it could. I am wondering how one would go about proposing a way to take into account the 'longue durée' as it can be read across structural lines that compound over and across various incidents, as your work itself demonstrates.

Nadine El-Enany In theory this kind of analysis of those connections could happen in a public inquiry, for example, if the terms of reference—which the Chair has the discretion to decide—include that. It's not a legal process, but it's part of the armoury of administrative justice. But that didn't happen, and there's a great chapter in the Grenfell book by Patricia Tuitt where she really analyses how or why that didn't happen.[1] So, I think that's important to bear in mind, even in a context where that could have happened.

Ghalya Saadawi I am wondering whether much of this might can come down to the question of if the law escapes the violence of its inception. Can the language of the law still be valid tool to fight against these struggles, in as much we may need it? Or should we go beyond the law, as it were, as a particular understanding of resistance?

Nadine El-Enany Yes, law is violence, and if we look at the history of colonialism and racism we see that the tools that colonists used were systems of categorisation, control, definition, referencing and filing that are key to law. We can see through history of colonialism how law, was operational on the ground and instrumental to the kind of colonial violence that you're talking about. I did argue in the paper that law is one of the forces of colonial violence, but I also don't think and would never argue that we can completely move beyond it. In fact, I always include at the end of

1 See Patricia Tuitt, "Law, Justice and the Public Inquiry into the Grenfell Tower Fire," in *After Grenfell: Violence, Resistance and Response*, Dan Bulley, Jenny Edkins and Nadine El-Enany, eds. London: Pluto Press, 2019.

my presentations this quote from Mari Matsuda talking about Angela Davis, where she says:

There are times to stand outside the courtroom door and say 'this procedure is a farce, the legal system is corrupt, justice will never prevail in this land as long as privilege rules in the courtroom'. There are times to stand inside the courtroom and say 'this is a nation of laws, laws recognizing fundamental values of rights, equality and personhood'. Sometimes, as Angela Davis did, there is a need to make both speeches in one day.[2]

Even if we recognize that law is violence, it is often the last bastion of hope for the most marginalised. If you think about the families I talked about and their seeking justice for their loved ones, there is almost a Fanonian idea of turning the law's violence on itself. I think that that's actually what they embody because they're powerful. There's a force in it.

Shela Sheikh

I wonder if we need to separate prevention and justice. From what you're outlining, it seems like there is no room for justice within a legal system, whereas I think we need to keep hold of the ecocide laws in terms of prevention for corporations carrying out these crimes. To go back the question about other forms of resistance, I'm thinking of the work of groups like 'BP or not BP', who do these theatrical actions at the British Museum against big oil sponsorship of the arts. This is also leading me to thinking that, in terms of the search for justice, the idea of reparations, perhaps might be more useful. I'm thinking about someone like the Martinican scholar Malcolm Ferdinand who makes the claim that that ecocide has to be understood in terms of slavery.[3] So, he's basically saying slavery is ecocide.

So, this is something that would be outside of the legal system, but it would be more in a kind of cultural system, this recognition that actually the plantation system, the movement of racialised bodies, is what brought us to the system that allows for ecocide and, therefore, justice would be making these demands for reparations, economic reparations, but cultural and let's say ethical. I am making these considerations to ask your opinion on where we find justice. Do we ever find justice within the legal system?

Nadine El-Enany

I agree with everything you said. I just can't imagine it at the level of legal drafting. It might be a limitation of my own imagination, or it might be having experienced multiple failures in seeking justice within the legal system. I try to think about justice as not just being limited to a successful court case, or a cop that killed your loved one going to prison. I think that's not what families feel either. For them justice is also about the fight, it is about keep fighting for justice until they've taken it as far as they possibly can. So, I think that there's something more to it than just that legal outcome. What they want is a recognition of the failure of the system, that it will fail until it is overthrown. That it will fail until something else comes.

2 Mari Matsuda, "When the First Quail Calls: Multiple Consciousness as Jurisprudential Method," Women's Rights Law Reporter II, no 1 (Spring 1989):8.

3 Malcom Ferdinand, "'Slavery as Ecocide': Beyond the Double Fracture of Modernity," *Fieldsights*, December 22, 2021. https://culanth.org/fieldsights/slavery-as-ecocide-beyond-the-double-fracture-of-modernity.

Lorenzo Pezzani I love this idea of justice not as the end point of a process but rather as an engine for struggle. I think your talk really addresses effectively the necessity to think the spaces within and without the court dialectically, not as existing in isolation from each other. but in tension with each other. In this sense, the power of mourning and grief opens up spaces where the issues that cannot be addressed in court can be finally heard and discussed.

Nadine El-Enany There's a memory I always reference to explain how justice and injustice are quite closely intertwined. In a police misconduct hearing, there is no opportunity for the family to speak—they can attend, of course—but the point of it is for the police officers and their representatives. So, I went with Kingsley Burrell's family and we sat at the back. For hours I just felt the family was completely absent [from the proceedings], even Kingsley was absent: the only presence was his name, written on the side of a white ring binder that the Independent Office for Police Conduct (IOPC) officer had with him. Then, all of a sudden, a very unexpected thing happened, which was the Chair said: Would the family like to speak?

This may seem nothing compared to the violence that this family has suffered: having to be silent, watching this process through which Kingsley was talked about as Black men are in these contexts, as being so strong and so big, he had to be restrained in this way. Kingsley's mother and sister were moved by that moment.

I felt actually that this was an almost perverse kind of moment of justice, a recognition that the Chair allowed to happen. We can interpret that in different ways. Some people might say that's like throwing a crumb. But I don't, because we felt the recognition in that moment, and that has to mean something.

Works cited

Ferdinand, Malcolm. "'Slavery as Ecocide': Beyond the Double Fracture of Modernity," *Fieldsights*, December 22, 2021. https://culanth.org/fieldsights/slavery-as-ecocide-beyond-the-double-fracture-of-modernity

Matsuda, Mari. "When the First Quail Calls: Multiple Consciousness as Jurisprudential Method." Women's Rights Law Reporter ll, no 1 (Spring 1989).

Tuitt, Patricia. "Law, Justice and the Public Inquiry into the Grenfell Tower Fire." In *After Grenfell: Violence, Resistance and Response*, Dan Bulley, Jenny Edkins and Nadine El-Enany, eds. London: Pluto Press, 2019.

FIELD NOTES

AS THE CROW FLIES

Beacon (noun): a light or fire in a place that is easy to see, such as on the top of a hill, that acts as a warning or signal.[1]

In this context, a rescue beacon is a tall pole topped by a powerful flashing blue LED light and secured to a mobile base—designed to be seen from far distances by people in distress and intended to be used by people who have crossed the border that separates Arizona in the United States from the state of Sonora, Mexico. Once that border is successfully crossed, what follows is a hike of upwards of 120 unforgiving rugged kilometres of largely (though not entirely) uninhabited desert to reach a designated pickup location on a main road, bypassing Border Patrol checkpoints located deep within U.S. territory and a thick web of surveillance and violent pursuit. Though it is not noted anywhere on the beacons installed across Arizona, they are built, installed, and maintained by the U.S. Border Patrol, and it is Border Patrol agents who respond to beacon activations and calls for help.[2] While they are designed for high visibility, Border Patrol does not share their exact locations, nor do they make public any data related to the beacons' total activations or ensuing rescues, apprehensions, and deportations. The term rescue should be called into question here.

In the spring of 2019, I began to map the beacons with the use of satellite imagery complemented by traveller blog accounts, and information received via Freedom of Information Act requests sent to the federal land management agencies who preside over the various jurisdictions where the beacons are installed. The laborious combing of public satellite imagery via Google Earth for rescue beacons produces its own visual logic and lexicon.

A round patch of earth, cleared of plant life and smoothed flat by Border Patrol dragging tires behind their trucks. A slender shadow cast by the 10 metre tall pole, punctuated by the hard angles of rectangular shadows of the call box. Greyish pixels of a concrete base, subtly contrasted against the warm hues of the desert floor. Always on a dirt road, which soon began to look increasingly distinct from a "wash" or "arroyo," a dry river bed that might run with water during the fierce monsoons of late summer months (though the roads can run like a river too, I have since learned).

1 "Beacon," Cambridge Dictionary, accessed 12 September 2022, https://dictionary.cambridge.org/dictionary/english/beacon.

2 Brittany Polliard and Ryan Ruegg, 'Rescue Beacons ('Panic Poles'),' *National Border, National Park: A History of Organ Pipe Cactus National Monument*, accessed 12 September, 2022. https://organpipehistory.com/orpi-a-z/rescue-beacons-panic-poles/.

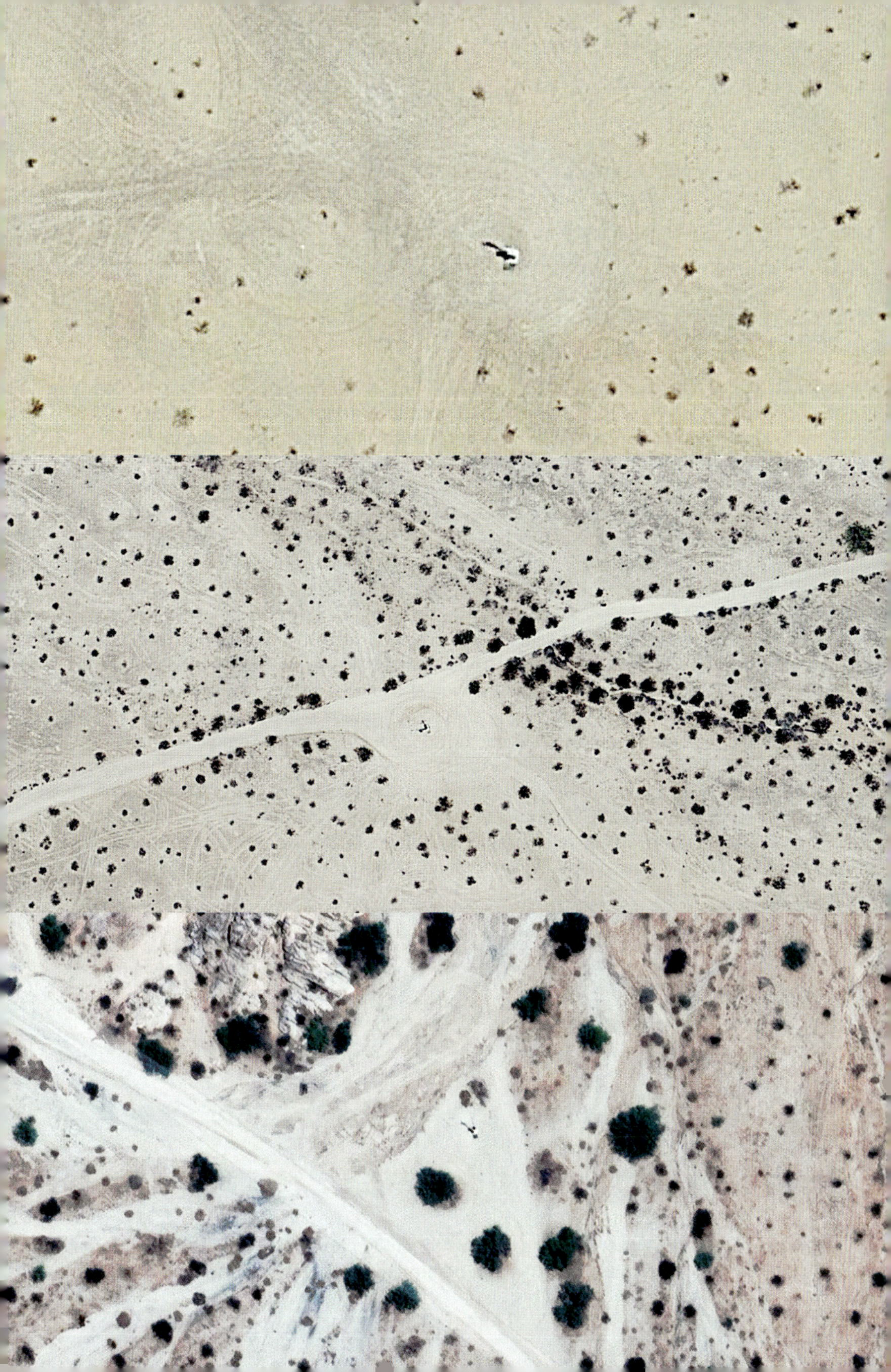

In April 2021, I published the Arizona Beacon Map, an online database that provides the coordinates for 45 of the 56 rescue beacons in Arizona. In June of that year, I travelled to the region to better understand how the map might be useful to advocates, activists, and humanitarian aid groups.

It is July in 2022 now, and I am still here, living in the small unincorporated community of Ajo, where I continue to map beacons while also collaborating with humanitarian aid and SAR (search and rescue/recovery) groups. Daily, there are reports of people who have gone missing in the desert, unable to walk any further or succumbing to heat related illnesses and exposure. Weekly, remains are found.

Photographs and videos are shared by those who are lost or by fellow travellers, who document where someone was left behind, sending this information to the family of the missing or via volunteer hotlines. These images are then disseminated across an ad hoc network of individuals with geolocation skills and longtime volunteers who have hiked hundreds of kilometres of trails, in an attempt to locate them.

I try to read the landmarks, the ecology, the shadows in tandem with digital landscape models and topographical maps to deliver a coordinate of where the footage or photograph was taken. Often, I fail. With a coordinate, Border Patrol might launch a search. Otherwise, the SAR groups –whose members work day jobs in San Diego, Phoenix, Albuquerque–will drive overnight to the area on the weekend and organise a search based on a best guess using the scant details they've received.

I try to match satellite vision with a grounded view. On one search, we are told a man was left next to a "big rock," thirty minutes before the rest of his group is apprehended by Border Patrol at a known coordinate. Halfheartedly, I searched for a "big rock" on satellite. By the time the information has come to us, it is watered down, confused, and hardly describes anything at all. If it is an accurate description, it is foolish to think I could find a big rock in the pixels of Google Earth (though I had thought the same about a beacon, a needle in a cactus field).

We hiked a few kilometres , to what I think could be a big rock. Instead, we find an enormous hole. I mistook the shadow of its depth to be stone. We guess what could have created it. My companion thinks, perhaps it is the remnants of a small copper mine or well. I feel more certain it is from an errant practice bomb, as we are surrounded by military air space and not far from a bombing range. As I am writing this, a jet fighter breaks the sound barrier above Ajo, a sound like an explosion, or like someone has slammed all the doors in the house at once, shaking the glass panes of the windows.

We found a healthy snake. We found a trail of many footsteps in a sandy wash. We found petroglyphs–Indigenous drawings carved into rock that are thousands of years old. We don't find who we are looking for.

A new lexicon has formed, developed in the senses, and in the body, and in language. I continue to learn to decipher: human-made path from animal trail; the age of a footprint that might suggest where humanitarian aid supplies should be placed; a truck's idiosyncratic groans as it climbs a rock ledge in 4-low from a rattle that requires immediate attention; human bone from animal bone; a sense of where to step when navigating a "cholla forest," where clusters of barbed-needle bushes threaten to latch on and dig in; what five miles “as the crow flies” (linear miles on a map) means for the soles of my feet, which are better protected than those who are walking much farther than that to reach safety.

Since publishing the Arizona Beacon Map, there have been two occasions where the now-known beacon locations have been key to finding a missing person, still alive. There is no metric of success here, and this minor technological interjection pales in comparison to what has been required to navigate the social-relational field of this space and this work, which comes with no map. I am now preparing to leave. I will be remote again, re-entering an academic milieu where the distance will likely be felt in values and tactics as well as in the perspective. Time will no longer be structured by the rhythm of the sun, which dictates an early rise in the coolest morning hours on a 42°C day, or by the ruggedness of a road, which turns 20 kilometres into a ninety-minute drive. Instead, it will be marked by the dates of available satellite imagery, and by deadlines, and benchmarks, and by what some might term a “critical distance” that perhaps comes at the cost of the being-in and the sitting-with.

Works cited

Cambridge Dictionary. “Beacon”. Accessed 12 September 2022. https://dictionary.cambridge.org/dictionary/english/beacon.

Polliard, Brittany and Ryan Ruegg. “Rescue Beacons (‘Panic Poles’),” National Border, National Park: A History of Organ Pipe Cactus National Monument, accessed 12 September, 2022. https://organpipehistory.com/orpi-a-z/rescue-beacons-panic-poles/.

HABITAT 2190

This essay presents excerpts, interviews, and research materials from the short film Habitat 2190 by Hanna Rullmann and Faiza Ahmad Khan.

[document][1]

Dear Mr Rullman. Thank you for your email on 9 May, in which you ask for information on the funding of the Fort Vert nature reserve in Calais, France. I can confirm that the Home Office holds the information that you have requested. We accept that the security arrangements in Calais and the surrounding region are of high interest to the public and media. However, we have carefully considered your request and have decided that we cannot disclose information on the whereabouts and funding of our investments. This information could provide criminals and terrorists with an overview of the strengths and weaknesses of the security measures we have in place in Calais and the surrounding area. Renewed attempts could then be made to penetrate security measures based on dedicated expenditure information.

[voice 1][2]

You have to imagine that 10 or 15 thousand years ago, the sea here was withdrawn, the sand was already present, but there were gusts of wind, and the dunes were created by the wind. Well, we are exactly in that state at the moment. Almost the whole area has been lowered by 20 centimetres or so. So these 20 centimetres of soil that were removed–it was also because when the state intervened here, they moved the soil to one side, then back to the other side, so we ended up with 20 centimetres of soil that was completely disturbed, soil with a lot of waste: pieces of wood, pieces of tent, a lot of stuff. So all of that was removed and now we find ourselves 20 cm beneath.

Having removed these 20 centimetres of soil, we can estimate that we have returned to the soil that existed–or that was exposed to the air–60 to 70 years ago. 60 to 70 years ago, for some of the seeds, it's the right time. We can imagine that we will find the same soil here, with the same kind of things. There will also be some seed reserves that are not from 10 thousand years ago, but that are still old and they will again be exposed to the light, or brought to the surface, and they will be redeveloped. What I mean by that is that we will start from scratch. Nature will fend for itself.

[document][3]

MUNICIPALITY: CALAIS, 1997
LOCALITY: MOULIN ROUGE
STATUS: COMMUNAL LAND, NATURAL ZONE OF ECOLOGICAL INTEREST, FAUNA AND FLORA (ZNIEFF), TYPE 1, NR. 72 (DUNES OF FORT VERT)

Characteristics of the observed area: The former quarry, near a body of water, is in the process of being colonised by creeping willows. On 13 July, 1997, the groundwater level was 42 centimetres from the surface. This site had 72 units of Liparis loeselii, including 29 flowers, 11 sterile and 32 young specimens. It was first discovered in 1997 by G. Terrasse.

1 UK Home Office in response to Freedom of Information request filed on 9 May 2017, at URL: https://www.whatdotheyknow.com/request/funding_of_nature_reserve_in_cal#incoming-1018862.

2 Authors' interviews with Alexandre Driencourt, former Conservation manager at Eden62, Calais. May 2017 and February 2018.

3 Xavier Dewalle and Gilbert Terrasse, *Liparis loeselii (L.) L.C.M. Rich dans le Nord-Pas-de-Calais en 1997: Répartition, Ecologie, Protection* (Bailleul, Lille : GDEAM, 1998): 11, 13, 24, 25.

Our subject was to try and have a
project without tension with anyone,

to restore the natural area
after the migrants left.

Taking into consideration nature, security,
inhabitants to be proud of their region, etc.

[voice 1]
In the 80s, when the Port of Calais was being expanded, they deposited the sand dredgings of the port here. So we have a deposit here that is effectively industrial waste, although it is sand only. Then, when all the big infrastructure was being built: the highway, the ring road, etc.; they came back here for sand to build this infrastructure.

The factories that are nearby have long been very large industries. Very, very polluting. When we put in the fence south of the water, we struggled, because there was rubble, rubble, rubble... and then a bit more rubble. We had to purge. We encountered phone towers, concrete slabs, all sorts of material.

[voice 1]
The land was bought by the regional government 2 years ago. To ensure protection, it was given to Conservatoire du Littoral [Conservation of Coastal Nature], to be able to take measures to preserve heritage that had already been identified; plants, swallows, plovers and amphibians. However, in between came the problem of the migrants. The state created a camp: in fact, they were a bit scattered everywhere and they wanted to concentrate the migrant's presence in one place, to be able to manage the migration problem. So they put them here, on a site that is protected.

[document][4]
Council directive 92/43
European Environmental Commission, 21 May, 1992
To ensure the restoration or maintenance of natural habitats and species of Community interest, it is necessary to designate special areas of conservation, in order to create a coherent European ecological network. Species of Community interest means species which are: (i) endangered, (ii) vulnerable, (iii) rare, (iv) endemic.

[voice 2][5]
We had board meetings with different people: the region, the hunters, the neighbourhood, the [UK] Home Office, also the state, the prefecture, the city. Our subject was to try and have a project without tension with anyone, to restore the natural area after the migrants left. I think it was a kind of symbol, a token, to try and make life come back to the site.

We tried to make a project for everybody. Taking into consideration nature, security, inhabitants to be proud of their region, etc. The hope we had to have different species was really compatible with security measures. In fact, the will of the city of Calais was compatible with the project, and the will of the [UK] Home Office and of the French state also. Everything was compatible, because when you try to build a reserve, you try to preserve the area from degradation.

[voice 1]
So the anti-intrusion elements are a fence, a ditch and a dyke. The ditches are made in such a way that the outer side is relatively steep, which we did not like, because making very steep ditches is not of biological interest. We wanted to bring a biological or ecological aspect to these ditches. On the other side, the interior ground is cut in an extremely soft slope, precisely so that, with the fluctuation of water, a variety of plants

4 Council of the European Union, 'Council Directive 92/43/EEC', *Official Journal of the European Communities*, No L 206, 22.7.92 (May 1992): 7–50.

5 Author's interview with Loïc Obled, former Manager at Conservatoire du Littorale, Nord–Pas–de–Calais, April, 2019.

can grow there. So that's it, a ditch, a fence and a dyke, mainly to prevent people and vehicles from going inside or passing through. The dykes also have another aspect, they are important because they interrupt the view, meaning that we can pass by and the birds inside will not be bothered by it, because the dykes obscure and create a quiet zone.

[voice 2]
There were dunes already, and our target was to improve the cliffs, so there was a multiplication of the cliffs by 3 or 4, and the same for the dunes. We also had to deal with the wind. As we cleaned the place, it was [exposed] to the wind, and there was a risk that the wind would take the sand back. So we also had to think about how the fact of digging, or building the cliff, was intelligent enough to prevent the wind from picking up the sand.

[document][6]
One plant species of European interest: Liparis loeselii (L.) Rich.
The site could be designated as a space for the Liparis loeselii, as part of the National Restoration Plan. Although it has not been observed recently, there is potential to develop the species with suitable ecological management, to facilitate the reappearance of the Liparis loeselii, it might be of interest to strip the soil. The existence of a bare soil surface is essential for the settling of orchid seedlings.

[voice 1]
Around the water here, the trees will be removed, to allow small plants to reappear, especially a small orchid that is protected at a European level: the Liparis loeselii. This is based on very old data. It was present here about 15 years ago.

[voice 2]
When we came back after the refugees left, there were a lot of onions growing there, and there were also some spots where we found invasive plants. We wanted to prevent those plants from growing. It was like waste, when we cleaned the surface, we also cleaned those plants.

I remember we went onto the site with a specialist of birds and a specialist of plants. One said, for the birds it would be perfect to have these plants, and the specialist of plants said no, we want to find the Liparis loeselii. To restore an ecosystem is always a choice. What do you want in this place? Do you want plants? Do you want birds, etc.? So we had to make a decision on what we wanted to find there. So that's it, to make nature come back.

Film: Hanna Rullmann & Faiza Ahmad Khan
Design: Tom Joyes
Commissioned by the Middlesbrough Institute
of Modern Art Supported by The Elephant Trust

6 Commission of the European Communities. *CORINE biotope manual, Habitats of the European Community. Data specifications* (Luxembourg: Office of Official Publications of the European Commission. 1991):2.

MUSTAPHA JUNDI: It's so great to finally meet you, even though it's online. I've been reading your work extensively and it has been very useful for highlighting the importance of water security and hydrogeology for my research.

MARK ZEITOUN: Of course, it's my pleasure. I was curious about the project when you described it in your email.

J Just to expand further on what I've mentioned in the email: my research examines the transboundary water disputes and power asymmetries between Lebanon and Israel with the focus on the underground. I'm interested in the different forms of gap and dissonance that condition these conflicts taking place in the Upper Jordan River Basin. As you very well know, that part of the basin in the region has witnessed several conflicts between Lebanon, Syria, and Israel in regards to water sharing and distribution.

Z nods in agreement with a slight smile.

J I first encountered the terms gap and dissonance in the context of transboundary water conflicts through your writing, and they immediately struck a chord with me in my research.

Z Yes, they were helpful for our work as we had to reconcile different forms of data with our knowledge of hydrogeology. Data from the three sides of the border was very poor. Even in Israel, it was not reliable. It was either not made public or simply missing for the lack of the infrastructure to produce it, thus the idea of a data gap. In parallel, dissonance is associated with the condition between physical river basin boundaries and political borders. We looked at the genealogy of border delineation in the region working with/against the multiple water flows, whether surface or subsurface.

J What are the limitations of its knowability in this process?

Z The process usually requires sampling wells for the study of water depth and quality but not its flow direction (this can be partly deduced from the geological faults). There needs to be 500 of them to construct a good picture in the Upper basin. Now there's approximately 4 only. It's totally a rough estimate because we don't know, but it can't be too far off; if there's a massive amount of water flowing through but is unaccounted for it would appear somewhere. What's peculiar here as well is that we're dealing with Karst geography which is very complex; water can disappear and go anywhere. You can never be sure in Karst geology. Therefore, what we did is mostly extrapolation.

J This truly complicates the mapping of ground water basin boundaries and water measurement. The Well and Karst are two forms of physical gap, working with and against water's knowability; the Karst transforms water's temporal flows through its abrupt location. The well, on the other hand, creates a link between the underground and the atmosphere, for either extraction or monitoring.

Z Yes, absolutely.

J And what I also know in hydrogeology is the relation between porosity and permeability where not every morphological connection necessarily translates into a hydraulic one. It's only when the voids in porous entities are connected that they become permeable, thus allowing water to flow.

Z Yes, that's true. What you should consider as well is the level of water that plays a role here, not just because of natural changes, but also due to extraction.

J So, here it's all about temporality and interconnectedness through which water is entangled in the underground. That brings me to the main conflict here–the 1990s Israeli claim that the Litani and Hasbani groundwater basins are hydrogeologically interconnected.

Z In the paper, we showed who argued for and against it and illustrated that there was no evidence to prove that there is any connection.

J My objective is to unpack the reasons for this controversy, although I'm not sure 'controversy' is the right term because it dilutes the existing power asymmetries; Israel remains the state with the strongest control over water and with better monitoring infrastructure in the basin [...] It is clear here that the unknowable was instrumentalised to build a subterranean imaginary through which Israel tried to expand its territorial project into Lebanon. Hence the resistance that was brought forth by the Lebanese scientific community. So, if we really focus on the characteristics of that hidden environment, how can we read that violent condition? How can we examine the leaky nature of water bearing entities?

Z You say 'imaginary', but people in social sciences would say 'discourse' or 'narrative'. Look into Todd Jarvis, a hydrogeologist who works on drowsing. He tried to imagine how they see underground water and there are enough similarities between this method and hydrogeology. The diviners not as a scientific match, but as an inherited practice that the community is dependent on.

J Sort of a sensing practice establishing a strong interconnectedness between communities and water.

Z Yes, exactly.

J What I am trying to do is to conceptualise and diagnose these different hydro-conditions, and to situate them within a spatial and visual practice. I wonder how one can rethink representation and mediation here?

Z I can easily see the value of such an inquiry and what the visualisation of these dynamics can add to their understanding. I would personally want to see that. In my opinion, you need to go out there and quietly ask people about this. Get the right contacts and go out there!

J As a researcher who's not part of any large organisation or public institution, I am not even granted access to the sites I am looking into. There is anxiety and trauma embedded in this borderscape. All this makes the research process much more complicated; it problematises what a gap is. It's not about lack of precision, but rather about working through the conditions that exist and are flanked by anxiety.

Z We were a team of four people with different expertise and nationalities, and we had various degrees of accessibility to the data and locations. We had to mitigate what was produced in Lebanon, Syria, and Israel. In your case, you could have chosen a much easier topic! (sonorous laugh)

J You're right! I'm in the midst of a methodological disconcertment.

I had been meaning to contact Zeitoun for more than a year before I managed to arrange an interview with him.[1] I had been closely reading his papers concerning hydropolitics and practices of hydro hegemony in the Upper Jordan River Basin and the analysis of water in relation to political ideology, border delineations and transboundary resource management. As his work moves across the social, political and biophysical processes in the basin, his analysis of the hydropolitical discourse of the Levantine region addresses the instrumentalization of hydrological/hydrogeological data for territorial expansion and its subsequent resistance.

I was reluctant at first to take part in a conversation with an expert on water and security. Through my initial research, it had become apparent that in order to unpack the dynamics of my field site, I would need to further engage the discipline of hydrogeology, to learn the scientific language through which hydrodynamics are examined and interpreted. This entailed a serious engagement with the existing literature around the transboundary water conflicts and governance in the region. In the process, gap and dissonance struck a chord in my research.

In June 2022, I set up my workspace at the library in preparation for the anticipated online meeting. At 1pm sharp, we began the conversation with the intent of finding a common ground for future conversations. I pointed out how data gaps and the resulting dissonance within such a context of occupation and violence manifest in the condition of invisibility that is simultaneously inherent in the underground as an environment of study and in the space of non-cooperation between the two states. As such, in this context pertaining to an impossibility or a complexity of knowing, I asked: Is there a potential for the not knowing[2] to become a mode of knowledge production? And can staying with the gap[3] operate as a productive epistemological methodology?

Although the conversation was short, its multi-layered narratives and complexities resonated with my own position as a researcher dealing with the anxiety, trauma and paranoia associated with the tensions at the border. Most importantly, it's a condition linked to my own arrest that took place in Beirut in June 2021, drawing links that implicated me even further in the conflict; a moment collapsing violence against my persona with geological violence, bringing together subterranean processes with body and psychological violations. As a consequence, the trauma generated by the arrest seeped into the border context, problematising that encounter, while simultaneously making palpable a border condition that is predicated on securitisation, obfuscation and warfare; intergenerational cycles of violence entangled in aquatic subterranean geographies. Against this background of multi-scalar forces, gap and dissonance become an operative lens between researcher and subject of study that is not simply a fieldwork condition, but a central concern of the project itself. As such, the unknowability of the site through distance and gap necessitates a different kind of attunement, away from the immediacy of physical experience; the separation of the body from the field. Simultaneously, the visceral effect triggered by the various violent histories brings back the body, collapsing the gap with the field. In that respect, a double bind emerges, intertwining new forms of attunement with viscerality while engaging with the complexities of a border environment. In their text

1 Mark Zeitoun is a Professor of Water Security and Policy at East Anglia University. His work encompasses the fields of political economy, political ecology, law, politics and hydrology. He addresses transboundary environmental governance in development contexts, focusing on the relationship between water and power in both the Middle East and Africa.

2 In reference to the "not knowing" as an ethnographic practice, proposed by Marisol de la Cadena.

3 This phrase alludes to Donna Harraway's book *Staying with the Trouble* .

Postcards from the Underground, Astrida Neimanis and Perditta Philips elaborate on their 'walkshop' where embodiment and 'proxy stories' are instrumentalized as methods for attuning to subterranean space through a feminist posthuman phenomenology and science.[4] They conceptualise the underground as a space that humans are incapable of seeing or inhabiting and they devise walking and sensing as an intertwined experience. On the one hand, the act of walking puts bodies in sensory contact with the underground's complex and inaccessible ecology. They build connections beyond the visible to focus instead on bodily modalities, drawing links between groundwater and the human body as a water entity. On the other hand, sensing technologies as proxies to the bodies are conceived as devices set within the scientific field that extend sensorial capacities. These scientific apparatuses don't substitute embodied knowledge, but they become its "amplifiers and sensitizers".[5] As such, attunement is practised at a close proximity to the inaccessible subterranean environments along watery connections and the parsing through scientific knowledge produced through the multiple sensory devices that mediate subterranean space and add to the embodied experience.

In the framework of my research, I build on the prompt to consider different forms of embodiment and distributed knowledge. First, I employ conversations as "proxy stories" to formulate a type of deferred attunement against the physical distance separating me from the field. As the body is withdrawn from the immediacy of the borderscape, attunement occurs through the engagement with someone else's experience. Other people's knowledge and scientific practices are narrated and shared along a structure of questions and triggers that sketch the contours of a spatial investigation. In this sense, conversations reconstruct the field by becoming a new sensory apparatus that amplifies one's engagement. This process unfolds through gauging the complexities in the field and the limits of knowability, inside/outside the field, drawing parallels between one's own process and conditions and others'; an act of transmission and leak unfolds.

Second, set against the background of trauma, anxiety and paranoia, I situate viscerality as a necessary labour to engage with the inaccessible and complex Lebanese-Israeli border geography. Unlike the direct physicality of the walking in Neimanis' and Philips' work, the body of the researcher is absent from these violent fields of various forces, divorced from any possible physical engagement. The body and field are dissociated from one another, preventing the immediacy of their interconnectedness, leakiness and watery connections. However, this process unfolds at a distance, through the visceral response to the field's conditions, coalescing different forms of violence. With trauma, anxiety and paranoia associated with its reality, a viscerality emerges as a response to its tremors. This brings back the body into the space of investigation, but through a collapsed distance; the body remains at work, labouring its engagement. This outlines an affective mode of research, one where attunement through proxies, viscerality and distant labour conjure a gap; a resulting dissonance that locates the visceral within the attunement to the ecology of the underground.

4 Astrida Neimanis, and Perdita Phillips. "Postcards from the Underground." *Journal of Public Pedagogies*, no.4 (2019).

5 IBID, 131.

Works cited

De la Cadena, Marisol. 'Not Knowing: In the Presence Of .' In *Experimenting with Ethnography: A Companion to Analysis*, edited by Andrea Ballestero and Brit Ross Winthereik. Durham, North Carolina: Duke University Press, 2021.

Haraway, Donna J. *Staying with the trouble: Making kin in the Chthulucene*. Durham, North Carolina: Duke University Press, 2016.

Neimanis, Astrida, and Perdita Phillips. "Postcards from the Underground." *Journal of Public Pedagogies*, no 4 (2019).

SUBSISTENCE, SURPLUS, AND THE EVERYDAY

This text was originally written as a response to Professor Arun Agrawal's lecture 'Everyay Border" delivered on 12 May 2022 in the context of the Border Environments event at Goldsmiths, University of London. Organised by the Centre for Research Architecture in collaboration with Het Nieuwe Instituut, Rotterdam.

Flier for an agricultural assembly hosted by the Coalition for a Democratic India in Cambridge, MA, with presentations by members of the agricultural working group followed by discussion with farmers, farmers' unions, agri-cultural scientists and professors. Source: Flier by Avi Varma. 2022.

I'd like to begin by departing from the ground of *the everyday*, a point of departure that I find incredibly generative, and use this response to reflect upon what happens when the spaces and conditions of everyday life become intolerable, when the intimacy of the everyday approaches the threshold of crisis. What are the rituals, protocols, techniques, habits of friendship, ways of being together, invocations, and movements that emerge in response to this crisis of the everyday? How do they offer possibilities of subjective transformation, a reweaving and regeneration of communities under attack? What are the very real risks that arise, in the name of some sort of emancipation and liberation, of reproducing the same of individuation, communal violence, partition, and ultimately fascizing structures of domination?[1] Beginning with a cross-section of my own partial imbrication in the agrarian crisis in the Punjab region of Northwest India, this text is a first stuttering towards an articulation of the epistemic violence that constitutes as other, excessive, and *surplus* to requirements, the lifeworlds of those that don't consent to the environmental engineering of modernisation. Since the winter of 2020, when a movement of over forty farmers' unions, the Samyukt Kisan Morcha (larger united front of farmers), occupied the highway borders around India's capital of Delhi, I have participated in a working group meeting to study agriculture in India. The group organised itself towards generating seminars, forums, and assemblies to share our study with farmers in India. Though a new formation and operating at a geographical distance from Delhi and Punjab, the school of thought informing many members of the groups' practices has a lineage that dates back to the Ghadar movement, as well as nearly a century of commitment to carrying on Bhagat Singh's legacy.[2]

The group has moved intimately alongside the Kisan Andolan (farmers' movement),[3] the hundreds of thousands of largely Punjabi farmers occupying the highway borders of Delhi, as they established largely autonomous encampments on the highways, blocking that infrastructural bedrock of neo-colonial capitalist circulation and transportation, with informal social infrastructures of food, housing, health, learning, care, and political assembly. Learning to learn from the Kisan

1 This essay is indebted to a number of intertwined processes of collective gathering and assembly that emerged during the most intense moments of lockdown during the Pandemic in 2020, to which I owe immense gratitude. First of all, the nearly seventy week long process of *Testing Assembling* hosted by 16beaver, alongside which, in the winter 2020 as the Kisans (farmers) began to habitate by the hundreds of thousands the borders of Delhi, I began participating in an agricultural working group hosted by the Coalition for a Democratic India, in Cambridge, MA. This last space was held as part of the many-decades long work of Hardeep Mann and Jaspal Singh. Through the work of the artist Jesal Kapadia, this process of learning from the agricultural struggles in the Punjab began to root with the insurgent learning practices of Annie Paradise and Manolo Callahan across multiple convenings of the Centre for Convivial Research and Autonomy. An important marker of this conjuncture appears in Manuel Callahan, 'The Politics of Autonomous Spaces of Learning – Instituting – New Alphabet School,' HKW– New Alphabet School, *Instituting*, 23 November, 2021, in which he considers, in his theorizations of autonomous learning spaces, the traditional Sikh practice of langar, feeding of the community, through the Ilichian lens of conviviality.

2 The Ghadar Movement was an early twentieth century anti-colonial movement composed of largely Punjabi immigrants, originating on the West coast of the United States, and centred on widely disseminated newsletters calling for Ghadar (Mutiny) through armed struggle against British rule. The Ghadar Movement exercised a deep influence on Bhagat Singh, the Punjabi revolutionary and martyr, whose secular, socialist, and anarchist vision of independence informs the living theories of resistance of the Kisan Andolan. In Bhagat Singh's analysis of the wellspring of the call for Ghadar, he identified the experience of racial violence of young Punjabi immigrant students in white supremacist America. For an analysis from a place of intimacy with the movement see, Jaspal Singh, 'History of the Ghadar Movement', accessed 4 August, 2022, http://www.panjab.org.uk/english/histGPty.html. Also, Harish K. Puri, 'Revolutionary Organization: A Study of the Ghadar Movement.' *Social Scientist* 9, no. 2/3 (1980): 53–66.; Harish K. Puri, 'Bhagat Singh and the Ghadar Movement.' *Anarchy India* (blog), 29 August, 2011, https://anarchyindia.wordpress.com/bhagat-singh/bhagat-singh-and-the-ghadar-movement/.

3 The amount of knowledge produced within and alongside the Kisan Andolan is far too massive to offer any comprehensive citation. However, May Day Rooms has a fairly comprehensive archive of material alongside a partial syllabus pertaining to the farmer's protest. Available online at https://maydayrooms.org/17617-2/.

Andolan required a movement in two directions—not only to reach out towards the Kisans, and certainly never to represent them, but to be transformed by these encounters. It is this collective refusal of the continued fragmentation, fracturing, and objectification of their subjectivity, and community that seemed to animate the Kisans against all odds. As the poet Surjit Patar wrote in the poem "It is a Festival", composed in the first months of the protest, "As far as I can see / And as far as I cannot / People are participating in this / People of this earth, of heaven, of the three worlds".[4] He continues,

It is a festival
In this, the earth is present, the trees, water,
and air are present
In this, our laughter, tears, our songs are present
And you don't even know who is present?
In this, the colorful history of our ancestors is present
In this, the mythology of the people's
imagination is present
In this, our faith, patience, our hopes are present
In this, shabad, consciousness, melodic tune,
and prayer is present
And you don't even know?
In this, the present, past, and future are present
In this, Hindu, Muslim, Buddhist, Jain, and
Sikh are present
Much is visible, and so much more invisible is present
It is a festival
It is a protest, a movement, but also a celebration ...
No, this is not a crowd, it is a sangat,
the collective of souls
These walking sentences have meaning,
they are the lines of shabad
This pilgrimage is different from a pompous parade
A caravan is conducting itself as the Gurus directed
Leaving I behind, to go to Us and We ...
When you leave here, much dullness will come
There will be much traffic, but no sangat
The rows of people eating and sharing food
will not be here
People rushing home will not have this hue
What will we do then
And my eyes teared up
What one-of-a-kind love is this
It is a festival[5]

4 Sarjit Patar, 'It is a Festival.' *Trolley Times, Voice of Kisan Protest 2020*, 1, no. 1, (December 2020).

5 IBID.

In the space of the festival, the carnival and caravan, encampment and often barricades, a different kind of lifeworld with a different kind of subject emerges. It isn't the conventional demo, with a speaker, a microphone, a chant, an audience, a fourth wall. "Who is present?" is the poem's refrain, and that *who* is not a single, identifiable, easily locatable, objectified, and exteriorised self–"Leaving / behind to go to Us and We". One threshold, one portal opened across space and time, by the Kisan Andolan, is towards a de-subjectification and re-subjectivisation–in its own way, what Spivak might call, "an aesthetic education", an "uncoercive rearrangement of desires", one "transforming the way in which objects of knowledge are constructed; perhaps also shifting desires in the subject".[6] In the spaces of the Kisan's movement, on the highways of Delhi, there was this kind of shifting in what a day can hold. It begs the question–what was the quality of the everyday and the self that needed transformation, what were the practices of such a shifting, and how do we unlearn our own privilege through understanding it as loss, as being lost into spaces and temporalities that reproduce this *I*, whose illusory nature the movement of Kisans cast off? To understand this, it's worth asking the question, "who is present?" outside the highways, on small farms less than three hectares, or rather, who was present before the caravan of tractors, trolleys, and carts arrived at Delhi's borders.

The farmers' protest arose in opposition to three anti-farmer laws passed by Narendra Modi's Bharatiya Janata Party (BJP) government. These laws removed a Minimum Support Price for farmers, liberalising the agriculture market, opening it to further control from Adani and Ambani-led agribusiness, allowing them to hoard food (laying the groundwork for a neo-colonial famine akin to the cyclic famines of British rules), and forcing farmers to negotiate contracts directly with corporations.[7] These are starvation laws, and there are two ways to frame their imposition.

On the one hand, they are an acceleration and expansion of Hindutva fascism in the form of an imperial fantasy of *Bharat Mata* (Mother India, a unified Hindu nation). Along with these laws is the abrogation of Article 370,[8] allowing for Indian settler colonial intervention into Jammu and Kashmir (as Union Territories) and the Citizenship Amendment Act (CAA) undoing Ambedkarite constitutional protections against religious and ethnic minorities. Of course, these are symptoms, not the disease itself.[9]
In "Notes on Nepal: The Long March Towards Maoism", the Nepalese anarchist collective Red Marriott describe the history of the Hindustani nation state as a

6 Gayatri Chakravorty Spivak, *An Aesthetic Education in the Era of Globalization*, (Cambridge, Massachussetts: Harvard Univ. Press, 2013): 108, 141.

7 Alongside the BJP's long–durée strategy of Hindutva, of Hinduizing India through the creation of a Hindu Rashtra (Hindu Nation), a political project whose ideology derived much from European fascism, has been a simultaneous integration of BJP, state–sponsored dispossession and liberalisation with an active courtship of corporate interests, such as those of the Adani and Ambani. Gautam Adani's wealth grew by nearly $50 billion in 2021, the year of the farmer's occupation. 'Hindutva and the Question of Who Owns India,' *The Wire*, accessed 28 July, 2022, https://thewire.in/communalism/hindutva–and–the–question–of–who–owns–india; 'Gautam Adani Added $49 Billion in Wealth in 2021, More Than Any Other Billionaire,' *The Wire*, accessed 28 July, 2022, https://thewire.in/economy/gautam–adani–added–49–billion–in–wealth–in–2021–more–than–any–other–billionaire.

8 For the ongoing Indian settler colonisation of Kashmir see *The Kashmir Syllabus*, 'The Kashmir Syllabus,' Stand With Kashmir (blog), accessed 28 July, 2022, https://standwithkashmir.org/the–kashmir–syllabus/.

9 For the feminist led protests against the Citizenship Amendment Act (CAA) and the National Register of Citizenship (NRC) and the state's violent repression of it, see, for example, 'We Are Seeing, for the First Time, a Sustained Countrywide Movement Led by Women,' *The Wire*, accessed 28 July, 2022, https://thewire.in/women/caa–nrc–protests–women.

"coercive environment",[10] whose political elite oscillate between representing themselves as "anti-colonial heroes on the one hand and heirs to the British raj on the other".[11] On the other hand, it is also possible to understand Modi's anti-farmer laws as an accelerated imposition of starvation wages in the global spirit of development and corporate governance–what the Zapatistas, since 1994, have been calling a daily, informalised, and gendered war on subsistence.[12]

This war on subsistence is also a war of counter-insurgency. It works on a daily, coercive, subjective and environmental level to fracture the possibility of communities to reproduce and regenerate themselves in ways that challenge the complex global unity of racial patriarchal capitalism: to remember their languages, to relate to the world outside the compartmentalised speciation of categories of human, to know the places their children have been buried, to eat healthy food, to be neurodivergent, to reclaim a time different from the futures imposed on us, to meet together in socialities that aren't corroded from within by the wage and commodity relation.

In the context of the Punjab, it is important to return to the scale of the village, community, tribe, and to focus on microhistories of the waterways, small plots of cereal grasses, and the introduction of technologies such as the tractor. The charismatic construction of environmental mega-projects such as dams can tend to obscure the near half-millenia repetition of small, violent acts of colonial dispossession and accumulation of land and water that precedes and produces these projects as inevitable. A prescient articulation of this process occurs in the early writings on ecocide, during the so-called ecological turn of the 1970s at the historical conjuncture of guerrilla warfare and the Green Revolution.[13]

Put simply, "ecocide was intended as a way to formulate how you don't have to kill the people, you can instead kill the environment that gives life to the people".[14] The U.S. in Vietnam stumbled upon a strategy for stamping out Maoist strategies of rural revolutionary insurgency and guerrilla warfare. Drive the population into cities: "It is [...] forced-draft urbanisation and modernization which rapidly brings the country in question out of the phase in which a rural revolutionary movement can hope to

10 Red Marriott. *Notes on Nepal*. accessed 11 May. 2022. https://theanarchistlibrary.org/library/red–marriott–notes–on–nepal.

11 IBID.

12 Manuel Callahan. 'Zapatista Civic Pedagogy in a Time of War,' *Ecoversities* (blog). 5 February. 2022. https://ecoversities.org/zapatista–civic–pedagogy–in–a–time–of–war/.

13 For example. Monsanto's well–documented contribution to the US herbicidal warfare through the production of Agent Orange. coincided with Monsanto's development. branding. and export throughout the post–colonial world of glyphosate as the chemical fertiliser Roundup. Its afterlife can be seen today in legal forums (as yet unsuccessful) such as the Agent Orange trial in France for victims of the Vietnam War : Alexander Durie. 'Agent Orange Case: After Defeat. Woman. 79. Vows to Keep up Fight.' May 12. 2021. https://www.aljazeera.com/news/2021/5/12/agent–orange–case–after–defeat–woman–79–vows–to–keep–up–fight. Likewise. the process of decoupling from chemical inputs such as glyphosate form one of the core principles of regenerative agriculture (still at industrial scale and within capital) and the more radical agro–ecology movement in peasant to peasant social movements. Mauricio Betancourt. 'The Effect of Cuban Agroecology in Mitigating the Metabolic Rift: A Quantitative Approach to Latin American Food Production.' *Global Environmental Change 63* (July 2020): 102075.

14 Jim Glassman. 'Counter–Insurgency. Ecocide and the Production of Refugees Warfare As A Tool of Modernization.' *Refuge: Canada's Journal on Refugees*. 12. no. 1 (June 1992). Accessed 25 June. 2020. https://refuge.journals.yorku.ca/index.php/refuge/article/view/21645: 27.

generate sufficient strength to come to power".[15] In a sense, it wasn't military victory that became the strategy of the state, but rather the destruction of the conditions of the possibility of extra-state social reproduction, be it in subsistence agriculture, opaque and unmapped forests, a connection to land whose intimacy became an ally in sheltering insurgents, and rapid ecosystem transformation through direct destruction of landscapes.

I open up these problematics of subsistence, agriculture, and environment by thinking through the conceptual framework of *surplus*. In classic Marxist theory, surplus(in the form of surplus population) is generated by accumulation through dispossession to drive competition and push down wages.[16] However, something slightly different is happening with the Kisans and the environmental violence that drove their year-long occupation of Delhi's borders. In the first place, the three anti-farm laws were imposed in an already generalised condition of landlessness and unemployment in India–a process that began with the East India Company and British Raj, continued through the Green Revolution and Indira Gandhi's Emergency–rather than to produce it. Those who can't subsist through working small plots they used to own but now rent, aren't finding work or even necessarily being driven to find work in cities. It begs the question: what's happening to them? From places like Bihar, the Sahel in Africa, or the Northern Triangle countries in Central America, people form societies in movement, caravans that cross or occupy geopolitical borders. In other cases, such as the breadbasket regions of India like the Punjab, people made surplus are dying.

According to Geeta Kumari, in the first issue of the Trolley Times, the revolutionary newsletter distributed among the kisans (farmers) at the Delhi border, three lakh (three hundred thousand) farmers have committed suicide.[17] Death, excess peoples, and land theft have a long history in Bhramanical supremacy and caste prejudice on the subcontinent. In the essay "Caste in India", Ambedkar writes that caste functions autopoietically, to maintain endogamy (marrying and reproducing only within the caste) and to regulate the social mobility of *surplus* group members through marriage to prevent them from intermarrying outside caste boundaries, and to prevent dispossession of wealth and land through complex mechanisms of inheritance, child marriage, and murder (in the form of *sati*).[18] *Surplus* also has another sense with regards to nature, of being synonymous to abundance, and this abundance is structured within domination. Even Marx falls prey to this sense of ecology as surplus, as exploitable abundance, when he conceives of Nature as freely giving itself over, giving itself up, as use-values, that will go into the making of social worlds: an original,

15 IBID.

16 As Aditya Bahl has written in reference to the disgraceful rates of hunger, anaemia, undernourishment and food insecurity in relation to the neoliberal accumulation of surplus grains: "a recent pamphlet jointly issued by Shramik Samvad (Nagpur) and Mazdoor Samanvay Kendra puts these damning numbers in perspective: 'the overflow (in production) is not due to surplus production, but the godowns are full because a large section of the Indian population is stricken by hunger ... The country has enough grain because the vast majority has been denied access to it". Aditya Bahl, 'The Postcolonial Autumn,' *Spectre Journal*, accessed July 27, 2022, https://spectrejournal.com/the-postcolonial-autumn/; see as well, 'Capital, Labour and the Farm Laws: Who Stands to Gain?,' *Radical Notes* (blog), 6 January, 2021, https://radicalnotes.org/2021/01/06/capital-labour-and-the-farm-laws-who-stands-to-gain/.

17 Geeta Kumari, 'Delhi and Movements.' *Trolley Times, Voice of Kisan Protest 2020*, 1, no. 1, (December 2020).

18 B. R. Ambedkar, *The Essential Writings of B. R. Ambedkar*, ed. Valerian Rodrigues (New Delhi: Oxford University Press, 2004): 241–262.

yet constant excess that provides both raw material and the means of production out of which all value necessary to social production comes into existence.[19] What and who ("who is present?") are culled in the savage sorting of the ecological episteme of surplus are those deemed non-productive, not in relation, not engaging in valorisation, occupying the space of an epistemological void, non-human. As Walter Rodney wrote describing the early British colonisation of Guyana, the coastline, the environment itself, needed "humanization".[20]

These brief analytics of caste, counterinsurgency, and naturality have of course taken up too much space in the form of critique–which as Fred Moten described, in conversation with the Otolith Group, Department of Xenogenesis, and which I paraphrase here–runs the risk of capturing us in a spiral of becoming more and more inventive, creative, productive in the act of narrating our own itineraries of displacement and dispossession.[21] That has not been my aim. In the context of anti-farmer, anti-minority, anti-dalit, and anti-earth communal violence and capitalist development on the subcontinent, I absolutely don't want to be "recapitulating the very language of separateness and division".[22] The spaces of the Kisan Morcha on the highways of Delhi were precisely the opposite of such a grammar of inevitable colonial subjection. Their social language and environmental form of being did not produce *surplus,* a *surplus* (once fabricated) that necessitates intervention, management, and infrastructural governance. Instead, the Kisan Andolan was a rupture within that common-sense of the everyday, creating social infrastructures of conviviality that wove people together, that replenished and nourished an existential struggle against these farm pricing laws.

Almost as a response to Surjit Patar's poem on the festival written in the first weeks of the protest movement, numerous authors began to weave together living theories of struggle from across the diaspora, inspired by the Sikh practice of *langar*, of feeding the community. Sarover Zaidi writes in "The Gift of Food".

19 Though in Chapter 7 of *Capital*, "The Labour Process and the Valorization Process" Marx critiques bourgeois economists who see the "earth's spontaneous productions" as a "gift of nature" for obscuring the labour process productive of surplus value as mere natural abundance and refuses the separation of human society from nature through his concept of metabolism. Nonetheless, he includes earth in the labour process only at a certain distance, still exteriorized, predicate, supplement, appendage to the central social trajectory of the creation of surplus–value. "Nature becomes one of the organs of his activity, which he annexes to his own bodily organs, adding stature to himself"; "The earth itself is a universal instrument of this kind", it provides the "objective conditions necessary for carrying on the labour process" but does not "enter directly into the process". Karl Marx and Ernest Mandel, *Capital: Volume 1: A Critique of Political Economy*, trans. Ben Fowkes, illustrated edition (London ; New York, N.Y: Penguin Classics, 1992): 285–86.

20 Walter Rodney, *A History of the Guyanese Working People*, 1881–1905, Johns Hopkins Studies in Atlantic History and Culture (Baltimore, Maryland: The Johns Hopkins University Press, 1981): 3; see Rodney, *Guyanese Working People*, 'Internal and External Constraints on the Development of Working People,' 1–30, for the full depth of his historical analysis of environmental transformation and subject–production.

21 The Otolith Collective, 'Department of Xenogenesis: Our Xenogenetic Gift: Thinking Octavia Butler with Fred Moten,' Fred Moten in conversation with Anjalika Sagar and Kodwo Eshun, LUX, *online lecture*, London, 13 February 2022.

22 Andaiye, *The Point Is to Change the World: Selected Writings of Andaiye*, ed. D. Alissa Trotz, Black Critique (London and New York: Pluto Press, 2020): 72.

The langar was originally introduced into the Sikh religion by its founder, Guru Nanak, who was possibly inspired by Chishtiya Sufis who also ran community kitchens. Cooking, serving, and eating food at the langar forms a central tenet of Sikh religious practices.

The langar is a community kitchen, a congregation, a form of serving the other, a socio-religious practice, a sacred tenet, and here a political formation, a practice, and a method and location of the protest.

The self begins to fold in while walking through the protest. Everyone is eager to feed you from makeshift kitchen stalls, and at some point, you become part of the protest itself, jumping into the kitchens to help stir large pots of chickpea curries, help roll the chapatis, or serve food to others.[23]

And the artist Jesal Kepadia wrote in a text-piece for Cooper Gallery in Dundee, reading the signs of what the farmers' movement was opening:

What is the time of devotion? Becoming a bhakt, singing the common sorrow, between seva and tequio, (muuch meyaaj, as Valiana taught me how to say it in the Mayan dielect), this is the time of the fiesta. The farmers have been gheraoing for nine months now. The langar is open and ongoing, no one will go hungry. There is a jinn in the air!*[24]

Rather than reproducing the logics of exclusion[25] in a study of bordering practices that, even in the name of social justice, recreates a world divided into those pushed back and those who rescue, I have explored instead the practices that emerge as the everyday becomes intolerable. Likewise, through recounting the continued destruction of the earth in Punjab, the literal ground of everyday life, through the Modi government's anti-farmer laws, it is possible to connect these conflicts to the long history of colonisation as ecological destruction. Throughout, I've sought to conceptualise and ultimately reject an ecological sense of abundance that frames divergent realities as *surplus,* in order to extract from or dispose of them. One model of such a refusal can be found in the assertion repeatedly made along Delhi's highway borders that everyone will be fed, even though the state might say no one was ever there.

23 Sarover Zaidi, 'The Gift of Food'. *E-flux Architecture*, accessed 11 May, 2022, https://www.e-flux.com/architecture/survivance/412221/the-gift-of-food/.

24 Jesal Kapadia, 'What am I reading now…' *A Space In-between*, Cooper Gallery, University of Dundee, accessed 27 July, 2022. https://sites.dundee.ac.uk/cooper-gallery-inbetween/what-i-am-reading-now/2021-2/.

25 On the "sociologics of exclusion", see Denise Ferreira da Silva, *Toward a Global Idea of Race*, Borderlines 27 (Minneapolis: University of Minnesota Press, 2007); Denise Ferreira Da Silva, 'Towards a Critique of the Socio-Logos of Justice: The Analytics of Raciality and the Production of Universality,' *Social Identities* 7, no. 3 (September 2001): 421–54.

Stills from Anand Patwardhan, *In Memory of Friends*, 1990, 60'. In this montage, Professor Jagmohan Singh explains the threat posed by Bhagat Singh's revolutionary, secular, and socialist ideas to the British colonial administration. The pervasiveness of Singh's image amongst the Kisan movement of recent years likewise speaks against any tendency to historicize anti-colonial struggle. Source: Image by Anand Patwardhan, reprinted with permission of the artist.

The British continued to sow disunity

even after the hangings

To finally annihilate
Bhagat Singh's ideas

Works cited

Ambedkar, B. R. *The Essential Writings of B. R. Ambedkar*, ed. Valerian Rodrigues. New Delhi: Oxford University Press, 2004.

Andaiye. *The Point Is to Change the World: Selected Writings of Andaiye*, ed. D. Alissa Trotz, Black Critique. London, New York: Pluto Press, 2020.

Bahl, Aditya. "The Postcolonial Autumn." *Spectre Journal*, accessed 27 July, 2022, https://spectrejournal.com/the-postcolonial-autumn/.

Betancourt, Mauricio. "The Effect of Cuban Agroecology in Mitigating the Metabolic Rift: A Quantitative Approach to Latin American Food Production." *Global Environmental Change* 63 (July 2020): 102075.

Callahan, Manuel. "The Politics of Autonomous Spaces of Learning – Instituting – New Alphabet School." HKW– New Alphabet School, *Instituting*, 23 November, 2021, https://newalphabetschool.hkw.de/the-politics-of-autonomous-spaces-of-learning/

Callahan, Manuel. "Zapatista Civic Pedagogy in a Time of War." *Ecoversities* (blog), 5 February, 2022, https://ecoversities.org/zapatista-civic-pedagogy-in-a-time-of-war/.

da Silva, Denise Ferreira. *Toward a Global Idea of Race.* Borderlines 27. Minneapolis: University of Minnesota Press, 2007.

da Silva, Denise Ferreira. "Towards a Critique of the Socio-Logos of Justice: The Analytics of Raciality and the Production of Universality." *Social Identities* 7, no. 3 (September 2001).

Glassman, Jim. "Counter-Insurgency, Ecocide and the Production of Refugees Warfare As A Tool of Modernization." *Refuge: Canada's Journal on Refugees* 12, no. 1 (June 1992). Accessed 25 June, 2020, https://refuge.journals.yorku.ca/index.php/refuge/article/view/21645.

Kapadia, Jesal. "What am I reading now." A Space In-between, Cooper Gallery, University of Dundee, accessed 27 July, 2022. https://sites.dundee.ac.uk/cooper-gallery-inbetween/what-i-am-reading-now/2021-2/.

Kumari, Geeta. "Delhi and Movements." *Trolley Times, Voice of Kisan Protest*, December 2020.

Marx, Karl and Ernest Mandel. *Capital: Volume 1: A Critique of Political Economy*, trans. Ben Fowkes, illustrated edition London ; New York City: Penguin Classics, 1992.

Patar, Sarjit. "It is a Festival." *Trolley Times, Voice of Kisan Protest*, December 2020.

Puri, Harish K. "Revolutionary Organization: A Study of the Ghadar Movement." Social Scientist 9, no. 2/3 (1980): 53-66.

Puri, Harish K. "Bhagat Singh and the Ghadar Movement." *Anarchy India* (blog), 29 August, 2011, https://anarchyindia.wordpress.com/bhagat-singh/bhagat-singh-and-the-ghadar-movement/.

Red Marriott, Notes on Nepal, accessed 11 May, 2022, https://theanarchistlibrary.org/library/red-marriott-notes-on-nepal.

Rodney, Walter. *A History of the Guyanese Working People, 1881-1905*, in Johns Hopkins Studies in Atlantic History and Culture. Baltimore, Maryland: The Johns Hopkins University Press, 1981.

Spivak, Gayatri Chakravorty. *An Aesthetic Education in the Era of Globalisation*. Cambridge: Harvard Univ. Press, 2013.

The Otolith Collective, "Department of Xenogenesis: Our Xenogenetic Gift: Thinking Octavia Butler with Fred Moten," Fred Moten in conversation with Anjalika Sagar and Kodwo Eshun, LUX, online lecture, London, 13 February 2022.

Zaidi, Sarover. "The Gift of Food." *E-flux Architecture*, accessed May 11, 2022, https://www.e-flux.com/architecture/survivance/412221/the-gift-of-food/.

"Hindutva and the Question of Who Owns India." *The Wire*, accessed 28 July, 2022, https://thewire.in/communalism/hindutva-and-the-question-of-who-owns-india;

"Gautam Adani Added $49 Billion in Wealth in 2021, More Than Any Other Billionaire." *The Wire*, accessed 28 July, 2022, https://thewire.in/economy/gautam-adani-added-49-billion-in-wealth-in-2021-more-than-any-other-billionaire.

"The Kashmir Syllabus." *Stand With Kashmir* (blog), accessed 28 July, 2022, https://standwithkashmir.org/the-kashmir-syllabus/;

"Capital, Labour and the Farm Laws: Who Stands to Gain?." *Radical Notes* (blog), January 6, 2021, https://otheraspect.org/2021/01/20/capital-labour-and-the-farm-laws-who-stands-to-gain/.

INVADING LANDSCAPES: A BIOGRAPHY OF A TREE IN PALESTINE

Mount Abu Ghneim covered with a forest planted by Jordan (before 1967) and Israel (after 1967), pre–March 1997. Bottom: Infrastructure works prior to construction of Har Homa settlement on the same mountain, June 1997. Source: Applied Research Institute in Jerusalem (ARIJ), "The Har Homa Settlement and the Uprooting of Abu GhnaimForest - POICA".

A FLYING TREE

In January 2021, I asked Imad Hussein–a Palestinian medical doctor interested in biology and earth sciences, who walks extensively in Palestine to document its flora and fauna–to talk to me about trees in Palestine. We went for a walk in an abandoned olive grove in Wadi Al 'Uqdeh, near Ramallah. Among our different encounters with trees was a single pine tree emerging between smaller shrubs. Recognising this tree, which is mostly found in Israel's planted forests, from my research, I was curious to know what brought it to rural Palestinian land in the West Bank. "This is *pinus halepensis*, it probably flew from the settlement," said Imad. It took me a moment to understand what he meant by "flew". I looked around to see if any settlement appeared on the horizon but couldn't find any. Seeing that I was a bit confused, Imad explained: "If you follow the valley to the West, in about two kilometres from here, you will be faced by an Israeli settlement called Dolev. The seed was probably carried from there by the wind." I picked one of the pinecones, curiously analysing its shape and trying to visualise how the seeds could have flown a distance of a few kilometres from the settlement to the grove.[1]

A collective walk guided by the author as part of the Al Block collective in a JNF pine forest planted on the lands of Suba, a Palestine village destroyed in 1948, 2022. Source: Image by Ailo Ribas.

Pinus halepensis is commonly known as Aleppo Pine (Arabic: شِيرق *qreish*, and Hebrew: אורן ירושלים *oren yerushalyim*), a name given by the English botanist Philip Miller to a tree species sampled in Aleppo in 1768.[2] This species has functioned as an agent of the Zionist settler-colonial project throughout the years. Through understanding this role, we can

1 Excerpt from video essay by author *A Walk in Wadi Al 'Uqdeh-Ramallah* (January, 2022)

2 Nili Liphschitz and Gideon Biger, "Past Distribution of Aleppo Pine (Pinus Halepensis) in the Mountains of Israel (Palestine)," *The Holocene* 11, no. 4 (May 2001): 427–36.

begin to unravel the politics of land and the incursion of colonial imaginary landscapes into Palestine. For this purpose, I will renounce the tree's scientific and common names and, alternatively, refer to it through the physical features that construct it as a political agent.[3]

In the first two decades of the twentieth century when Palestine was still under the Ottoman rule, the Jewish National Fund (JNF),[4] a non-governmental organisation established by the Zionist movement in 1901, started planting trees in Palestine with the principal intention of holding newly purchased lands for the arriving Jewish settlers. According to Ottoman law, if privately-owned land was left unused, it would constitute an opening for others (i.e. the Arab communities) to utilise the land and thus claim possession.[5] In the early 1900s, the JNF planted olive trees for their biblical significance but soon realised that, while olives didn't demand much labour, planting them wasn't the simplest and cheapest method for holding the purchased lands.[6] Together with other species, *the fast-growing tree* proved to be well-suited for this purpose, because of the moderate ecological requirements.[7]

The "Olive Tree Fund" certificate by the Jewish National Fund from the early twentieth century, from Elissa Rosenberg. 2018. "'Something from Nothing': Constructing Israeli Rurality". Landscape Research 44(5):1–15. / The "Tree Fund" certificate by the Jewish National Fund. In 1913, as the JNF planted other tree types, the word "olive" was omitted from the fund's name, changing it to "Tree Fund". Source: United States Holocaust Memorial Museum, courtesy of Victor Glasberg.

After 1948, planting forests became a large-scale national project for the newly established Israeli state.[8] The JNF, which then acted as a quasi-governmental organisation, planted millions of trees on Palestinian land, transforming the existing landscape and mobilising the Zionist settler-colonial project. Joseph Weitz, the long-

3 To prevent confusion, other species mentioned in the essay will be referred to with their English common name.

4 The JNF was established as the product of the congresses of the World Zionist Organization held in Europe in the last years of the nineteenth. It was the Zionist institution responsible for purchasing land in Palestine and developing it for settlement by the Jewish community.

5 Shaul Ephraim Cohen, *The Politics of Planting : Israeli-Palestinian Competition for Control of Land in the Jerusalem Periphery* (Chicago ; London: The University of Chicago Press, 1993), 49.

6 Shaul Ephraim Cohen, T*he Politics of Planting*, 47–49.

7 Liphschitz and Biger, "Past Distribution of Aleppo Pine."

8 In the early years of the Israeli state, Prime Minister Ben-Gurion spoke publicly of the importance of afforestation and its role in building the state, calling to afforest a quarter of the area of the state. The role of afforestation was a major element in the foundation of Israel used for security, aesthetic and land-holding purposes. See: Cohen, *The Politics of Planting*, 60–74.

serving afforestation director at the JNF, known as the 'father of the forests', wrote in his book *Forests and Afforestation in Israel*, describing the natural landscape of the area:

> The so-called trees in the scrub are of little worth economically or even ornamentally. This is because the great majority of them lack that primary characteristic of the forest tree—an erect trunk branching out either pyramidally or in a round-shaped crown, according to the natural growth form of the particular species [...] But over the rest of the area, man could step in and convert the scrub into forest capable of functioning as such, possessing a natural beauty, providing nesting sites for songbirds and ranges for forest animals, as well as a place for man himself to wander and refresh his spirit.[9]

In his writing, Weitz described the existing landscape as incomplete without Jewish labour and modern tools. He saw the natural 'shrubs' as not sufficiently trees in the western sense of the word and therefore believed they should be replaced with forest trees. *The fast-growing tree* with its erect trunk was well-suited to transform that 'faulty' landscape. It materialised imaginaries of the Palestinian landscape as populated with Europeanised forests.[10] Moreover, *the fast-growing tree with an erect trunk*'s hemispherical crown worked well as a mask for covering the remains of the Palestinian villages on which they were planted, after their destruction in 1948. By hiding the traces of these villages from the Israeli public, the tree carries "the heavy burden" of seeing the Palestinian ruins without recognizing them.[11]

After 1967 and Israel's occupation of the West Bank and its continual seizure of land beyond the Green Line[12] for settling Jewish populations, *the fast-growing tree with an erect trunk and a hemispherical crown* performed again its function as a landholder for future settlement. In her book *Planted Flags*, the Israeli legal scholar and ethnographer Irus Braverman examines how the 1858 Ottoman Law was employed and manipulated to transform vast tracts of land in the West Bank into Israeli state land.[13] Trees, being a visible marker in the landscape, have been key to establishing legally recognised control over territory. In many cases, they have been planted around Israeli settlements or on lands designated as green areas in order to draw borders, preventing Palestinians from claiming these lands and holding them for the future expansion of the settlements.[14]

9 Joseph Weitz, Shlomo Levenson, and Isaac Arnon, *Forests and Afforestation in Israel* (Jerusalem: Jerusalem Massada Press, 1974), 43.

10 Irus Braverman, *Planted Flags: Trees, Land, and Law in Israel/Palestine* (New York: Cambridge University Press, 2014), 88–90.

11 Of the 150 forests managed by the JNF, 46 forests cover ruins of 89 Palestinian villages—87 destroyed in the Nakba and two in the 1967 war. Trees growing where towns once stood are guarantors that those expelled have nothing to which they can claim a return. Eitan Bronstein Aparicio, "Most JNF – KKL Forests and Sites Are Located on the Ruins of Palestinian Villages," April 2014, https://www.zochrot.org/en/article/55963.

12 The Green Line, (pre–)1967 border, or 1949 Armistice border, is the demarcation line set out in the 1949 Armistice Agreements between the armies of Israel and those of its neighbours after the 1948 Arab–Israeli War. It served as the *de facto* borders of the State of Israel from 1949 until the Six–Day War in 1967.

13 The Ottoman Law stating that continuous cultivation of state land grants ownership to the cultivator has been turned on its head by Israel, entailing that all uncultivated lands, whether privately owned or not, return to the hands of the state. As a result, many Palestinians were required to prove that they had cultivated the land for at least 10 years to claim ownership. Braverman, *Planted Flags*, 165.

14 "The Har Homa Settlement and the Uprooting of Abu Ghnaim Forest–POICA," Applied Research Institute in Jerusalem (ARIJ), Monitoring Israeli Colonizing activities in the Palestinian West Bank and Gaza, March 18, 1997, http://poica.org/1997/03/the-har-homa-settlement-andthe-uprooting-of-abu-ghnaim-forest/.

The planting of the first saplings in the Martyrs Forest, commemorating the victims of the Holocaust. The saplings were planted on the lands of Kasla, a Palestinian village destroyed in 1948, January 1953. Source: Avraham Malevsky – The Jewish National Fund Photo Archive. Pictures of the affected area before and after the August 2021 wildfire in Jerusalem environs showing agricultural terraces revealed by the fire. Source: Image courtesy of Tarek Bakri.

My recent encounter with a *fast-growing tree with an erect trunk and a hemispherical crown* while walking through a Palestinian olive grove in the West Bank, with no visible settlement on the horizon, reveals another layer of the tree's role as a political agent. The tree has small winged seeds that allow them to fly with the wind over long distances and grow on lands hundreds of metres away from where it was initially planted. The saplings that are planted by the JNF are mostly grown from seeds, not collected from local wild trees, but rather brought from different sites across the Mediterranean Basin, and have a genetic composition that is essentially different from the wild populations.[15] While the planted *fast-growing trees with erect trunks, hemispherical crowns and small winged seeds* might have biologically invasive qualities that enable them to spread easily and colonise new land, I am not concerned with proving the trees' invasiveness or indigeneity, as much as I address the invasive approach of the settler-colonial project that plants them.

If we go back to the tree's common names, we can expose the different approaches towards land that are carried in language. The Arabic common name is قريش *qreish*, meaning crunchy, which refers to its small crunchy seeds traditionally

15 Alon Rothschild, "The Need to Stop Afforestation in Sensitive Natural Sensitive Ecosystems in Israel, and Conserve Israel's Natural Landscapes" (The Society for the Protection of Nature in Israel (SPNI), 2019).

used in the making of ملبن *malban,* a Palestinian sweet made from grapes in the last days of summer.[16] The Hebrew common name is אורן ירושלים *oren yerushalayim*, meaning 'Jerusalem pine', stressing its significance as the main tree in the Israeli planted forests, and ties it to the biblical image of Jerusalem as 'originally' surrounded with forests, turning into a 'desert' after thousands of years of 'exile' and being 'reforested' by Israel.[17] While one name reflects a certain relationality between the local Palestinian communities and land materialised in the crunchiness of the tree's seeds, the other originates from the Zionist settler-colonial project in Palestine that views land as a separate 'other', a land*scape* ripe for invasion with imposed imaginaries.

Winged seeds of Aleppo Pine, from Nili Liphschitz and Gideon Biger. 2016. "Past Distribution of Aleppo pine (Pinus halepensis) in the Mountains of Israel (Palestine)." The Holocene, 11(4), 427-436.

16 Imad Hussein, "A Walk in Wadi Al–'Uqdeh", interview by Areej Ashhab, January 12, 2022.
17 Liphschitz and Biger, "Past Distribution of Aleppo Pine."

Work Cited

Aparicio, Eitan Bronstein. "Most JNF – KKL Forests and Sites Are Located on the Ruins of Palestinian Villages," *Zochrot*, April 2014, https://www.zochrot.org/en/article/55963.

Ashhab, Areej. A Walk in Wadi Al 'Uqdeh– Ramallah (January 2022).

Braverman, Irus. *Planted Flags: Trees, Land, and Law in Israel/Palestine*. New York: Cambridge University Press, 2014.

Cohen, Shaul Ephraim. *The Politics of Planting : Israeli-Palestinian Competition for Control of Land in the Jerusalem Periphery*. Chicago ; London: The University of Chicago Press, 1993.

Liphschitz, Nili and Gideon Biger. "Past Distribution of Aleppo Pine (Pinus Halepensis) in the Mountains of Israel (Palestine)," *The Holocene* 11, no. 4 (May 2001): 427-36.

Rothschild, Alon. "The Need to Stop Afforestation in Sensitive Natural Sensitive Ecosystems in Israel, and Conserve Israel's Natural Landscapes" (The Society for the Protection of Nature in Israel (SPNI), 2019).

Weitz, Joseph, Shlomo Levenson, and Isaac Arnon. *Forests and Afforestation in Israel*. Jerusalem: Jerusalem Massada Press, 1974.

Applied Research Institute in Jerusalem (ARIJ). "The Har Homa Settlement and the Uprooting of Abu Ghnaim Forest – *POICA*," Israeli Colonizing activities in the Palestinian West Bank and Gaza, March 18, 1997, http://poica.org/1997/03/the–har–homa–settlement–andthe–uprooting–of–abu–ghnaim–forest/.

This photograph shows an early cattle—wire border fence and an agent patrolling the line on horseback. Source: ASI Archives, National Agricultural Library.

The geographies of the U.S.-Mexico border wall system are shaped not by state security intentions alone, but also by grounded environmental formations (including nonhuman actors and environmental relationships) that affect boundary infrastructures. The earliest barriers installed for the purpose of controlling migration in the U.S.-Mexico borderlands were not meant for humans alone, but also animals and microbes. Such was the case at Organ Pipe Cactus National Monument, which lies athwart the international boundary between Arizona, U.S. and Sonora, Mexico. Though not founded for the purpose of boundary enforcement, environmental imaginaries which constructed American nature as preserved from human contamination sanctioned land managers to protect the land through boundary fortification.[1] To stop cattle from grazing in the park and spreading hoof-and-mouth disease, the National Park Service, Bureau of Animal Industry, and International Boundary and Water Commission together funded and installed the first federally-constructed border fence of Southwestern Arizona (much like the fence pictured above).[2] That cattle-wire fence, and the border it marked, impeded Organ Pipe's Native residents (the Hia-Ced O'odham) from freely accessing and tending their land on the other side of the barrier– "green colonialism" manifest.[3] At other early cattle fences along the border, quarantine measures and fumigation

1 Paul Outka, Race and Nature from Transcendentalism to the Harlem Renaissance (New York: Palgrave Macmillan, 2008).

2 Jessica Piekielek, "Creating a Park, Building a Border: The Establishment of Organ Pipe Cactus National Monument and the Solidification of the US—Mexico Border," *Journal of the Southwest* 58, no. 1 (2016): 5.

3 Interview with Miguel Velasco in The Quitobaquito Cemetery and Its History, by Fillman Bell, Keith M. Anderson, and Yvonne G. Stweart, United States Department of the Interior, National Park Service (Tucson, 1980): 535—538. See also Piekielek, "Creating a Park, Building a Border."

were imposed upon Mexican cowboys travelling with their cattle, exemplifying how environmental formations bled into the construction of race in certain places.[4] The cattle-wire fences scattered across the borderlands testify to the imperial domination and racialisation which initially carved out, and continue to structure, the borderlands. Parts of the Organ Pipe cattle-wire fence were not fully replaced until the so-called Trump wall construction in 2019.

Legacy pedestrian fence made from corrugated steel landing mats recycled from U.S. war in Vietnam. Source: Brandon Quester and Castañeda.

Borders are "highly selective" technologies that differentiate along lines of belonging.[5] A border barrier's materiality is central to that difference-making because it determines what or who can or cannot cross the line. However, for border barriers to endure, they must be designed to consider the dynamic terrain on which they are built. From 2004-2006, the National Park Service designed and installed 30 miles of single-layer vehicle fence along Organ Pipe to stop vehicles from driving across the boundary while allowing "water and animals… to safely roam their natural ranges uninterrupted."[6] When the U.S. Department of Homeland Security later added bulkier pedestrian barriers around the international port of entry in the park to further deter humans from also crossing on foot, those walls included flood openings and gates to accommodate flooding and pre-empt catastrophic breakages.[7] Nonhumans impact the material bounds of the nation in both destructive and co-constructive ways: destructive because geophysical events occasionally take down border barriers, and co-constructive because those same forces affect humans to engineer designs that take dynamic terrain into account.

4 Mary E. Mendoza, "Treacherous Terrain: Racial Exclusion and Environmental Control at the US–Mexico Border," *Environmental History* 23, no. 1 (2018): 119.

5 Andrew Burridge et al., 'Polymorphic Borders,' *Territory, Politics, Governance* (Taylor & Francis, 2017): 244.

6 National Park Service, 'International Border Vehicle Barrier – Organ Pipe Cactus National Monument,' last modified May 13, 2018, https://www.nps.gov/orpi/planyourvisit/barrier.htm.

7 National Park Service , 'Effects of the International Boundary Pedestrian Fence in the Vicinity of Lukeville, Arizona, on Drainage Systems and Infrastructure, Organ Pipe Cactus National Monument, Arizona,' last modified August 2008, https://www.nps.gov/orpi/learn/nature/upload/floodreport_july2008_final.pdf.

Barriers' materialities also connect to networks of imperial militarism that extend beyond the present borderlands in both time and space.[8] Some pedestrian barriers installed throughout the '90s-'00s were constructed from portable helicopter mats recycled from the US war in Vietnam.[9] Today, drones/UAVs and security systems that surveil the borderlands are "field proven" by Israeli settlers against Palestinians, as per Israeli manufacturer Elbit systems.[10]

Source: Kingsville Vulture Deterrence RFI.

Virtual fencing like the kind sold by Elbit Systems uses remote sensing technologies to help border authorities detect, visualise, and respond to human movement between ports of entry. Ecological disruptions are aplenty, however: desert heat distorts visuals; uneven landscape evades visual penetration; and animals set off ground sensors.[11] Dynamic terrain sometimes disrupts the state's attempts to make it legible to the "Smart Border".[12]

In 2020, the United States Customs and Border Protection lost control of an entire radio tower when a flock of over 300 vultures decided to call it home. The condors subsequently disrupted radio communications when they covered the tower

8 Harsha Walia, *Border and Rule: Global Migration, Capitalism, and the Rise of Racist Nationalism* (Chicago: Haymarket Books, 2021); Todd Miller, *Empire of Borders: The Expansion of the US Border around the World* (New York: Verso Books, 2019).
See also Ian Graham, Ronald Shaw and Majed Akhter, 'The Unbearable Humanness of Drone Warfare in FATA, Pakistan,' *Antipode* 44, no. 4 (2012): 1502.

9 Victoria Hattam, 'Imperial Designs: Remembering Vietnam at the US–Mexico Border Wall' *Memory Studies* 9, no. 1 (January 2016): 27–47.

10 Will Parrish, 'The U.S.. Border Patrol and an Israeli Military Contractor Are Putting a Native American Reservation Under "Persistent Surveillance,"' *The Intercept*, August 25, 2019, https://theintercept.com/2019/08/25/border-patrol-israel-lbit-surveillance/.

11 Juanita Sundberg, 'Diabolic Caminos in the Desert and Cat Fights on the Rio: A Posthumanist Political Ecology of Boundary Enforcement in the United States–Mexico Borderlands,' *Annals of the Association of American Geographers* 101, no. 2 (2011): 319; Geoffrey A. Boyce, 'The Rugged Border: Surveillance, Policing and the Dynamic Materiality of the US/Mexico Frontier,' *Environment and Planning D: Society and Space* 34, no. 2 (2016): 245–62.

12 Boyce, 'The Rugged Border.'

in corrosive faeces, urine, and vomit.[13] Hoping to overcome the birds, Customs and Border Protection issued a Request for Information (RFI), indicating their plan to install a "Vulture Deterrence Netting System" for the purpose of making the towers less attractive to roosting condors.[14] The final price of such a netting system, and the total funds dedicated toward its installation, remains unknown. The RFI implies that the impositions of environmental constraints are never final. As nonhumans thwart barriers, state actors advocate for increased funding to overcome the disruption. The financial expansion of the military-border industrial complex is therefore partially mediated by nonhuman activity.[15]

Source: Fernando Sobarzo Robles and Cuenca Los Ojos.

Source: KYMA.

13 Katherine J. Wu, 'Hundreds of Vultures Roost on U.S. Border Patrol Texas Radio Tower,' *UPI*, January 13, 2020, https://www.upi.com/Top_News/US/2020/01/11/Hundreds-of-vultures-roost-on-US-border-patrol-Texas-radio-tower/9501578768484/.

14 Department of Homeland Security (DHS) U.S. Customs and Border Protection, 'Kingsville Vulture Deterrence System for Radio Tower Request for Information' *Department of Homeland Security*, 2020, 1. https://www.documentcloud.org/documents/6615777-Kingsville-Vulture-Deterrence-RFI.html.

15 This is Sundberg's argument in "Diabolic Caminos," 319.

Nonhuman breaches partially explain where Trump wall segments stand. Trump's walls are uniform-material segments made out of reinforced 33' or 18' (approximately 10 m or 5.5 m) steel bollards, each spaced 3-4" (approx. 8-10cm) apart, connected at the top with a thin metal plate. In 2020 in California, winds over 30mph toppled a 40 metre segment of Trump's newly constructed border wall, tumbling the structure into Mexico.[16] Just months after their installation, segments of privately-built barriers along the Rio-Grande stood shakily on eroded and cracking foundations. At the San Bernardino National Wildlife Refuge in Southeastern Arizona, 5.5 centimetres of summer monsoonal rainfalls blew the hinges off of six hinged metal floodgates in the wall, leaving gaps.[17] These openings among others–caused by breaches, tumbles, cracked foundations, or simply areas left unfinished when construction workers on a strict timeline to finish building by the end of Trump's administration met with rocky terrain–were not the outcome of human-designed tactical logic. Rather, the bric-a-brac spatiality of the border wall system partially emerges from attempts to install a homogenous structure upon a heterogeneous and ever-changing borderland.

Rick Wilking in Chen, 2019. Source: Reuters.

The boundary set by the U.S. and Mexico in 1853 divides the traditional homelands of over 36 Native nations recognized by the U.S. government (including the Tohono O'odham, Kumeyaay, Pai, Cocopah, Yaqui, Apaches, and Kickapoo people)[18] and peoples not yet recognized (like the Hia-Ced O'odham).

Native sovereignty in the borderlands impacts the spatiality of the border wall system. The vehicle barrier at the southern edge of the Tohono O'odham reservation (VF300) is an outcome of government-to-government negotiations between the Tohono O'odham and U.S. Department of Homeland Security. According to Tohono O'odham Governor Verlon Jose, the fence was built to allow the passage of wildlife and cattle,

16 KYMA News Team, 'Portion of New Border Wall Falls in Mexicali,' *KYMA*, January 29, 2020, https://kyma.com/news/2020/01/29/portion-of-new-border-wall-falls-in-mexicali/.

17 Paul Ingram, 'Monsoon Floods Damage Border Wall near Douglas,' *Tucson Sentinel*, August 21, 2021, https://www.tucsonsentinel.com/local/report/082121_border_wall_damaged/monsoon-floods-damage-border-wall-near-douglas/.

18 Christina Leza, 'How a Border Wall Would Separate Indigenous Communities,' *Pacific Standard*, accessed September 1, 2022, https://psmag.com/social-justice/a-border-wall-would-separate-indigenous-communities.; Vanda Felbab-Brown, 'The Damage Trump's Wall Causes in Mexico,' *Brookings* (blog), July 20, 2020, https://www.brookings.edu/blog/order-from-chaos/2020/07/20/the-damage-trumps-wall-causes-in-mexico/.

in line with Tohono O'odham way of life.[19] Like all O'odham, they maintain sacred relationships with their lands, particularly Saguaro cacti. Though the boundary there is a straight line, parts of the fence along the Tohono O'odham reservation swerve between Saguaros, deviating from the boundary as if pushed off course by the standing cacti. The Saguaros' positions, and their reciprocal relationships with the Tohono O'odham, mould the border wall system in material ways.

19 Molly Hennessy–Fiske, 'Arizona Tribe Refuses Trump's Wall, but Agrees to Let Border Patrol Build Virtual Barrier,' Los Angeles Times, May 9, 2019, https://www.latimes.com/nation/la-na-arizona-tribe-border-patrol-trump-wall-20190509-htmlstory.html.

Works Cited

Bell, Fillman, Keith M. Anderson, and Yvonne G. Stewart. *The Quitobaquito Cemetery and Its History*. Western Archeological Center, National Park Service Tucson, 1980.

Boyce, Geoffrey A. 'The Rugged Border: Surveillance, Policing and the Dynamic Materiality of the US/ Mexico Frontier.' *Environment and Planning D: Society and Space* 34, no. 2 (2016): 245-62.

Burridge, Andrew, Nick Gill, Austin Kocher, and Lauren Martin. 'Polymorphic Borders.' *Territory, Politics, Governance*. London and New York: Taylor & Francis, 2017.

Felbab–Brown, Vanda. 'The Damage Trump's Wall Causes in Mexico.' *Brookings* (blog), July 20, 2020. https://www.brookings.edu/blog/order–from–chaos/2020/07/20/the–damage–trumps–wall–causes–in–mexico/.

Hattam, Victoria. 'Imperial Designs: Remembering Vietnam at the US-Mexico Border Wall.' *Memory Studies* 9, no. 1 (January 2016): 27-47. https://doi.org/10.1177/1750698015613971.

Ingram, Paul. 'Monsoon Floods Damage Border Wall near Douglas.' *Tucson Sentinel*, August 21, 2021. https://www.tucsonsentinel.com/local/report/082121_border_wall_damaged/monsoon–floods–damage–border–wall–near–douglas/.

KYMA News. 'Portion of New Border Wall Falls in Mexicali.' *KYMA*, January 29, 2020. https://kyma.com/news/2020/01/29/portion–of–new–border–wall–falls–in–mexicali/.

Leza, Christina. 'How a Border Wall Would Separate Indigenous Communities.' *Pacific Standard*. Accessed September 1, 2022. https://psmag.com/social–justice/a–border–wall–would–separate–indigenous–communities.

Mendoza, Mary E. 'Treacherous Terrain: Racial Exclusion and Environmental Control at the US–Mexico Border.' *Environmental History* 23, no. 1 (2018): 117-26.

Miller, Todd. *Empire of Borders: The Expansion of the US Border around the World*. Verso Books, 2019.

National Park Service. 'Effects of the International Boundary Pedestrian Fence in the Vicinity of Lukeville, Arizona, on Drainage Systems and Infrastructure, Organ Pipe Cactus National Monument, Arizona,' August 2008. https://www.nps.gov/orpi/learn/nature/upload/floodreport_july2008_final.pdf.

National Park Service. International Border Vehicle Barrier – Organ Pipe Cactus National Monument.' Accessed September 1, 2022. https://www.nps.gov/orpi/planyourvisit/barrier.htm.

Outka, Paul. *Race and Nature from Transcendentalism to the Harlem Renaissance*. Springer, 2010.

Parrish, Will. 'The U.S. Border Patrol and an Israeli Military Contractor Are Putting a Native American Reservation Under "Persistent Surveillance."' *The Intercept*. August 25, 2019. https://theintercept.com/2019/08/25/border–patrol–israel–el–bit–surveillance/.

Piekielek, Jessica. 'Creating a Park, Building a Border: The Establishment of Organ Pipe Cactus National Monument and the Solidification of the US–Mexico Border' *Journal of the Southwest* 58, no. 1 (2016): 1-27.

Sundberg, Juanita. 'Diabolic Caminos in the Desert and Cat Fights on the Rio: A Posthumanist Political Ecology of Boundary Enforcement in the United States-Mexico Borderlands.' *Annals of the Association of American Geographers* 101, no. 2 (2011): 318-36.

Walia, Harsha. *Border and Rule: Global Migration, Capitalism, and the Rise of Racist Nationalism*. Chicago: Haymarket Books, 2021.

Warren, Scott. 'In Defense of Wilderness: Policing Public Borderlands.' *South Atlantic Quarterly* 116, no. 4 (October, 2017): 863-72. https://doi.org/10.1215/00382876–4235073.

Wu, Katherine J. 'Hundreds of Vultures Roost on U.S. Border Patrol Texas Radio Tower.' *UPI*. Accessed January 13, 2020. https://www.upi.com/Top_News/US/2020/01/11/Hundreds–of–vultures–roost–on–US–border–patrol–Texas–radio–tower/9501578768484/.

"Kingsville Vulture Deterrence RFI – DocumentCloud." Accessed September 1, 2022. https://www.documentcloud.org/documents/6615777–Kingsville–Vulture–Deterrence–RFI.html.

SMOULDERING GROUNDS

On the 8th of September 2020, large fires broke out at the migrant camp of Moria, in the frontier island of Lesvos, Greece. The fires burned the camp to the ground, forcing the relocation of the thousands of people detained there to a newly built facility on the island, and transforming the epicentre of the EU's carceral migration regime into ruins. Yet, this recent, devastating fire, was not an unusual phenomenon; in fact, it was only the last out of more than a hundred outbreaks that occurred in and around the camp since it was established in 2013.

Through these fire occurrences, which were far from singular, decontextualised incidents, the migrant camp of Moria could be said to have existed in a constant state of smouldering; not merely because of the ubiquitous presence of the provisional fires migrants necessitated for cooking and warmth, but also due to its tendency to erupt into these frequent, often detrimental, conflagrations.

Notwithstanding fire's recurrent emergence, one of the most common questions surrounding these outbreaks was that of direct causation. Where did the fire start, what was the physical source of ignition? Was it the collapsing electrical infrastructure that creates tangles of often deteriorated cables dwindling from the flimsy tents and leading to regular episodes of power outage? Was it the volatile moment of contact between the flammable fabric of the shelters and the deficient heating devices that migrants resorted to during the cold winter months? Was the fire caused by spontaneous ignition due to elongated droughts and heatwaves that more and more frequently afflict Southern Europe as a consequence of rapidly changing environmental conditions? Or did the fire start as an act of protest on the part of the migrants against enforced containment and deplorable living conditions?[1]

All these hypotheses are concerned predominantly with the identification of straightforward causalities, the fleeting moment of the outburst. However, the staggering reiteration of fire outbreaks in and around the camp, rather than being a sum of isolated incidents or 'regrettable accidents', should be understood as unravelling multi-scalar patterns and demonstrating the simultaneous collapse of diverse forms of operation and causalities–from the failure, inadequacies and overlapping complexities of the humanitarian infrastructure (such as the precarious 'housing' system or parts of the supply networks, like electricity and the provision of food), to the violence of the legal, administrative and bureaucratic framework that operates to restrict, channel and immobilise migrants; from the split second of the failed cable, to the macroscale of rapid climate change and its effects on wildfires.

Similar to its emergence, fire's aftermath always appeared enmeshed in political complexities which affected and, in turn, were reshaped by its meaning and interpretation, whereby public and legal discourses reified racist narratives of criminality, thus maintaining the (re)production of migrant 'illegality'. Since 2015, dozens of migrants had been indicted and prosecuted with the accusations of arson, accompanied by a complete lack of substantiating evidence, and by severed, if not non-existent, legal aid and judicial provisions. This violent scapegoating, which often took the form of collective punishment against resistance and direct action, culminated

1 This essay is accompanied by a public investigative platform that archives fires outbreaks as gathered from social media, official accounts, and sources living in the camp at the time, and locates them spatially and temporally: smouldering-grounds.com.

in the wrongful conviction of six young asylum seekers for the fires of September 2020, a still ongoing legal process whose trials have been characterised "a parody of justice."[2]

Within the inadequate and erroneous judicial register, the structural conditions of the border regime that produced and sustained such a tense, volatile and flammable environment remain largely ignored; where zones of presumed protection are turned into areas of abandonment that not only bear witness to detrimental fires, but are also left criminalised for them.

OSINT ARCHIVE SELECTION

On 19 September, 2016, during expansive conflagrations that lasted almost one day, adjacent olive groves and a significant part of the camp were burned, alongside tents and shelters that accommodated around 1000 people.[3] Only several months after the EU-Turkey Statement that enforced an array of containment policies alongside geographical restrictions on the island, the fire also took place against a backdrop of far-right extremism. According to various accounts amongst activist and migrant groups,[4] when people were trying to flee the camp to Mytilene, they were confronted by the police. One of the two main roads to Mytilene was blocked by a racist mob, and several people were attacked. Most of the shelters that were burned were 'Better Shelter' units, the sponsored output of a partnership between the United Nations High Commissioner for Refugees (UNHCR) and the IKEA Foundation.[5] These shelters were installed in the camp in 2015, but UNHCR ordered their redesign and withdrawal, after they were criticised for insufficient fire safety provisions along with other design flaws (which had been already identified during field trials but were omitted in the original reports "for fear of losing funding").[6]

2 Helena Smith, 'Jailing of Afghans for Lesbos migrant camp fire a 'parody of justice', *The Guardian*, 13 June 2021, https://www.theguardian.com/world/2021/jun/13/jailing-afghans-for-lesbos-moria-migrant-camp-fire-parody-of-justice.

3 'Timeline', Dimitra Andritsou, accessed 2 August, 2022, https://smouldering-grounds.com/Timeline

4 No Border Kitchen Lesvos, 'A Rough Night: Protests for Freedom, Moria on Fire and Fascist Attacks', 21 September 2016, https://noborderkitchenlesvos.noblogs.org/post/2016/09/21/a-rough-night-protests-for-freedom-moria-on-fire-and-fascist-attacks/; Legal Center Lesbos, '#7 – Lesvos on Fire', (19 September 2016), accessed 2 August 2022, https://soundcloud.com/legalcentrelesbos/lesvos-on-fire?fbclid=IwAR1ZiFT6xD_yN45YJ06uzP1Ndbw3WtuRzAgfHoJKm8POLIh4aYPvXrM9qBU.

5 I was able to reach this conclusion through mapping the zones of the camp that were burned, and cross-referencing them with the zones that housed most of the Better Shelter units, as captured in photographs and videos before the incident in question.

6 Cameron Sinclair, as quoted in: Marcus Fairs, 'Ten Thousand IKEA Refugee Shelters Left Unused over Fire Fears, United Nations Admits', *Dezeen*, 29 April 2017, https://www.dezeen.com/2017/04/29/united-nations-admits-10000-ikea-better-shelter-refugees-mothballed-fire-fears/.

I3505 / Twitter @HumanityCrew
19 September, 2016
13:30–23:00 (GMT+2)
Location: Zones 4 & 5

On the 24 October, 2016, a fire broke out in the section of the camp which housed the offices of the European Asylum Support Office (EASO).[7] More than two years after the incident, Sohel M., a politically active figure on the island defending migrant rights, was indicted on felony charges related to the fire without any evidence.[8] These charges were a part of a wave of criminalisation of migrants confined on Lesvos and other Greek islands, often taking the form of collective punishment.

I3905 / No Border Kitchen Lesvos
24 October, 2016
10:05–11:10 (GMT+2)
Location: EASO Offices

On 31 October, 2016, a fire blazed for more than 12 hours in the surrounding olive groves of the camp.[9] The fire brigade assumed that a potential cause of the fire was the burning of crop residues and branches, which expanded beyond control due to strong winds and the elongated droughts.[10] While the fire service published official reports disassociating the fire from the hotspot, dominant narratives circulated online around the fire, targeting and scapegoating migrants.

7 'Timeline', Dimitra Andritsou, accessed 2 August, 2022, https://smouldering-grounds.com/Timeline

8 'Defender of Migrant Rights Arrested and Facing Criminal Trial in Lesvos', *Legal Centre Lesvos*, 22 January 2019, https://legalcentrelesvos.org/2019/01/22/defender-of-migrant-rights-arrested-and-facing-criminal-trial-in-lesvos

9 'Timeline', Dimitra Andritsou, accessed 2 August, 2022, https://smouldering-grounds.com/Timeline

10 'Πυρκαγιά –άσχετη με το hot spot– στη Μόρια', *ThePressProject*, 31 October 2016, https://thepressproject.gr/purkagia-asxeti-me-to-hot-spot-sti-moria

I4002 / Lesvos News
31 October, 2016
16:15–12:00 (next day) (GMT+2)
Location: Surrounding olive groves

On the 24 November, 2016, an expired gas canister used for cooking exploded inside a tent in the camp.[11] The explosion caused fatal injuries to a 66-year-old woman and her 6-year-old grandchild who were sleeping inside the tent, as well as serious injuries to two more members of the family.[12] Riots and protests all around the hotspot broke out after that, with more than 10 different reported sources of fire in diverse sections of the camp.The largest part of the camp was later evacuated by the police, who also forced 15 arrests. Up until this day, there has not been any official investigation into state accountability for the deaths.

I4404 / Facebook European
Council on Refugees and Exiles
24 November 2016
22:10–07:00 (next day) (GMT+2)
Location: Zones 2, 4 & 5

On 16 January, 2019, A. sent me images and videos, captured on his phone, of a fire that broke out that day, rapidly burning a large polyester tent in the surrounding olive groves of the camp. Activist sources stated that the police violently drove around 50 migrants to the police station and warned against any video recordings, even by confiscating people's phones. The burned shelter was in close proximity to an electric panel, which inadequately provided power to (at the time) almost 1200 people living in the olive groves, and which was subject to frequent overcharging and short-circuits. Only four days before that incident, I had received another message about a burning

11 'Timeline', Dimitra Andritsou, accessed 2 August, 2022, https://smouldering-grounds.com/Timeline
12 The two people that were fatally injured were not identified by name in any of the media reports or social media posts that were located. They were merely identified by age and nationality.

container inside the camp – in the so-called 'safe zone,' a separate, fenced-off section run by a UNHCR partner that hosted unaccompanied minors.

V10205 / Personal Archive
16 January, 2019
10:00–14:00 (GMT+2)
Location: Rubhall, South
Olive Grove

On 29 September, 2019, a large fire reportedly initiated by deteriorating faulty wiring burned several prefabricated containers within the camp, and led to the death of at least one person, Faride Tajik.[13] More than 12,000 people were stranded in the camp at the time, which amounted to more than four times the official 'accommodation' capacity. This was the 113th fire that broke out in the camp and its surroundings since it was established in 2013.[14]

V11301 / Twitter @ahampay
29 September, 2019
17:30–19:30 (GMT+2)
Location: Zone 4

13 'Timeline', Dimitra Andritsou, accessed 2 August, 2022, https://smouldering-grounds.com/Timeline

14 Hellenic Republic, Ministry of Citizen Protection, National Co-ordination Centre for Border Control, Immigration and Asylum, 'National Situational Picture Regarding the Islands at Eastern Aegean Sea', (September, 2019).

FIELDWORK

Captured through fieldwork in April 2019, the images depict the amassing of combustible materials within the pyrophilic agricultural landscape of the olive groves surrounding the official camp of Moria, almost one year before the camp burned down completely. Within the camp's institutional hotspot, the provision of electricity was persistently maintained at a liminal, inadequate state. At the makeshift camp in the periphery of the centre, electricity was supplied irregularly through a network of wires, plugs, sockets, and flimsy connections hanging on the trees. The electrical panel attached to the tree served as the main power source, distributing electricity through an ad-hoc, faulty wiring system, while concomitantly operating as a lurking risk node. Traces of provisional fires as well as fire outbreaks could be seen on the ground and the olive trees at the overspill camp. Olive trees, which are the predominant type of vegetation surrounding the camp, are quite resilient to fire, so their trunks bear the traces of several fire occurrences before being completely burned.

INTERVIEWS

During fieldwork in 2018-2019, I conducted semi-structured interviews and informal conversations with a diverse array of actors, including migrants residing in the camp at the time, humanitarian workers, governmental officials, and firefighters. Part of these interactions also included drafting maps of fire occurrences and relevant incidents as they were recorded by migrants and humanitarian workers by memory. At that time, people were generally restricted in their movements and made to stay on the island for at least one or two years before receiving permits to travel to the mainland, and so most of them would have experienced numerous fire outbreaks in and around the camp. An output of such interactions can be seen in this annotated map, which depicts in different colours the areas where several fire outbreaks took place between 2016 and 2019. Fire outbreaks were not singular incidents with momentary influence, but they reorganised life in the camp; it was not uncommon for internally displaced people after a fire to then be spatially re-accommodated in other sections according to shared nationality or ethnicity. Additionally, as can be seen on the map, one can identify unfolding spatial patterns; within the institutional hotspot, the areas more 'vulnerable' to fiery outbreaks are the ones which were occupied with more 'precarious'" humanitarian infrastructure – for example, zones 4 and 5 in the centre of the camp. While this by no means implies that a mere infrastructural 'upgrade' could serve as a 'technical solution' while the underlying structure remained ignored, it is nonetheless important in its manifestation of the "(re)produced and enacted"[15] precarity that encompassed life on the camp. The ubiquity of the fires–not only in its 'eruptive' emergence, but also through its everlasting presence for heating and warmth–unravels yet another, less visible but highly consequential effect; that of the propagated toxicity that encompassed the burning of fuel, and which persisted long after the quenching of the fire. As A. recounted, in January 2019, there were two days that they witnessed freezing temperatures, but the liminal electrical provisions were on a constant outage; "Moria [the administration] did nothing. They didn't care. No one had heating in the tent."[16] He continued, explaining that for these days, in order to sleep, they were burning olive wood in an iron-steel fireplace inside the tent close to the entrance. "It was very dangerous. Too much smoke. I didn't want it. When power was back, we stopped. It was warm but not good for our health; difficulty breathing."[17]

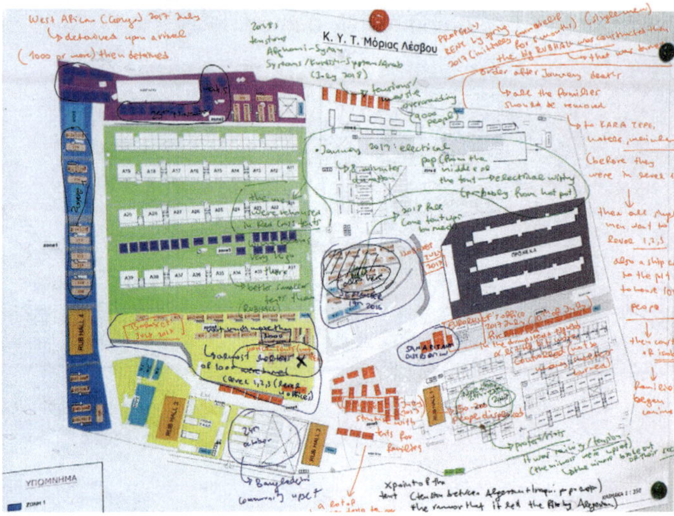

REMOTE SENSING

The moisture index illustrates the burn scar after a fire outbreak on the north of the camp on 19 September, 2016. By viewing moisture index maps from different dates in succession, it becomes clear that fires in the camp manifested patterns and temporalities of recurrence, albeit volatile and variable. A certain recurrence resonated with the so-called 'anti-fire' season in Greece – a six-month period whereby mechanisms are in place to prevent conflagrations due to the higher temperatures. In the context of rapid environmental destruction, this period, characterised by prolonged heatwaves and droughts, witnesses more and more conflagrations that may erupt out of spontaneous ignition. This period corresponded – albeit not strictly – with the 'migration season' as well; whereby sea temperatures and weather conditions appear more auspicious in order to facilitate the sea passage.

15 Kate Coddington, Deirdre Conlon, and Lauren Martin, 'Destitution Economies: Mapping Relations of Enforced Precarity', *Society & Space*, 11 December, 2018, http://societyandspace.org/2018/12/11/destitution-economies-mapping-relations-of-enforced-precarity/.

16 Author's interview with A., in Moria Camp. April 2019.

17 IBID

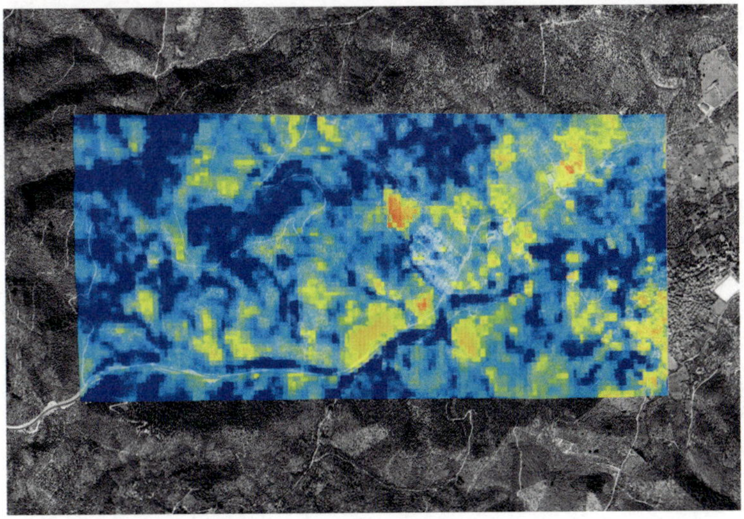

Sentinel–2 L1C satellite imagery from 25 September 2016, band combination (B8A – B11)/(B8A + B11) [moisture index], with warm colours corresponding to the driest vegetational areas and cold colours to the most humid ones. The moisture index image, courtesy of Sentinel–Hub EO Browser, is superimposed onto Google Earth terrain. (Composition by Dimitra Andritsou. 2019.)

Works cited

Andritsou, Dimitra. 'Smouldering Grounds' , smouldering–grounds.com.

Coddington, Kate, Deirdre Conlon and Lauren Martin. 'Destitution Economies: Mapping Relations of Enforced Precarity', *Society & Space*, 11 December, 2018, http://societyandspace.org/2018/12/11/destitution–economies–mapping–relations–of–enforced–precarity/.

Fairs, Marcus. 'Ten Thousand IKEA Refugee Shelters Left Unused over Fire Fears, United Nations Admits', *Dezeen*, 29 April 2017, https://www.dezeen.com/2017/04/29/united–nations–admits–10000–ikea–better–shelter–refugees–mothballed–fire–fears/.

Hellenic Republic, Ministry of Citizen Protection, National Co–ordination Centre for Border Control, Immigration and Asylum. 'National Situational Picture Regarding the Islands at Eastern Aegean Sea'. Athens, 29 August 2019.

Legal Center Lesbos, '#7 – Lesvos on Fire', (19 September 2016), accessed 2 August 2022, https://soundcloud.com/legalcentrelesbos/lesvos–on–fire?fbclid=IwAR1ZiFT6xD_yN45Y–J06uzP1Ndbw3WtuRzAgfHoJKm8POLIh4aYPvX–rM9qBU.

Legal Centre Lesvos, 'Defender of Migrant Rights Arrested and Facing Criminal Trial in Lesvos', 22 January 2019, https://legalcentrelesvos.org/2019/01/22/defender–of–migrant–rights–arrested–and–facing–criminal–trial–in–lesvos/

No Border Kitchen Lesvos, 'A Rough Night: Protests for Freedom, Moria on Fire and Fascist Attacks', 21 September 2016, https://noborderkitchen–lesvos.noblogs.org/post/2016/09/21/a–rough–night–protests–for–freedom–moria–on–fire–and–fascist–attacks/;

The Press Project, 'Πυρκαγιά -άσχετη με το hot spot– στη Μόρια', 31 October 2016, https://thepressproject.gr/purkagia–asxeti–me–to–hot–spot–sti–moria

Smith, Helena. 'Jailing of Afghans for Lesbos migrant camp fire a 'parody of justice', *The Guardian*, 13 June 2021, https://www.theguardian.com/world/2021/jun/13/jailing–afghans–for–lesbos–moria–migrant–camp–fire–parody–of–justice.

AN INTERROGATION OF TERMS

Compiled by Anya Edmond–Pettitt, Hanieh Fatouraee, George Ridgway, Hanna Rullmann, Borbála Soós and Aslı Uludağ, members of the Border Ecologies Network.

To comprehend the interconnected violence produced by the emergent instrumentalisation of environmental forces and practices in border securitisation, we need to develop inventive critical frameworks and approaches for tackling and addressing this intersection. This essay is our contribution to this endeavour, taking the form of a glossary-without set definitions-it operates as an opening of lines of enquiry and modes of analysis. Each term provides a specific lens through which to understand this conjuncture.

BORDER ECOLOGIES

Both as an umbrella name under which we cluster our work, as well as an operative concept, we continually rethink and redefine border ecologies collectively and through our individual practices. We are interested not only in what various borderlands may have in common–bringing them into conversation across their specific geographical and political contexts–but also aim to understand how they remain distinct and linked to specific ecological and historical processes. This means, for example, investigating how national borders have become an increasingly complex agglomeration of conflicting policies and technologies which produce border landscapes as a patchwork of differential mobility regimes for human and other-than-human species. The security infrastructures deployed in these increasingly militarised conservation/border-zones both instrumentalise and disturb natural ecologies in their restrictions on human movements. They are also increasingly legitimised through the dual environmental and migration crises and their accompanying rhetoric, including invasion, protection, stewardship, endangerment, pollution and naturality. This work also extends to broader concepts of borders as regimes of exclusion and inclusion, for example, social-political categories of "native", "alien", and "invasive" across human and other-than-human landscapes; delineation through classification and environmental policies; or links between species, landscapes and national or regional identities.

COMMONS

Commons have been understood traditionally as sets of cultural and material resources belonging to and having effect upon a local community. Operating between practices of inhabiting ecologies, the commons are not 'things' or necessarily material entities, but sets of socio-ecological, interspecies relations.[1] As such they are not merely a resource but a social practice and ongoing commitment held between entities inhabiting ecosystems. They attend to the upkeep of care and the well-being of living entities as well as the various forms of managing the material components that constitute them in collective ways. The commons are born inherently out of localised relation and valuation, signalling relations of reciprocity, and a responsibility for reproduction of shared

1 Silvia Federici, *Re-enchanting the World: feminism and the politics of the commons*. Oakland, California: PM Press / Kairos, (2019), 93–94.

wealth. Acknowledging the commons as sites of resistance, we understand them as oppositional to enclosure and borders across various forms: of space (and spatial occupation), of species, of use, of knowledge systems and of temporal understandings. These interspecies relations oftentimes are not reflected in land-based practices, including habitat conservation and species protection practices where care for individual species are valued over relational and co-constitutive formations of care, labour and sociality. How might understandings of the commons be extended to other spatial domains, for example, to rethink sonic environs as socio-ecological spaces?

CONSERVATION

Conservation pertains to the practice of maintaining the structure and make up of the component parts of a system. Its application within environmental and ecological contexts has largely been to call for the preservation of identified species or habitats deemed at risk by human interventions. In the context of natural habitats, resources, biodiversity, cultural heritage, landscape, and other categories– it generally requires a delineated understanding of the environment and a number of shared assumptions of certain terms (e.g., what is to be considered natural, native, alien, invasive, endangered) put forward by an authoritative entity–private, state, community, or otherwise. It is ultimately a set of practices, activated by the implementation and enforcement of rules and regulations as they relate to the intended goals of that authority.

Conservation constitutes a demarcation of boundaries–of species and habitats, but also of space and access. Acting as a division between what is included and protected in an ecosystem, and what is not–it is often organised through what is considered to be of value: that which is rare, endemic and endangered. These values drive the mechanisms and tools that legitimise and enable conservation: classification, endangered species/habitat lists, biodiversity, protection funding schemes and social relationships to the land. Concealed within these schemes are political decisions that are often presented under a veil of neutrality. Understanding critically the designation of a conservation area requires attending to how choices determine who the area is accessible to, how it may be used and by whom, as well as what landscape is preserved as a moment in time. Within current ecological breakdown, conservation inhabits a conflicted domain, as these borders and value systems coexist with necessary methods of co-curated care and the taking seriously of other-than-human life.

CRIMINALISATION OF SOLIDARITY

The criminalisation of solidarity refers to recent policy changes in many countries towards the increased policing of individuals and NGOs who provide assistance to migrants in various forms,[2] e.g., through search and rescue operations, distributing food, help with housing or education. It is part of a larger policy drive to create hostile environments[3] for migrants, and to discourage people on the move to travel to certain countries. It is a tool to control and criminalise alternative relations, including simple acts of humanity, and to confine and destabilise forms of

2 https://www.amnesty.org/en/latest/campaigns/2020/03/free-to-help/, accessed 3 Oct 2022.

3 JCWI, "The Hostile Environment Explained," https://www.jcwi.org.uk/the-hostile-environment-explained, accessed 3 Oct 2022.

organising outside the logic of the state's border regime.[4] Often, punishments are excessively harsh so as to act as a deterrent to others considering providing assistance, thereby leaving displaced people even more vulnerable. Under this system "border defence, not the protection of life, remains the priority at Europe's frontiers".[5] In some cases, criminalisation seeks to silence journalists, activists and lawyers in order to control narratives and render invisible the state's neglect and cynical necropolitics on the borders.

(IN)VISIBILITY

At the intersection of environment and bordering practices, visibility and invisibility are central concerns. We are living in unprecedented times in which displaced people have never been more surveilled. Fingerprints and biometrics are taken at borders, phones used as tracking devices, the multimillion-pound surveillance industry providing drones and infrared cameras, and even deforestation in the pursuit of making visible and trackable those who attempt to cross borders irregularly. Simultaneously, we are seeing migrants pushed out of sight. Physical barriers such as walls and fences are being erected at borders and around refugee camps to hide residents from the view of the general public,[6] informal camps are being moved further and further from population centres and increasing numbers of offshore processing and deportation arrangements are being made,[7] all of which function to invisibilise 'people on the move'. At the same time, we are interested in the power and control structures that perpetuate hidden violence under the veil of conservation, classification and other environmental regulations, as well as through landscape and terrain. (In)visibility functions as a condition through which border ecologies may be interrogated: what is made to be seen as well as hidden? What ecological relations are made visible by borders? How do we remain critical of our methodologies and visualising practices, such as remote sensing, in shaping the perspectives through which we approach and communicate our work? How can both visibility and invisibility be implemented as tools for control but also resistance? What is obscured or exposed by landscapes? How do governing forces use and abandon landscapes to exert control?

MILITARISATION

Mobilisations of landscape, as a (neo-) colonial practice of territorial defence or expansion, play a significant role in border governance, not only through instrumentalising and manipulating terrain, but also through surveillance. In his text Legal Terrain, Stuart Elden notes how "a military commander views a landscape [...] as a strategic and contested medium, rather than a passive backdrop or simply the stake of struggle".[8] In its conception as a strategic medium, landscape is shaped through military demands for control of mobility and visibility. Techniques first

4 Deanne Dadusc and Chiara Denaro, "Criminalising Solidarity: Silencing Critical Voices and Erasing the Critical Gaze on Border Violence," *Border Criminologies Blog. Faculty of Law, University of Oxford,* 16 April, 2021, https://blogs.law.ox.ac.uk/research–subject–groups/centre–criminology/centreborder–criminologies/blog/2021/04/criminalising.

5 Daniel Trilling, "Should we build a wall around North Wales?," *London Review of Books*, 39, No. 14, 13 July 2017.

6 Elisabeth Vallet, "The World Is Witnessing a Rapid Proliferation of Border Walls," Migration Policy, 27 September 2022, https://www.migrationpolicy.org/article/rapid–proliferation–number–border–walls.

7 Webber, Frances. (2017). "Europe's Unknown War," *Race & Class*, 59(1), 36-53.

8 Stuart Elden, "Legal Terrain - the political materiality of territory," *London Review of International Law*, 5, Issue 2, 2017, 199-224: 202.

conceived in the military domain have expanded in recent years to become omnipresent in border landscapes, as fortification against unwanted migration. Examples of this are extensive: the removal of trees along highways leading to Calais, France, for the benefit of surveillance,[9] the flooding of the surrounding area of the Eurotunnel, preventing access,[10] building of electric fences and walls manned by armed border enforcement in Poland, Hungary, Croatia, Greece, Serbia, and beyond Europe in Libya, Morocco, Sudan and Tunisia,[11] as well as the numerous cases of 'push backs' throughout the continent[12]. Operating both on a material and discursive level, militarisation turns border landscapes into agents in 'migration management'. As an ideological practice, it highlights a produced national unity, criminalisation and illegalisation of the 'other' through the proliferation of nationalistic anti-migrant sentiments—mobilising and securitising societies against a perceived collective 'invasive' enemy. If border landscapes are, in some instances, produced through military logics, in what way do those same logics produce ideas around national identity and culture through landscape? How do military logics enter discourse around nature? For example, as Stuart Elden points out, in military context, strategic landscapes are often conceived to be "devoid of life"[13], both human and non-human.

TOXICITY

Toxicity is not a quality inherent to certain substances. It is, rather, a condition, a relational matter between existents. It functions as an intervention into an existing field of relations—a potential for intensive differentiations, reorganisation and repositioning. It is a potential event that brings to the fore the topological surfaces that both contain and connect; the blurry distinction between animate and inanimate, life and nonlife;[14] invisible ecological flows, connections and blockages; and the mechanisms of purity and immunity (rhetorical or material) that bind a body through controlled permeability. Toxicity is a matter of establishing borders and implementing them.

As an investigative tool, toxicity functions as a manifestation and a trace. However, it is only functional above a certain threshold, when it is sensible,

9 Meynen, Nick. "Belgian authorities slash trees to istop migrants hiding!" *The Ecologist*, April 27, 2018, https://theecologist.org/2018/apr/27/belgian-authorities-slash-trees-stop-migrants-hiding-writes-nickmeynen.

10 Oliver Gee. "Eurotunnel adds moats to keep refugees away." *The Local*, 13 January 2016, https://www.thelocal.fr/20160113/eurotunnel-adds-moats-to-keep-refugees-away/.

11 See: Lorenzo Tondo "Poland starts building wall through protected forest at Belarus border." *The Guardian*, January 27, 2022, https://www.theguardian.com/world/2022/jan/27/poland-starts-building-wall-through-protected-forest-at-belarus-border., Marton Dunai, "Hungary builds new high-tech border fence-with few migrants in sight." *Reuters*, March 2, 2017, https://www.reuters.com/article/us-europe-migrants-hungary-fence-idUSKBN1692MH., Zeljko Trkanjec, "50 more kilometres of razor wire on the Croatian borders." *Euractiv*, March 4, 2021, https://www.euractiv.com/section/politics/short_news/50-more-kilometres-of-razor-wire-on-the-croatian-border/, Jennifer Rigby and James Crisp, "Fortress Europe." *Telegraph*, https://www.telegraph.co.uk/global-health/fortress-europe-borders-wall-fence-controls-eu-countries-migrants-crisis.

12 "Push-back." ECCHR, accessed September 6, 2022, https://www.ecchr.eu/en/glossary/push-back.

13 Stuart Elden, "Legal Terrain - the political materiality of territory." *London Review of International Law* 5, no. 2 (2017) 199–224: 202.

14 Elizabeth A. Povinelli, *Geontologies: A Requiem to Late Liberalism*. (Durham: Duke University Press, 2016).

such as rot in fruit, a yellow tint in the air, stench in water and cancer in cells. As novel manifestations (as opposed to naturalised states of things) these articulations function as traces of events that are registered and expressed by matter. Following these traces across matter makes visible the imperceptible flows and connections existing in between.[15]

Toxicity is a gradient. Though it is certainly inclusive of it, it is not solely an absolute risk of terminal disintegration. It gathers things, triggers new encounters and relations, generates other modes of being and togetherness, in solidarity. Conceptually, it gives rise to questions regarding queer relationality[16] and nonhuman/nonlife agency. However, the generativity of toxicity as a concept and an investigative tool should not override the harm and the challenges that it may bring when above the aforementioned threshold. After the investigation, toxicity, more often than not, remains because toxicity is irreversible even when remediated. Then, returning to queer relationality, we must ask: how do we exist within toxicity?

WEAPONISATION OF NATURE

The weaponisation of nature is the utilisation of natural terrains of separation like rivers, deserts and mountain ranges through surveillance technology and militarisation in order to generate forceful governance on migration. The infrastructures, military activities and technologies implemented on border regions are strategically instrumentalised as violence against mobility and usually evolve into other complex forms of, for example, environmental violence. Considering that borders are technological apartheid systems enforcing organised deterrence methods for certain peoples of the Global South, they are usually highly securitised terrains that are strategically taken advantage of by intensifying the existing difficulties of navigating through natural terrain[17–18] to implement life-threatening conditions for crossings. In these circumstances, crossings become reasons for drowning, getting lost, dying from extreme heat or cold, hunger or fatigue. These regions of hostility can also consist of extended terrains, where a whole nation might play the role of a buffer zone frontier to neocolonial politics,[19] as the nation-state came into existence to protect specific power assemblages. The methods connected to the weaponisation of nature are authoritarian practices that are politically implemented and sustained by obfuscating the public understanding of migration by criminalising migrants.

15 Susan Schuppli, *Material Witness: Media, Forensics, Evidence*. (Cambridge, Massachusetts: MIT Press, 2020).

16 Mel Y. Chen, "Toxic Animacies, Inanimate Affections," *GLQ: A Journal of Lesbian and Gay Studies* 17, no. 2-3 (June 2011): 265-86.

17 Gastón Gordillo, "Terrain as Insurgent Weapon: An Affective Geometry of Warfare in the Mountains of Afghanistan", *Political Geography* 64 (May 2018): 53-62.

18 Jason De León, *The Land of Open Graves: Living and Dying on the Migrant Trail*. (Oakland, California: University of California Press, 2017).

19 Nivi Manchanda, "Rendering Afghanistan Legible: Borders, Frontiers and the 'State' of Afghanistan," *Politics* 37, no. 4 (November 2017): 386-401.

Works cited

Chen, Mel Y. "Toxic Animacies, Inanimate Affections." GLQ: *A Journal of Lesbian and Gay Studies* 17, no. 2-3 (June 2011): 265-86.

Dadusc, Deanne and Chiara Denaro. "Criminalising Solidarity: Silencing Critical Voices and Erasing the Critical Gaze on Border Violence." *Border Criminologies Blog. Faculty of Law, University of Oxford.* 16 April, 2021, https://blogs.law.ox.ac.uk/research-subject-groups/centre-criminology/centreborder-criminologies/blog/2021/04/criminalising.

De León, Jason. *The Land of Open Graves: Living and Dying on the Migrant Trail.* Oakland, California: University of California Press, 2017.

Dunai, Marton. "Hungary builds new high-tech border fence - with few migrants in sight." *Reuters*, March 2, 2017, https://www.reuters.com/article/us-europe-migrants-hungary-fence-idUSKBN1692MH,'

ECCHR. "Push-back." Accessed September 6, 2022, https://www.ecchr.eu/en/glossary/push-back.

Elden, Stuart. "Legal Terrain - the political materiality of territory," London Review of International Law 5, no. 2 (2017): 199–224.

Federici, Silvia. *Re-enchanting the World: feminism and the politics of the commons.* Oakland, California: PM Press / Kairos, 2019.

Gee, Oliver. "Eurotunnel adds moats to keep refugees away." *The Local*, 13 January 2016, .https://www.thelocal.fr/20160113/eurotunnel-adds-moats-to-keep-refugees-away.

Gordillo, Gastón. "Terrain as Insurgent Weapon: An Affective Geometry of Warfare in the Mountains of Afghanistan." *Political Geography* 64 (May 2018): 53-62.

JCWI, "The Hostile Environment Explained." https://www.jcwi.org.uk/the-hostile-environment-explained, accessed 7 October 2022.

Manchanda, Nivi. "Rendering Afghanistan Legible: Borders, Frontiers and the 'State' of Afghanistan." *Politics* 37, no. 4 (November 1, 2017): 386-401.

Meynen, Nick. "Belgian authorities slash trees to 'stop migrants hiding." *The Ecologist*, April 27, 2018, https://theecologist.org/2018/apr/27/belgian-authorities-slash-trees-stop-migrants-hiding-writes-nickmeynen.

Povinelli, Elizabeth A. *Geontologies: A Requiem to Late Liberalism.* Durham, North Carolina: Duke University Press, 2016.

Rigby, Jennifer and James Crisp. "Fortress Europe." *Telegraph*, https://www.telegraph.co.uk/global-health/fortress-europe-borders-wall-fence-controls-eu-countries-migrants-crisis.

Schuppli, Susan. *Material Witness: Media, Forensics, Evidence.* Cambridge, Massachusetts: MIT Press, 2020.

Tondo, Lorenzo. "Poland starts building wall through protected forest at Belarus border." *The Guardian*, January 27, 2022, https://www.theguardian.com/world/2022/jan/27/poland-starts-building-wall-through-protected-forest-at-belarus-border.

Trilling, Daniel. "Should we build a wall around North Wales?." *London Review of Books* 39, no. 14, 13 July 2017.

Trkanjec, Zeljko. "50 more kilometres of razor wire on the Croatian borders." *Euractiv*, March 4, 2021, https://www.euractiv.com/section/politics/short_news/50-more-kilometres-of-razor-wire-on-the-croatian-border/.

Vallet, Elisabeth. "The World Is Witnessing a Rapid Proliferation of Border Walls." *Migration Policy*, 27 September 2022, https://www.migrationpolicy.org/article/rapid-proliferation-number-border-walls.

Webber, Frances. "Europe's Unknown War." *Race & Class*, 59, no. 1, (2017): 36-53.

BIOGRAPHIES

Dimitra Andritsou is an architect and investigative researcher. In 2019, she completed the MA at the Centre for Research Architecture, where her work revolved around the spatial politics of migration. She has been working with Forensic Architecture since 2019 and is currently the Research Coordinator for the organisation's Berlin-based sister agency, Forensis.

Areej Ashhab is an architect and spatial researcher. Her work examines the role of the more-than-human in decolonising land practices. Ashhab completed her MA in Research Architecture in 2022. Together with a group of Jerusalem-based Palestinian artists, she co-founded Al-Block collective that experiments with walking as a research practice to document the transformation of the Palestinian cultural and natural landscapes under settler-colonialism.

Riccardo Badano is an architect, researcher, and editor working at the intersection of migration circulations and critical ecologies. He is a Tutor on the MA City Design programme at the Royal College of Art. Badano completed his masters at the Centre for Research Architecture where he is currently undertaking his PhD.

Border Ecologies Network is a platform that brings together researchers, activists, artists and other practitioners investigating relations between nature and borders.

Nadine El-Enany is Reader in Law at Birkbeck, University of London, where she co-directs the Centre for Research on Race and Law. Her current research focuses on questions of race and justice in death in custody cases, and the role of law in addressing health inequalities arising from environmental harm. Her book *(B)ordering Britain: law, race and empire* was published in 2020.

Mustapha Jundi is an architect and artist. His research examines shifting borders in relation to environmental conditions such as water, meteorology, and extractive practices. He received his MPhil at the Centre for Research Architecture in 2022

Faiza Ahmad Khan is a documentary filmmaker and activist based in Mumbai. She completed her MA at the Centre for Research Architecture in 2018.

Stefanos Levidis is a spatial investigator and visual practitioner. He is an Advanced Researcher at Forensic Architecture/Forensis, where he oversees the agency's work on border violence and migration. He completed his PhD at the Centre for Research Architecture on the entanglement of border defence strategies and the natural environment at the external borders of the EU.

Tomas Percival is an artist and researcher. His work critically examines the intersections of space and security, with a particular interest in regimes of assessment, risk governance, prison infrastructures, criminal justice data, asylum administration, and forensic bordering. He is a Lecturer in Research Architecture.

Lorenzo Pezzani is an architect and researcher, whose work explores the spatial politics, visual cultures and political ecologies of migration and borders. He is co-director of Border Forensics, an agency mobilising spatial and visual analysis to investigate border violence. Between 2016 and 2022 he was Lecturer in Forensic Architecture at the Centre for Research Architecture. In 2022 he joined the Department of the Arts at the University of Bologna as Associate Professor.

Tara Plath is a visual and spatial researcher. Her projects look at the technologies and rhetoric of rescue in the Arizona–Sonora borderlands. She completed her MA at the Centre for Research Architecture in 2019, and is currently a PhD student in Film and Media Studies at the University of California, Santa Barbara. Plath is a member of the Border Ecology Network and a Researcher at the Border Forensics agency.

Hanna Rullmann is a researcher, filmmaker, and designer, whose practice engages questions of ecological restoration, environmental histories, environmental policy, and legal/political production of natures. She graduated with an MA from the Centre for Research Architecture in 2018. She is a member of the Border Ecologies network.

Susan Schuppli is an artist–researcher whose work examines material evidence from war and conflict to environmental disasters and climate change. Her current work is focused on Learning from Ice. Schuppli is the author of *Material Witness: Media, Forensics, Evidence* (MIT Press 2020) and is the Director of the Centre for Research Architecture as well as Board Chair of Forensic Architecture.

Ariadna Serrahima is a publisher, researcher, and designer. Her research explores struggles around autonomous spaces, and the production of collective insurgent learning. She co–founded the graphic design studio Oficina de Disseny, L'Automàtica cooperative print shop in Barcelona, and I.F Publications. She completed her MA in Research Architecture in 2018 and is a PhD candidate in Visual Cultures at Goldsmiths.

Juanita Sundberg is a geographer examining nature conservation, border security, and militarization. Her work seeks to foster conversations between feminist geopolitics, political ecology, more–than–human geographies, anti–racist theory, and Latin American Studies. She is an Associate Professor of Geography at the University of British Columbia.

Ishita Sharma is a researcher operating between between activism, academia, and artistic practice. Her work focuses on the intersection of land, dispossession, territoriality, and resistance. She has also worked as a facilitator and researcher with youth and feminist organisations in South Asia. She is currently a PhD candidate on the Topological Atlas project at the Technical University of Delft.

Avi Varma is an artist–researcher. His work takes as its departure point the nexus of ecology, epistemic violence, and anti–colonial struggle in the contexts of the U.S. southwest and India. He completed his MA at the Centre for Research Architecture, where he is currently a doctoral candidate.

Gabrielle Wolf is a geographer and radical cartographer researching the US–Mexico border. Her work is broadly concerned with the complexities surrounding how borders are drawn and maintained. Originally from Los Angeles, she lives and studies in Vancouver, B.C., which occupies the unceded lands of the xʷməθkʷəy̓əm (Musqueam), Sḵwx̱wú7mesh (Squamish), and səlilwətaɬ (Tsleil–Waututh) First Nations.

A Centre for Research Architecture
series exploring pedagogy,
politics, and practices

Series Editors:
Riccardo Badano
Tomas Percival
Susan Schuppli
Ariadna Serrahima

Border Environments

Editors:
Riccardo Badano
Tomas Percival
Susan Schuppli

Graphic Design:
Oficina de disseny
(Ariadna Serrahima
and Diego Bustamante)
Copyediting:
Sanjana Varghese
Image correction:
Xavier Tulleuda

Printed in the EU

Published by:
Spector Books
Harkortstrasse 10
04107 Leipzig
www.spectorbooks.com

The publication has been made possible
through the generous support of the
Graham Foundation for Advanced
Studies in the Fine Arts, the Het Nieuwe
Instituut, and the Department of Visual
Cultures at Goldsmiths, University
of London.

Graham Foundation

Additional Image Sources:
Juanita Sundberg (p. 40),
Francesca Volpi / Médecins Sans
Frontières (p. 78),
Finnbarr Webster Editorial / Alamy
Stock Photo (p. 94),
Tara Plath (pp. 116–119),
Hanna Rullmann & Faiza Ahmad Khan
(pp. 122, 124).

Distribution:
— Germany, Austria:
GVA, Gemeinsame Verlagsauslieferung
Göttingen GmbH & Co. KG,
www.gva-verlage.de
— Switzerland:
AVA Verlagsauslieferung AG, www.ava.ch
— France, Belgium:
Interart Paris, www.interart.fr
— UK:
Central Books Ltd, www.centralbooks.com
— USA, Canada,
Central and South America, Africa:
ARTBOOK / D.A.P., www.artbook.com
— South Korea:
The Book Society, www.thebooksociety.org
— Japan:
twelvebooks, www.twelve-books.com
— Australia, New Zealand:
Perimeter Distribution,
www.perimeterdistribution.com

First edition: 2023

ISBN 978-3-95905-686-1